The Roaring Eighties and Other Good Times

The Roaring Eighties
and Other Good Times

Norman Snider

Exile Editions

Publishers of singular
Fiction, Poetry, Essays, Drama, and Graphic Books
2007

Library and Archives Canada Cataloguing in Publication

Snider, Norman, date

The roaring eighties and other good times / Norman Snider

ISBN 978-1-55096-093-8

I. Title.

FC600.S63 2007 C814'.54 C2007-906323-3

Design and Composition by Homunculus ReproSet
Typeset in Garamond at the Moons of Jupiter Studios
Printed in Canada by Friesens

The publisher would like to acknowledge the financial assistance of The Canada Council for the Arts, and the Ontario Arts Council–which is an agency of the Government of Ontario.

Conseil des Arts du Canada Canada Council for the Arts

ONTARIO ARTS COUNCIL
CONSEIL DES ARTS DE L'ONTARIO

Published in Canada in 2007 by Exile Editions Ltd.
144483 Southgate Road 14
General Delivery
Holstein, Ontario, N0G 2A0
info@exileeditions.com
www.ExileEditions.com

Canadian Sales Distribution:
McArthur & Company
c/o Harper Collins
1995 Markham Road
Toronto, ON M1B 5M8
toll free: 1 800 387 0117

U.S. Sales Distribution:
Independent Publishers Group
814 North Franklin Street
Chicago, IL 60610
www.ipgbook.com
toll free: 1 800 888 4741

As always,

For F.M.

CONTENTS

INTRODUCTION

ANXIOUS MONSTERS

I was with Tom Hedley, in the offices of *Toronto Life* magazine. At the time, he was that publication's editor. Hedley had a set of moves I hadn't seen before. No underdog, he looked like a veteran ad exec type. With his penchant for a hybrid mix of high and low, unlike most Toronto editors, Hedley had a talent for putting out magazines that had sexual glamour. He had moved from the old *Toronto Telegram* to *Esquire*, in its irreverent golden age, where, as the youngest editor in its history, he sent quality-lit icons William Burroughs, Jean Genet and groovy Terry Southern to report on the Democratic party convention in turbulent 1968.

That day, Hedley and I discussed a profile of Glenn Gould I was working on, one of the first articles I had undertaken for *Toronto Life*. I was new to journalism, in thrall to its tawdry romance, a complete captive. In some recess of my mind, I kept the image of the Broadway boulevardier reporter of yesteryear – a flower in his buttonhole, spats on his shoes, a quip on his lips, keeping a hoodlum's coffee warm for him at the booth in Lindy's, as the dude goes out to meet his doom on the steps of the cathedral. That's who I wanted to be. That guy. Little did I know, but nothing could stop me from trying. And here we were, right on the cusp of the Roaring Eighties.

Fascinated by celebrity himself, Hedley was the kind of guy people talked about. Other men tried to emulate him. Like Jay Gatsby, Hedley had sprung out of some Platonic ideal of himself.

Originally from a military background out west, he acted as if he came from vast wealth. In his mid-thirties, Hedley looked like he had attended some Eastern U.S. boarding school and cultivated a socialite-on-a-spree style, tall, always pushing a Kennedyesque hank of hair off his forehead. He had the air of a nineteenth-century aesthete, possibly of noble lineage, and liked to edit manuscripts in bars and restaurants. Other editors went home every night to dull wives serving up roast chicken and mashed potatoes. Hedley prowled the night-life in the company of glamorous women and visiting notables, acting as if he was still immersed in the high life of Manhattan. He was a master of the grand gesture: sending bottles of good champagne to friends in restaurants. He would order up a limo in a moment. He considered extravagant, expensive gestures as his form of rebellion against the typical pinched Protestant sense of caution. Nobody in Toronto acted like this in 1980. It would be a few years before others caught on.

In New York, Hedley had absorbed the brawling manners of the White Horse Tavern and Cedar Bar where artists and writers cared enough to throw guys through plate-glass windows over differences of opinion. They were just that serious. Out on the tiles, Hedley loved to mess with dangerous people: transvestite rough trade, small-time Mafiosi drinking in low bars, their gorilla chests festooned with bling-bling. A writer had to step out and look around. Those were the kind of places you found good stories. Not every night ended in Emergency or a brawl, but enough did to keep it interesting.

More importantly, as an editor, Hedley stood in pugnacious opposition to the cramped style of much of Canadian media. He loved Andy Warhol and Pop Art, magazines were just part of a hip mix that included novels, movies, comics, you name it; an article could reflect it all. The key was to structure your piece like a novelist or short story writer by using fiction's technical arsenal: point of view, panorama and scene. Out reporting, you had to be on the alert for items of dress, decor and especially spoken idiom. Sharply observed details were what gave a story conviction. Reading a great novelist like Raymond Chandler you knew exactly what a hotel lobby off Wilshire Boulevard was like in 1946, what kind of belted camel-hair coat the gigolo wore as he walked in, what the pink marble registration desk looked like. In order to write prose like this, you had to have a novelist's insight into character, his feeling for rage and sorrow. And any good novelist had his own voice. I wanted my voice to be sharp and bright as a razor, like Coltrane's tenor sax.

A few years previous, I had lived in a cool loft on Spadina, neighbour to the painter Gordon Rayner. I had occasionally sat in on bass with the Artists' Jazz Band and had met the painters Graham Coughtry and Robert Markle, Hedley's good friend. These painters were known for their uninhibited figure studies, riots of sensual gorgeous colour, and I didn't see why journalism couldn't have the same colours too. The way they lived downtown also served as example. (Nearly thirty years later all those condo dwellers would follow in their antic footsteps, all unawares.) The Toronto painters were inner-city frontiersmen, searching out the ethnic restaurants, strip bars. Toronto was not New York or Paris, neither was it insignificant.

Of course there was much talk of the New Journalism at the time, of Wolfe, Thompson, Mailer, and Capote. But journalism that aspired to the status of literature was of far more ancient provenance. There were those very boulevardier New York reporters of the 1920s and 1930s whose outfits Wolfe sought to emulate with his white suits and double-breasted waistcoats. A forgotten New York newspaperman named Hickman Powell had written a wonderful book about Lucky Luciano called *Ninety Times Guilty* that read as well as any novel. Going back to the early nineteenth century, Thomas De Quincey would get loaded on tincture of opium, climb on the top the fastest stagecoach he could find and, with the wind rushing through his Byronic locks, just you know, thrill. Then he recorded the whole wild experience for the *Edinburgh Review* in a pioneer piece of personal journalism titled "The English Mail Coach." Much more recently, there was Albert Goldman's novelistic biography of Lenny Bruce. It portrayed magnificently the greasepaint and gonorrhea world of small-time nightclub showbiz from which Bruce emerged. Writers like these were my inspiration.

Newspapermen hated all of this. They were often solemn freshwater owls who thought magazine articles were long, overwritten news stories. Hedley had returned to Toronto to elevate the genre. Unlike most editors, Hedley actually liked writers. He encouraged new voices and he urged you to find your own – the more original and startling, the better. And he had patience with writers' blocks and alcoholism and chronic depression and bad girlfriends and raging egos and all the rest of the ailments of the literary life. Just so long as you wrote well. He wanted you to forget everything you thought you knew about good magazine writing. He wanted you to loosen up.

"If Burroughs was doing this," he told me, "there'd be purple monsters coming out of the toilet."

This was too good to be true.

After that invitation to freedom, I needed little prompting. Like thousands of others, I had made it through adolescence with the Beats, especially the Burroughs of *Naked Lunch*, as spiritual guide and example, minus the heroin addiction and gay sexuality. As far as I was concerned, in those days, he was the greatest writer since James Joyce. Kerouac and Ginsberg celebrated the joyous freedom of The Road but compared to Burroughs they were sentimentalists. Burroughs was an authentic literary outlaw, a gimlet-eyed observer of the absurdities and horrors of the Cold War era. Like Kerouac and Ginsberg, he was possessed of an incomparable vision of freedom. And like Bruce, he was funny, funny. For brave young writers of the era, the notion was: nothing is too horrifying to write about. *Nothing human is foreign to me*. What is that naked item dangling on the end of every cafeteria fork? Bring it on. Then there was Vladimir Nabokov and his dictum: *There is nothing as exhilarating as Philistine vulgarity*. Like these writers, I subscribed to the notion that audacity was the key to art; in a media-saturated age a bold approach was the only method that allowed you to be heard.

Much of Burroughs' first novel, *Junkie*, had taken place around Times Square in New York. The Yonge Street strip in Toronto was fully the equivalent of Times Square. A few years before, I had been an enthusiastic habitué of the clubs on the strip as a teenage jazz fan. The Town Tavern, the Friars, The Colonial, Le Coq d'Or: that was my nightly turf. Top-drawer jazz musicians out of New York played those clubs every week. Miles Davis, Wayne Shorter, Cannonball Adderley, Bill Evans. These men were as remarkable for their personal style as for their adventurous music. They had, well, *an irreverent view of life*. Except for Davis, they were approachable. At that time, jazz musicians were social outlaws, regularly jailed for narcotics offences, pilloried in the press as degenerates.

The bar at the Colonial was also the lair of black pimps who lined up three deep. In its rhythms, their argot resembled the jazz coming from the bandstand. It was a poetic language, fabricated by men who were cut off from society, as Sartre says, invented to describe states of ecstasy unknown to most whites. Back then, I thought every black cat was another Charlie Parker and every black woman Sarah Vaughan. As much as the musicians, the pimps provided a valuable course in street sense, one not offered by my teachers and professors at the university. (The conventional education proffered in the schools, then as now, was nothing if not hypocritically Pollyanna, about as well-suited to the *realpolitik* of actual life as an upbringing in a convent.) I had also met Muddy Waters on Yonge: he was benign, indulgent, vastly amused that a roomful of white kids had come out to hear his rowdy blues. His music and its grit was like the soundtrack to inner-city Toronto, just as much as Chicago. The pimps at the bar were hipsters and the kids were hippies. Battling racism every day of their lives, the pimps were tough-minded realists, but the hippies were middle-class naifs, who had jettisoned middle-class prudence and so were quickly in thrall to all the predators in the jungle, and whatever religious or political charlatan came down the pike. I preferred the pimps' viewpoint. I was also fascinated by the way they cultivated their highs, connoisseurs of exquisite states of consciousness. The hippies used drugs like fraternity boys drank beer: party 'til you're paralyzed.

Down the block, Le Coq d'Or was a rounder's paradise: it was a *Beggar's Opera* cast and every bookie and bank robber in town hung there. Foreign sailors came up the St. Lawrence in freighters that docked in Toronto's harbour. Le Coq d'Or was their last call on shore. There were spectacular bar fights. The dishwashers in the kitchen all carried lead-weighted saps in their back pockets. The local papers occasionally printed reviews of the performances at the clubs, but for them it was marginal, not worthy of attention. The whole mad scene just lay there, like the lady in Chekhov, begging to be described.

As much as I appreciated the view from street level, it was severely limited. The boys at the bar, push come to shove, believed might was right. They were constantly working an angle on you. One way or another they were, to a man, looking for a Mr. Big and the direction and focus he would provide their ambitions and desires. God knows what happened to them all.

It was only a five-dollar cab ride from Le Coq d'Or to the heart of Rosedale but they were like separate universes. An early marriage had sent me exploring amongst the corporate lawyers and tycoons and politicians of the Anglo-Protestant establishment. I wanted to bring the hard-eyed wit of the boys from the Colonial Tavern to bear on them.

One of my first wife's ancestors had been a Father of Confederation, her mother had worked with Lester Pearson in

London during World War II, her father had been on General Montgomery's staff. These guys fascinated me just as much as the Yonge Street denizens. They were the descendants of the Anglo-Scottish gentry who had always run Canada. Part of the country's remaining British heritage was a Tory belief in the inherited privileges of social hierarchy. What enabled people like them to maintain these privileges in the face of so much egalitarianism? Why did they love chintz so? Why were their family lives so often a disaster? I wanted to find out and I wanted to write about it.

Between Rosedale and the Yonge Street bars, I was running my own little game of high and low. Glenn Gould was not only one of the world's leading piano virtuosos, he was also the most interesting musical mind on the planet. Notoriously, legendarily, iconically reclusive, he seldom granted interviews. I had written him a wonkishly earnest letter. McLuhan, who had conceptualized hybrid energies, was the rage and I had thrown in some questions on the influence of recording techniques on the direction of music itself. I suppose the letter sparked Gould's interest. He had kindly assented to a phone interview and it had gone well. Hedley's direction freed up my style and the article appeared. Then, the great Glenn Gould took to phoning me at all hours from his penthouse on St. Clair Avenue and launching into extended verbal arias about obscure composers. I guess he needed somebody to talk to. It was only after his death that I learned from his biographers that Gould had been cross-addicted to uppers and downers, worse than any jazz junkie in the Yonge Street demi-monde. After a few two-hour monologues, bored with topics like the music of Ernst Krenek, I hesitantly ventured a couple of notions of my own. Gould wasn't interested. He stopped calling, but that article taught me how to write all the others.

For me, in those years, writing for *Toronto Life* under Tom Hedley, and later Don Obe and Marq De Villiers, gave me the keys to the city. I could enter any world. I wrote what were called "profiles." To me they were portraits. The question that always fascinated me was: "Who is this man? Who is this woman?" I wrote about the burgeoning scene on Queen Street West. I wrote about Eddie Greenspan and his murder trials, I wrote about cocaine dealers, television executives, murdered heiresses, fashion models and advertising tycoons. I was the art critic for a time, I wrote about pop music. I wrote travel pieces. I covered the waterfront.

Opposite the *Toronto Life* offices on Front Street, there was a little basement bar called Café des Copains, now long gone. There, Hedley and Don Obe, Marq De Villiers, and writers such as Paul William Roberts, Barry Callaghan, Stephen Williams, and other buccaneer journalists would belly up to the bar. Yes, I admit it was a boys' club, but far from being a clique. These guys were the ruggedest of individuals. Nobody was ever tossed through a window, but people were often not on speaking terms, sometimes for years. Each guy acted as if he were already a star, a household name at the very least. Occasionally, Barry would bring in his dad, the illustrious Morley Callaghan, our living link to Hemingway and Fitzgerald. Morley talked about "Scotty" as if he had just left the room. Fitzgerald had been the original yuppie, sixty years before. We believed in Hemingway's romance of professionalism. Often enough, in our case, the code devolved, in blackly comic fashion, into disgrace under pressure. In any event, there were assignments to

Africa and Egypt and Latin America. Rivalry was rampant. Ambition was high. Guts were at a premium. Later on, Roberts covered both the 1991 and 2003 wars in Iraq for *Harpers* and wrote one of the best books about Saddam Hussein's regime, *The Demonic Comedy*. Stephen Williams wrote *Invisible Darkness* and *Karla*, the best books about the Bernardo-Homolka murder case, and got himself thrown in jail for his efforts.

Jazz was also a feature at Café des Copains but it had plainly changed since the heyday of the Yonge Street strip. Great musicians, like John Lewis of the MJQ and the pianist Kenny Barron, played the bar, but solo, bereft of a rhythm section. Jazz was no longer so adventurous and rowdy, but rather more polite, a genteel light classical music. Far from being the outlaws of yore, its musicians were college professors who dressed like undertakers. The cops didn't hunt jazz musicians like they did in the 1950s; drug use was far more discreet, but then, so was that of corporate lawyers.

Another hangout was the 22 Bar of the Windsor Arms Hotel. Then there was the Courtyard Café. The era saw the explosion of the restaurant and bar scene in the city. If you cared to you could live a café life, just as if you were in Paris. And you had to develop a certain manner of café style, in the continental manner. You always ate at the bar, tables were for the tourists. You cultivated the friendship of the owner and the waiters. If you liked a spot, you became an insider there, you ran a tab, took your business meetings there, did your interviews there, and arranged your romantic assignations there, had staff take messages for you, made it your centre of operations.

Michael Enright, at *Quest* magazine, sent me to Las Vegas to cover the heavyweight championship fight between Larry Holmes and the current Canadian champion, big Trevor Berbick. It was a measure of the times that a smallish publication would even spend the money to send a writer to Las Vegas to cover a fight. Berbick was a country boy from Port Antonio, Jamaica, via Halifax. Media trained? Never even heard of it. He didn't care if some writer hung around with a notebook while he enjoyed Vegas to the hilt and incidentally fought for the world heavyweight title. He was happy for the company.

My chief advantage as a reporter was that I had put in much time hanging with various worthless types. I was good at it. Hanging out was an art in itself. Now, it became most useful. Your average reporter came on like the cops, asking a lot of aggressive questions that only caused street dudes like boxers and rockers to shut the hell up. The art was to blend into the subject's world like you belonged there, get all the sights and sounds down, while you waited for dramatic scenes to present themselves. Find out something about your subject that your readers didn't know. They called it saturation reporting. It took a light touch.

As a dues-paying introvert, I had to duck into a psychological phone booth somewhere en route to the assignment and suit up in my extrovert schmoozing-reporter personality. There was always the anxiety that the subject, whoever it was, would clam up, shut you out. Or that you would spend days hanging around, spending the magazine's money, and nothing worth writing about would happen. Home you would come, empty-handed. Hunter Thompson and Norman Mailer solved this particular problem by becoming the story themselves.

Conscious of themselves as public performers, they would *make* something happen. Of course, the nominal subject of the piece would tend to get lost in the process.

One of the keys was to concentrate on what other reporters deemed unimportant. Most professional athletes encased themselves in an armour of cliché and kept their real thoughts to themselves. This was not the case with heavyweight fighters. His whole career lived in the shadow of Muhammad Ali, Larry Holmes felt unappreciated in comparison. After every workout he would rant and rave into a microphone about it. The beat reporters, who had heard it all too many times before, left for the bar. I stayed and listened, fascinated, even though Holmes lacked a scintilla of Ali's wit. After he finally finished, I somehow floated with his sparring partners into Holmes' locker room, digging the fighters' juke and jive. Readers ought to know what it was like in the dressing room of the world's champion. I was a camera. Holmes' little brother Mark was trying to be a fighter. He was having problems. "You gettin' some bad habits, man," said Holmes. "It's like eatin' pussy. Once you start, you cain't hardly stop."

Berbick himself was determined to meet every available lady in Las Vegas. He wasn't shy. He didn't care that I was writing it all down. Three hours before the fight, against every known maxim of training, he went out for a mammoth Chinese meal. He then fought fifteen rounds with the great Larry Holmes and almost beat him. It all went in the notebook. Somewhere along the line, possibly at the blackjack table at Caesars Palace at three o'clock in the morning, I thought: *This is what I was born to do*. When the article appeared, Berbick appeared at the offices of the magazine. Enright, himself all courtly tolerance and encouragement, feared revenge; a titanic wrecking of the office. The entire subject of what he was pleased to call "prizefighting" made him nervous. But Berbick was full of surprises. The Canadian champ loved the piece. He just wanted to tell somebody.

Enright next sent me to Winnipeg to write about federal politics at the Conservative leadership convention. Joe Clark was not about to let me into his locker room but a political convention was a Nabokovian feast, no, a veritable banquet of philistine vulgarity. Reporting on politics was a challenge; major politicians were besieged by the press every day of their lives; substantial access was tough to come by.

More than any other field, the beat reporters in national politics were a clannish lot. They didn't much like outsiders on their turf, especially guys from the big city who favoured red shoes rather than blue blazers. Their relationships with politicians and their handlers were painstakingly cultivated, sometimes over a period of years. Half of the Parliamentary gallery cultivated social relations with politicians, especially those in power. It pleased their image of themselves to dine often with the prominent; they soon became part of the woodwork, part of the permanent Ottawa establishment. The other half wished they could live like Hunter Thompson but their jobs obliged them to write pure C.P. wire service. At the same time, the atmosphere around big time politics was toxic, immersed in great gusts of bad feeling from both journalists and politicians. The closest thing I could compare it to was the atmosphere in a maximum security penitentiary. Everybody was playing hardball. Politics were closer to the fight world than appeared at first glance. Successful politicians were bruisers. So were front-line reporters. All the damage was done with words instead of fists. I did the same thing I did in the world of boxing: paint portraits. The grand currents shaping society were important; but I was more fascinated by individual men and women and their impact on events.

Five minutes after I arrived at the hall in Winnipeg I encountered a couple whose radiation of brilliant expensive glare had almost a physical quality. I didn't know who they were so I made inquiry. Brian and Mila Mulroney, somebody said. He was as handsome and slick as Bugsy Siegel. They were the Roaring Eighties made flesh incarnate. The decade had truly arrived in Canada and I was to disappear into its politics for the next five years.

In some ways I was a latecomer. Just as I had to settle for writing about for Larry Holmes rather than Muhammad Ali, I wrote about Jean Chretien rather than Pierre Elliott Trudeau. Like Holmes, Chretien was underrated in comparison to his illustrious predecessor. Still, it was an opportunity to explore some large themes. Unlike most political writers, I had no ideological agenda. Too many writers arrived at extreme political positions, left or right, as a means of self-dramatization, as a way of creating a role for themselves in the political drama.

By the time I started writing about politics, political correctness was the order of the day on the left. It was a repressive creed that focused on gender and race. To me, it was the return of the tight-ass prig, only in a political, rather than religious guise. If you weren't a minority, you were an oppressor. On the right, neo-conservatism was transparently selfishness and greed disguised as principle. I was neither utopian nor cynic. I was an Annex liberal, mildly progressive.

Still, I wanted to comprehend politics and politicians in a way that transcended the merely partisan. Again I wanted to portray the process. My interest was in describing what politics looked and sounded like. What it was like in the premier's helicopter or the enormous sexual feeling that was generated during election campaigns. I wanted, as far as possible, to look into the souls of the men and women who sought power to see what beasts and angels lurked within.

The first political piece I had ever written was about the Ontario NDP, for "Fanfare," a section of the *Globe and Mail* wistfully directed at the young audience. The NDP, in their eternal socialistic humorlessness, were always ripe for satire. I didn't forget that razor. I spared no one. I got a congratulatory call out of the blue from one Larry Zolf at the CBC, who was still laughing. Zolf knew all of the movers and shakers in Canadian politics. He knew all the riding presidents, the backroom guys, the ward heelers. He was on the phone culling people like Mulroney for tidbits. He also knew more about Canadian political history than anybody outside of a political science department. Zolf was also completely outrageous, which suited me fine. Worse luck, he was almost family. Zolf hailed from North Winnipeg and so did my mother and father. He was in-your-face Jewish. My very respectable uncles all disapproved of him. He was giving the tribe a bad name. I planned to do the same. In his heyday, Zolf had more nerve than anybody in the country. A more portly Lenny Bruce, with specs. His best stuff, naturally, never made it onto the air: *Zolf walks into a café in Yorkville, spots a couple of blond Teutonic types, says a friendly hello. Quoth Zolf, in his booming radio announcer's voice: "Vee Nazis and Jews must stick together!" . . . Zolf walks into a Austrian schnitzel emporium in the west end. Quoth Zolf: "Two seats by the ovens, pliss!"*

It was a long leap from Tom Hedley to Larry Zolf but I intended to bridge the gap. I had that razor and I was getting a rep as somebody who didn't mind using it. An editor would tell me, "You're the only guy who'll write something honest," and I would ride off in my own quest for unflinching beauty, autumn in my heart, and make three more lifelong enemies. I became the journalistic equivalent of the hockey brute whose coach tells him "Go get him," and who promptly jumps off the bench and rams the other guy's head into the boards. After the piece appeared, the same editor would inform me, "You're getting a rep as a bad actor in print." In my naiveté, I had failed to realize that I was messing with people's reputations and their reputations were only slightly less dear to them than their bodily health. Bad publicity could kill a livelihood. Not everybody appreciated my sense of humour.

At the same time as I was venturing out to championship fights and political conventions, I was immersed in the world of books. If I went to the island of Cyprus to write about the Canadian peacekeepers there for *Weekend*, I lugged a stack of books. I was reviewing for the *Globe and Mail* and the editor there was a hard-nosed Irishman named Ed O'Dacre who cherished unvarnished opinion. O'Dacre was the most incorruptible editor I ever met. He rode his motorcycle in from the suburbs to the newspaper every day. He socialized with neither writers nor their subjects and did neither favours. Once, the very famous Patrick Watson published a novel. In my review, I said as a novelist he was a great broadcaster. Watson went on television and threatened to beat the shit out of me, should we ever meet. Watching, I wondered how a guy defended himself against an older, one-legged man. It was hard to come out ahead, win or lose. *Snider beat up an old guy with one leg?* Or – *Snider couldn't even beat an old guy with one leg!* I resolved to avoid Patrick Watson. Then, his good friend, Marshall McLuhan, phoned up O'Dacre and demanded my head. My idol, Marshall McLuhan, wanted me fired!

These were the perils of appearing in the public prints. Some time in the 1980s, the *Globe* asked me to write a regular column analyzing and defining trends coursing through the culture. While I made a point of deferring to the personalities I depicted in magazine journalism, the column became a vehicle for my own opinions, thoughts, attitudes. With my photo appearing every week, I became a minor figure on the media scene, occasionally recognized in public. I also had strangers who phoned to insult me. The price of notoriety. But, as they say, it all went with the territory.

This is not a story where everybody leaves the theatre grinning. The New Journalism got old fast. Freedom all too soon turned to licence. Self-portraits can be beautiful; they're just hard to do well. The writer is obliged to look hard into the mirror and explore every disfigurement and mole he or she finds there. Scott Fitzgerald started the trend in the modern era, with "The Crack-Up," first published in *Esquire*. Fitzgerald delved deep into his alcoholism and his crumbling marriage with Zelda. Hemingway thought such unsparing self-revelation shameful, but to me there was something courageous about baring the soul, especially when it was done in Fitzgerald's eloquent language. There were endless journalistic memoirs about broken marriages, hellish divorces, failed relationships, bad childhoods, what it was like to be a new mother or father. But somehow, they all managed to be self-exculpatory rather than unsparing. A good writer could spend three pages describing the metaphysical reasons why he didn't care to answer the telephone but lesser talents made heartbreak boring. Because the techniques of fiction were employed in this style of journalism, newspaper guys often accused us of piping it, just making the whole deal up. It was not something I ever needed to do, there was too much weird shit out there. Nonetheless, it happened. In fact, one of the best-known pieces of the genre, by Nik Cohn, "Tribal Rites of the New Saturday Night," which appeared in *New York* magazine and which formed the basis of the movie *Saturday Night Fever*, turned out to be fiction from beginning to end. Not for nothing did Balzac title his book about journalism and ambition *Lost Illusions*.

Gradually, the freedom promised by "New" Journalism was lost. Political correctness from one direction, and conservatism, in the form of business writing, from another, put the squeeze on freedom of expression. These forces were opposed to each other in everything but a shared prudishness. Political correctness had a genteel aversion to anything unmentionable in a Victorian parlour. As a creed, it stemmed from the "correct political line" of Soviet Marxist ideology. Like all ideology, political correctness refused to gaze on anything it might find unpleasing to its sight. As a result, much of uncouth reality was ruled inadmissible in print. In the world of PC, a minority group member never did anything wrong; white males could do little that was admirable. From the right, neo-conservatism loathed everything they considered "countercultural"; that is to say any non-servile attitude. Relatively poorly paid writers assumed their bosses' attitudes to the lower orders. So, the rich and mighty were never in the wrong. As a result, writers with independent voices became an endangered species. With businessman's bounce the order of the day, editors began enforcing formulas. The prospect of lawsuits terrified them; they started asking for blow jobs on suburban construction tycoons, wannabe Barons of Brampton or Earls of Etobicoke. Original voices were not wanted. Service journalism was: where to buy a top-dollar meal, wardrobe, renovation, you name it. Failing that, celebrity gossip was required, soap-opera-style escapism. Few new writers appeared with the taste for saturation reporting, or the stamina. Unlike Tom Hedley, the new editors often didn't like writers, especially free-booting types like Roberts or Williams, who didn't take easily to formulaic, corporate prose. There were no Canadian magazines left that could send writers abroad on assignments. Nor were the new editors interested in original voices. As far as they were concerned, they, the editors, were the stars of the show and you would write the house style or not at all. Often you had the sense these editors were just biding their time until they could get a real job, say, in corporate P.R. or teaching at Ryerson. Journalism was losing its allure for me. If you were compelled to write characters and scenes, you were far better off writing novels or screenplays, where you could find genuine artistic freedom.

Worse, working as a freelance in Canada put you on a fast track to poverty. The editors you worked for all had good salaries and nice lives but a writer had zero security and was always one step from the street. Those writers loyal to literary non-fiction moved full time into book-length projects. Originality popped up again on the Internet but bloggers showed little inclination towards fine writing and any piece of writing longer than a paragraph seemed tedious on the computer screen. The Internet, finally, promoted an even shorter attention span than television.

Finally, the economics of the business wrote *finis* to the entire story. *Quest* folded, so did *Weekend*, so eventually did *Saturday Night*. In a strip bar named Gimlet's around the corner from Café des Copains, Tom Hedley found inspiration for the movie *Flashdance*. The atmosphere of the city in the 1980s found its way into the screenplay I wrote with David Cronenberg that later became *Dead Ringers*. William Burroughs, in person, expressed his admiration. More Hollywood screenplays followed. The real New York and Hollywood and Paris became the scenes of my activity. Yet, the urge to step out there and report never quite left me. Books and screenplays often required research in the field. I had experiences in places like San Francisco and Buenos Aires and the American South that more than lived up to my early romantic fantasies. But that's another story.

Defining life in decades is all too often glib and trite. Even though they are close to thirty years in the past, the 1980s are still too near to be seen clearly. Perhaps that is because they are still very much with us. The contours of 1980s are less clearly defined than the wartime Forties or Depression Thirties. The "Me Decade" or the "Greed Decade" often serves as brusque shorthand.

Yeats envisioned history as a whirling gyre oscillating back and forth as it propelled forward in time. The conservatism of Mulroney and Reagan did reach its limit as the gyre turned once again by decade's end. If that impulse receded slightly in the years of Clinton and Jean Chretien, it was only by a little. In the next historical turning, it was replaced by an even more vicious variety of conservatism; that of the religious right. As the sage Burroughs observed, there is no sonofabitch like a religious sonofabitch.

At the other end of the spectrum, political correctness became a permanent, if hypocritical, feature of the social landscape. The prigs who regarded pejorative terms for minorities as a new kind of unacceptable obscenity were the identical sorts unlikely ever to invite a member of the same minorities into their own living rooms. Even worse, the unthinking guardians of cultural relativism were asking that we extend our tolerance even to the medieval shibboleths of barbaric religions, which sought to punish hard-won freedoms with terrorist violence. The pressure from both left and right resulted in a Disneyfication of writing. Much that was human was suddenly foreign, "too dark" for readers to contemplate. The general run of humanity is content to move with the conventional wisdom wherever the twists and turns of history may take it. Journalists, writers of literary non-fiction, have a separate obligation. For them, the only remedy for the distortions of conventional wisdom is a good dose of honest street sense and a renewed skepticism and irreverence. The new piety is no more deserving of their respect than the old. No writer with self-respect should be its dupe. An irreverent stance, however, is more likely to bring down condemnation from the orthodox than previously. An irreverent view is now uncommon but though our numbers may be few, we remain a happy few.

Toronto, July 2007

THE ROARING EIGHTIES AND OTHER GOOD TIMES

CRONENBERG GOES TO HOLLYWOOD

We left Toronto at seven a.m. bound for Los Angeles. I was travelling with David Cronenberg, the writer and director. We'd been friends since college. I had acted in one of his underground films. He had directed a show I'd written for the CBC.

A few days before, Cronenberg had locked himself into his three-year-old daughter's bedroom and crouched in front of the red Contemporaphone for a long time, concentrating, summoning up all the considerable ambition of a man in his early thirties. He had long Prince Valiant hair, a thin, ascetic face, and specs that made him look like a detached scientist. Fighting off fear rushes, he had phoned Hollywood and had asked to speak to Roger Corman, the legendary producer and director. Corman was reputed to be the richest producer in Hollywood, an unrivalled spotter of talent, the man who'd given Jack Nicholson his chance, and Peter Fonda and Martin Scorsese as well. The saint of the New Hollywood, he filled every tank town drive-in on the continent and he was still the darling of those European intellectuals who compare him to Poe and Blake.

The winter of 1974 had been a lean time for feature film in Canada. It was tough to get any film made unless you had distribution in the United States. Corman had read a Cronenberg script called *Shivers* and he had liked it. The script had at first been called *Orgy of the Blood Parasites*. It was a strongly original take on the horror genre. Cronenberg succeeded in getting Corman's secretary on the line. He told her that he was coming out to Los Angeles. Would he be able to see the great man and talk to him about distribution?

"Sure," said the secretary. "Come on out. Roger would love to talk to you. Why, you can talk forever."

I had been working in television. Cronenberg invited me along but I was in a state of dread. This was my first time to California and I imagined the worst: American abrasiveness, urban gore under a setting of palm trees, lost angels in a city of spiritual maniacs. *California: Tomorrowland Facing the Future*.

In our media age, we think we know a great deal about a place without having been there. We have other people's images, stored in the memory. When the topic comes up we can talk about it with apparent knowledge and conviction, but in point of fact we don't know a thing about the reality. I did know this: I was obsessive about film and Hollywood was the vortex. I was curious to know how a real film industry worked, how it was really done. We had introductions from a film editor who had worked with Corman. As Cronenberg saw it, the trip could turn out either of two ways: the boys from Toronto could descend from the north to conquer or they would be handed their hats by a famously mean town.

As advertised, the first Southern California fact is the automobile. The second is the luxury automobile. Los Angeles is a wealthy city. There were a vast number of Alfas, Jags, Dino

Ferraris. And there were plenty of resuscitated vintage cars – '40 Cadillac LaSalle Coupes, '56 Thunderbirds with Landau tops, '51 canary-yellow Jaguars. I had understood that it was a prime law of life in Hollywood that everyone had to be beautiful but I didn't know it also applied to cars. Coming in from the airport, we saw a scruffy dude having his dishevelled, rusted-out car pushed down the street. Normal street scene, some poor guy having his car pushed out of the way – except in Hollywood, the car was an Alfa Romeo.

Of course, there wasn't much of a public transportation system in Los Angeles. The auto manufacturers had made certain of that decades ago. But was it an accident that all the benches at the bus stops were provided by a funeral home? Or did the users of mass transit just die of exhaustion or old age while waiting for a bus? If you didn't drive in L.A., you didn't exist, so we rented a 1974 candy-apple red Mustang. Perfection! The all-American car!

Cronenberg driving, me navigating, we gingerly entered the city of Los Angeles. What happened next was disaster; the one that usually befalls those dumb enough to rely on friends to put them up without phoning ahead first. You call from that strange booth in the strange city, flipping through all those scribbled names and addresses, and you come up empty. It had happened before in my travels around the globe and it was always flat terrifying. The most important thing to do when you hit a new city was to establish a beachhead, a centre of operations. A new city was a mystery and a puzzle. It was one of the great pleasures of travel to delve into the mystery but it was all the more difficult if you had the sensation that you were living in the street, or in this case a red Mustang. We had driven straight from the airport to Hollywood and now we were on the corner looking for a place to stay.

All the same, our being out on the street brought back the ghost of Jack Kerouac and those 1960s road pilgrimages that everybody in my and Cronenberg's generation had to go through like they did the measles when they were kids. Any travel I had done in recent years was the sort you did on assignment, when you have a healthy expense account and all the details are taken care of by somebody's office, no worries. All you can do, after the job is done, is spend the expense money on restaurant food, and drink too much. It was more comfortable, no doubt, but it just didn't have the same buzz when you set off for Marrakech in 1968 in a '59 Volkswagen with just a few dollars in your pocket. Now, you didn't just hit the road on a whim. You only did it on a professional basis, for pay, by Boeing 707. Anything else was low hippie status. But this time, Cronenberg and I were travelling on our own dime and there was no expense account. We were depending on the good graces of friends, and the friends all had answering services and the answering services had no idea where they were. There were a few bleak hours until somebody came to our rescue. An older couple, friends of Cronenberg's pianist mother and writer father, who had moved out to California years ago to work in the movies, generously agreed to put us up in their small apartment, a mere block from the Sunset Strip.

Somebody once wrote a rock tune called "New York City, You're a Woman." In a sense, all great cities have an almost sexual fascination. When you first hit town, it's exactly like the beginning of a great love affair. You want to know everything about the lady, all her history, stories of the men who have known her. So, you want to immerse yourself in the new city, pore over maps, talk to its people, check out its energies, feel the pulse. You want to do everything, all at once.

While we were cruising around searching for a place to stay, I had noticed a hotel on a hill in Hollywood, its name painted on the side, "Chateau Marmont." I knew the same sort of underground legend had grown around the Chateau Marmont that surrounded the Chelsea Hotel in New York. Scott Fitzgerald, Lenny Bruce, Bob Dylan; plenty of the cult greats we both admired had all stayed there. The hotel was built in the style of a French chateau but, instead of the Alps, it was nestled in the Sunset Hills. It had a rundown look, but that only added to the glow. The Chateau Marmont was a fabulous remnant of the Golden Age of Hollywood in the 1940s when the town was Eden in the popular mind of America and the world. The Marmont had porticos and cloisters, and in the early evening it was dipped in a wonderful golden light. If California was the Promised Land to our film pilgrims, then this was one of the holy places.

Cronenberg's friend at the Marmont was Lorne Michaels. He was staying there and he invited us up. Michaels had previously produced a network variety show for the CBC. Now, he was in Los Angeles working for Lily Tomlin, producing television for her. Tomlin had made a national reputation in America as the dotty phone operator on *Laugh-In*. Now, she was becoming a hip comedienne, her activities followed in places like *Rolling Stone*. Hip had come to Hollywood about ten years earlier and it had conquered, at least for the time being. The rock musicians stayed at the Hyatt House, a half-block down the Strip from the Marmont. There, all the musicians' Babylonic pursuits were indulged – ruined rugs restored, smashed colour TVs replaced. House-trained freaks, marginally more civilized, television and film writers and directors stayed at the Marmont.

We were in the hotel lobby, asking about Michaels' room number. There, among the plants and the grand piano, was Maximilian Schell, the German actor. He was in Los Angeles to promote his current film. It was Cronenberg, a fan, who recognized him. Just at the moment, Schell appeared slightly harassed. Naturally, running into star performers would be a recurring note of our stay. You catch yourself halfway between a hick delight at seeing celebrities in the flesh and a desire to stay cool and unimpressed. I had to admit that, at bottom, I felt as thrilled to be in Los Angeles as a seven-year-old.

At first glance, the room in which Michaels lived looked fairly ordinary. An old hotel room like any other. It could have been one of the rooms in the old Park Plaza back home. The thrill of it was that Michaels' room was populated by presences. He told us that Dorothy Parker had lived in the room, Tony Perkins as well. Jim Morrison had gone out the window and broken an arm. Some cultural historian should agitate for a row of plaques.

Michaels had changed entirely. He was darker, there was a kind of intensity about him, and he was much thinner. "It's illegal to be fat in L.A.," he joked. He lay on the hotel room bed, chain-smoking Marlboros, talking on two telephones at once – one his number at the hotel, another private. As we talked, he took calls from friends, colleagues and, who else, his mother. "Yes, I do have time to talk to you, dear. After all, you are my mother." You could tell Michaels loved telephones, he held virtuoso conversations on them. At the same time, he went into a pyrotechnic "Canada-is-terrible" rap. It's an old song, but Michaels sang it well. For show-biz bravado, it was absolutely unmatched.

It was a scene from a Mordecai Richler novel – the one where the hometown Canadian boys come to their pal who is making it in the big time in London and listen to the wonders he has found there and to talk about that obsessive place they all come from. We were all three of us Jews, we inhabited vaguely the same worlds as Richler, we even had a friend or two in common with him, uncle figures. But this was Hollywood, not London, and we were another generation.

While Mordecai Richler had voyaged to England in the 1950s and meditated on Karl Marx's grave about the prospects those stones held out to Canadian Man, we have journeyed to California to consider the future. Los Angeles has become the city out on the edge of the future. Was there any fad or cult that showed up in Toronto that didn't have its first stirrings here? All those books, documentaries, movies were there to proclaim: the twenty-first century belongs to L.A.

"You know," said Michaels, "we thought we were going to be the first generation that was going to be able to stay home in Canada and do it. When Expo was happening and there was all that excitement. But it didn't happen. You're going to have to come down here and so will your kids."

I was going through the eight phases of jetlag, a situation not helped by a jug of California wine. As the talk went on, I sat there in that clear space beyond exhaustion where you achieve a kind of meditative clarity – just before you fall out of your chair. I was thinking about what Michaels had said. I had never before thought of enthusiasm for Canada as a relic of the 1960s along with all the other idealistic enthusiasms that had recently died. But we wanted to make feature films, and there were exactly no Canadian feature films that were being made just at the moment. The old law seemed to hold: they'll reject you at home until you go somewhere else and make something happen. Then Canadians won't be able to love you enough. I had written a film called *Partners* for the Canadian director Don Owen that had been on the brink of production at least three times. Cronenberg had been trying to get *Shivers* off the ground for a couple of years now. The purpose of his visit was, after all, securing American assurances about his project so that back home they would have the confidence to go ahead with it. So at the moment, we were both ready to talk about our disappointment with film in Canada.

The calls continued to come in, the talk went on, and the room began to fill up with people. Roz Michaels, Lorne's wife, with her zaftig good looks, had arrived. And Moses Znaimer, head of CITY-TV, came in. Znaimer had Brando features in miniature. He was our own homegrown whiz-kid media tycoon. Roz Michaels was doing "a five-day intensive" at Arica, a California-style spiritual organization. She had been through just about every movement of that type there was to be found. So she just had to come to Los Angeles. The place was a spiritual candy store. It was the dot in the centre. But all her friends kept warning her again and again: Rosie, don't get involved in a cult. It was the standard vision of California: Charles Manson heart-snatching cults, suntanned, baby-eating zombies. It's a happy surprise when the story turns out altogether different. Znaimer was down from Toronto buying television programming but I had a suspicion that he just wanted to have a good look around. Once you have a taste of California, if you're in the media business, the question is always there to haunt: Should I come down here for good?

Michaels was discussing the geography of Los Angeles. He pointed vaguely south and east. "Downtown's that way, man. But forget it, nobody's been there for twenty years."

He reminded us of that other world out there, the Los Angeles that had nothing to do with showbiz, Orange County chock-full of right-wing white-collar workers, people who worked in defence factories, East L.A. with its Chicanos, Watts, the world-famous ghetto that burned during those hot 1960s summers.

Outside, it was a Mediterranean night and I was reminded of other nights in Mexico. It was the beginning of spring and the cypresses were a dark green, the overhanging hills full of perfume. The hills would turn a hazy brown in the summer but now they were a dusty gold. We drove to Dan Tana's restaurant on Santa Monica. It was the kind of place you saw Cher, squired by David Geffen. It was the sort of restaurant that had a gone excitement; that sort of place a picky celebrity could get spinach salad at three a.m. People who did a lot of night-crawling came here. Moses Znaimer took a look at Dan Tana's, the heavy social scene inside, and said, "Hey, this is no snackin' around." And it wasn't. I was getting my first lessons in California manners. There were a dozen subtle degrees of casualness, each masking an equal number of states of dead-serious formality.

Once we were seated and eating, Cronenberg continued the "Toronto-is-terrible" litany. He described the bureaucratic hassles he had with the Canadian Film Development Corporation, the absurd twists of committee decision-making. Znaimer was unsympathetic. Cronenberg's bitching was spoiling his mood.

"Maybe," he told him, "they just don't want to hurt your feelings."

Znaimer had to go back to Canada. He launched into a thorough-going put-down of Cronenberg and his Quixotic idea of making feature films in Canada. They were a complete waste of time. The CFDC phoned him, Moses Znaimer, a couple of times every month, asking him to produce movies. Features in Canada? He wouldn't touch them with a ten-foot pole. Cronenberg should have become an accountant or a plumber because, in effect, he's been unemployed three years putting *Shivers* together. And what for? Ninety minutes on a screen somewhere? Forget it. But all the same, Dave was a sweet guy. "You're a sweet guy, Dave." Sweet guys finished last in Znaimer's league.

Next morning, it had to be Schwab's for breakfast. Tradition demanded it. But it was tradition too late. The place was nondescript: an old-fashioned drugstore with the usual lunch counter. The bacon and eggs were pretty good and a few actors still hung out there. But Schwab's was soon to disappear, one of the last of those great American drugstores of the 1930s and 1940s: drugstore cowboys, Lana Turner waiting to be discovered. Schwab's was the quintessential example of the genre.

What made Schwab's different from other meeting places were the cosmetic and grooming possibilities it offered to adolescents, actors and star directors. In other words, anybody profoundly concerned with defining themselves through appearances and illusions. David Cronenberg, for instance. For him, it was paradise. He could spend two hours in the morning cleaning and polishing himself to perfection, as if he were fine-tuning exquisite and delicate machinery. It wasn't just vanity, for him it was a deep-seated spiritual matter.

At Schwab's drugstore, the blonde clerk in the cosmetics department dug him perfectly. She was ideally helpful. Should he use baby shampoo, he wanted to know, his hair being so fine and all? Perhaps some marvelous new products had been developed in Hollywood that haven't hit the market in Canada? The blonde at Schwab's was willing to discuss these little matters all morning, if need be, until Cronenberg made his selection. She was used to guys like him. In Toronto, Cronenberg was solitary, a freak of narcissism, but at Schwab's in Hollywood he was just another paying customer.

As for Cronenberg, he had taken one look at Schwab's drugstore and fallen in love. As the week in Hollywood progressed, it was hard to keep him away from the place. Whenever there was a lull, he would say, "Let's go to Schwab's." The pull was irresistible.

Then, after making his purchases, after getting himself absolutely straight, he disappeared into one of the classic wooden telephone booths in the drugstore, the seats worn smooth over the years by shoestring agents and unemployed actors, and he began to track down Roger Corman. The guy was proving to be not quite so easy to see as his secretary had promised.

In fact, the secretary who had supposedly set up Cronenberg's meeting with Roger Corman was out job-hunting. Hmmmm. Not such a good sign. Had he been suckered by those deceptively casual Californian manners? After further telephone discussions it turned out that we would see Roger Corman's script editor and his publicity man, but not the great man himself, not yet. Tomorrow, who can tell, said the voice on the phone.

"But that's not what Sharon said . . ."

"Uh, Sharon's not here anymore. What did you say your name was?"

Call me Kafka. And I need to talk about my case.

Cronenberg decided to go down and bird dog Roger Corman, on the spot. The offices of New World Pictures were in a penthouse high above Sunset Strip. As you went up in the elevator you could see Los Angeles spread out below; hills and smog, billboards on the Strip. The rest of the decor was like the elevator, medium slick. Like the headquarters of a not-quite-first-rate men's magazine with bright red wall-to-wall broadloom. As we walked in, Cronenberg said, "Now I understand why Napoleon fainted just before he took over."

At the reception desk sat the woman who'd taken over for the secretary who was now looking for a job. Her Brooklyn accent scraped the nerves. She was torturing the mailboy. Sadistic games, disguised as organizing his work. It was the American Imperial state of mind. Nobody wants to be a mere citizen; everybody needs to be a God.

Roger Corman's publicity man turned out to be a young film enthusiast named John Davison. Davison was talking to Cronenberg because it was a freewheeling organization here and everybody did a little of everything, none of that old style pegs-in-a-slot, stick-to-your-function arrangement. Beyond an open door lay Corman's office. At the same time as he talked to Cronenberg, Davison was on the phone to Ingmar Bergman's agent about the great Swedish director's film *Cries and Whispers*. No American distributor would pick up the film until Corman did. It had turned out to be Bergman's most popular film. Davison had read Cronenberg's script and liked it. Looking over his shoulder to Corman's desk, he said, "Yes, Roger will definitely want to talk to you."

Davison talked freely about his boss. Corman was still producing low-budget exploitation films. He was using the profits to distribute European art films like Bergman's. But he wasn't directing. According to Davison, he was going to a shrink. "You see, ever since those European critics took him seriously he can't make a movie. He's paralyzed with self-consciousness and he's afraid to direct."

It was a Friday afternoon. After consultation with Corman's script reader, the word came down: Monday. Roger will see you Monday. That left us with a Hollywood weekend. We were driving along the Santa Monica Freeway in the red Mustang, the radio blaring out the Beach Boys. *Help me Rhonda, help help me Rhonda!* It was the playing out of a long cherished dream. Growing up in Toronto, you had the idea that the best place to be a teenager was in California. There was a moment, travelling along at high speed, listening to rock 'n' roll, there was a moment where it was like coming home. Your real home.

That same night, Lorne Michaels had invited us to a party at the home of the British *Vogue* correspondent in Hollywood. The address was in the Hollywood Hills and the house wasn't easy to find. The street numbers were confusing but we thought we had found the place and were just getting out of the Mustang when this beautiful redhead with porcelain skin came strutting toward us and sirens started going off all over the place in my head. Uninhibited, flamboyant, a goddess! First thing she said was, "I just saw a plane go down."

Wha?

Second thing was, "Can I go to the party with you?"

Well, I guess so.

She was an actress, Gwen Welles. Currently shooting an Altman film called *California Split*, she had appeared in *Playboy*. She couldn't find the party either and was driving her sky-blue VW convertible around like crazy, marching right up to doors and knocking on them. Of course, in the Hollywood Hills, that *knock, knock* may be a God-knows-who blood-crazed zombie coming to call but we found the party by following the music and sidled in the front door without knocking. Nobody seemed to care. Not the aging gays, the fading blondes, the regal blacks, the Vegas-style studs boogalooing manically in plum velvet. Just the slightest bit intimidating for a couple of boys off the farm of Bay and Bloor. Especially after a bracing encounter with one of Corman's writers, a grizzled, hard-bitten vet of the movie wars. A kid screenwriter was just the guy he didn't want to meet. But not to worry. After a couple of drinks, they began to look like old friends.

At that point, for me, the party shifted from the tableau of revellers to a close-up in high focus of frustration: Cronenberg talking to Tom Baker, the star of biker movies like *Angels Die Hard*. Cronenberg feels about motorcycles the same way others feel about religion. Intense. His eyes narrow. His lips go dry. He was verging on a heavy discussion about bikes. But no dice. Baker said, "Are you kidding? Are you kidding? I had to get drunk every time I even got on one of those things."

At the party Friday night we met Lorne Michael's landlady, the British actress Barbara Steele, who had been in the Fellini classic *8-1/2*, a number of Corman's movies, and about a dozen European horror films. She was tall, thin, and witchy;

the Vampira look. But a gracious lady. So, Sunday, on her invitation, we drove the Mustang out along the Pacific Coast Highway, past all the beach houses to Malibu. Brunch was being shared out on the patio of Barbara Steele's beach house.

Facing the blue horizon, eating *huevos rancheros*, drinking wine, was a young dude from New York, a writer named Ilya. I never did get his last name. Ilya had published one book of journalism and then he had taken an advance from his publisher to do a book about the Black Panthers in exile. And off he'd gone to Algeria. Instead, he told me, he came up with 800 pages, partly about the Panthers but mostly about a creature called Aqbal. The creature was a young Algerian Cyclops and Ilya's book is about his adventures. Ilya told us how he had rigged up photographs of the young Cyclops, including one with him wearing one cool lens of his shades on his one eye. The publisher rushed around with excitement and was making big plans to bring Aqbal the Cyclops to the United States. He had just got to the point where he was booking Aqbal on the Johnny Carson show when Ilya took pity on the guy and broke the news that Aqbal wasn't for real. Ilya had tricked out an Algerian kid with putty makeup and one false eye and doctored the photos. The publisher sagged. And that's when problems with Ilya's book began. How do you market a book that's partly about the Black Panthers and partly about Aqbal the imaginary Cyclops?

At any rate, Ilya now found himself in Hollywood, drumming up work. He claimed to have quite a bit lined up. His friend François was a producer working on an adaptation of

Larry McMurtry's latest novel. The number of film possibilities seemed as infinite as the waves in front of us. And there was the tar parade as you walked the beach. An ordinary woman passed us by, hardly noticeable – Doris Day. An effete-looking guy in a bathing suit – head of ABC programming.

Out at Malibu you began to notice the climate working its spell on you. You slowed down, you began to feel your body in a new kind of way. Ambling along the beach you could foresee a state of metabolism where bodily well-being reigned supreme and that nervous part of yourself, the part with the busy head, would atrophy and drop off altogether. One was on the way to becoming . . . cooled out. But Southern California was the land of extremes and if Malibu was a little breeze from heaven, we were very soon to feel a gust of the hot breath of hell.

That evening we were driving through Westwood Village when I spotted a patrol car beside us on the road. I studied the cops for a few seconds. I was curious about the notorious L.A.P.D. I was very shortly going to find out more about them than I would ever want to know. When the two cops in the black-and-white patrol car returned my look with a hard, ugly stare, I glanced away quickly, a bad mistake.

Suspicious.

I was acting suspicious.

Right away the cops were motioning us over to the side of the road. The one drawback with candy-red Mustangs is their high visibility factor. I told myself, *Take it easy, we don't have any drugs, we're innocent.* But, I have this automatic response to police, customs men, anybody in uniform. Whatever it is they're looking to find, I've got. Whoever they're looking to catch, I'm him.

No matter how innocent, I'm guilty.

The two cops were a wonder. Big and muscle bound, they wore khaki uniforms with military-style plastic nameplates on their shirts. Jablonski and Brenner. A couple of snout-face meat-yards. The first cop came up to the driver's side of the Mustang.

"Open your mouth," he said to Cronenberg.

"Open my mouth?"

Cronenberg open his mouth slightly, as if he were at the dentist. Jablonski shone his flashlight in.

"There's nothing there," he said.

His tone was aggrieved. Jablonski sounded surprised. He had been absolutely sure he was going to find a drug stash. These guys lived to find a stray joint. They loved power, orders, punishment. Some other day they might have been in luck but at this time and place they were out of luck. At any rate, they forced us out of the car and made us spread against it. The traffic passed by and all the nice people were watching L.A's finest nail a couple of degenerate drug dealers.

Well, I guess we did have long hair. That alone made us a couple of criminals in their eyes. I was thinking, *Hey, somebody should take a picture, suitable for framing.* And here I am being frisked in L.A.

I was alternating between amusement and panic, waiting for the planted package and the disaster that would follow. Jablonski and Brenner were smooth, practiced, and extremely thorough. All the time they were looking for the drugs they kept up a line of patter that was painfully polite but clearly scripted and rehearsed.

"You don't have any weapons on you?"

"No."

"Guns, knives?"

"Nothing like that."

"You sure you don't have any weapons?"

They were certain we were bad guys. We asked them what it was all about.

"Wait a minute," they said. "We'll tell you in a minute."

While they checked my breast pocket, they put a hand on my chest, to check out my heart rate. Naturally, my heart was whacking away like a jackhammer, I was so sure they were going to plant drugs on us. Jablonski made a heartbeat motion, thinking I couldn't see, to his partner. Then they searched the car even harder. See, the guy's nervous and if he's nervous, he must be guilty. So they pressed onward, looking for track marks on arms and legs. They pulled apart cigarette packages.

"What's it all about?"

"Tell you in a minute."

Finally, after searching every last nook and cranny of our bodies, belongings, and car, they gave up.

"There's no reason to think these gentlemen are anything but what they say they are," said Brenner. He had been sure he had a couple of real bad guys. Armed smack peddlers, at least.

"Okay," said Cronenberg, "what was this all about?"

"Well," said Jablonski, weakly. "It's the massage parlors. There's a lot of guys getting ripped off."

"So?"

"Well, the black guys are doing the robbing and the white guys are selling the dope."

"What does that have to do with us?"

"I thought we were making your friend nervous here."

Right.

As the new week started, Roger Corman was having root canal work done. *"But he wants to see you."*

While we waited, we started the rounds of the studios, seeing producers. We saw a producer on the Paramount lot, saw him very easily. He owned some land in British Columbia and thought that Canadians were a bit purer than the inhabitants of Bullshit City. He invited us to a screening of his latest. As we walked through the lot to the screening, a stately blue Mercedes went past, a gnome-like figure at the wheel, Roman Polanski, a particular hero of mine. Why, a girl at the party said I looked a bit like him. (Maybe that's who Jablonski and Brenner were looking for.) In all, there was a sense here in the capital of film that making a movie was an easy, everyday act. Not a goal that had to be struggled toward for years at a time.

We got an idea of what the film *avant-garde* were doing in an unlikely place: the porn houses on Hollywood Boulevard. We saw a film on the lower half of a double bill with *The Devil & Miss Jones* that was reminiscent of the dear, dead days of the New York Underground of the 1960s. Although the main reason for making hard-core porn had to be financial, there were some fascinating aesthetic considerations at work here. Porn was freed from conventional dramatic structure by the obligation to show sexual gymnastics as frequently as possible. There's a kind of freedom in this bondage. A section of *It Happened in Hollywood* was a take-off on the Samson and Delilah story and it was as funny as any of William Burroughs' comic routines in *Naked Lunch*. What was particularly interesting was the acting. The actors in hard-core displayed an exaggerated operatic fervour that was as much a parody of sex as the more conventional sort of hamming was a parody of the emotions.

We never did see Roger Corman.

On the flight home, in the airline comfort of the DC-10, it was necessary to reflect on the seductive appeal of Los Angeles. In homage to the city, Cronenberg had bought a gloriously tawdry rainbow T-shirt that announced "L.A." in glitter. The best you could do with it was tack it up on the wall in your apartment back home, as a kind of perverse totem.

Cronenberg would return to Toronto to see his film go into production that summer. We had had our pilgrimage to the capitol of Film, our glimpse of the vortex, the dot in the centre and now would sit at home thinking, *Should I make the move for good?*

Postscript 2007

This article was published in the July 1974 issue of Saturday Night. *When* Shivers *appeared the following year, the editor, Robert Fulford, made his notorious attack in the same magazine on David Cronenberg. "You Should Know How Bad This Film Is,*

You Paid For It." Fulford was trying to destroy Cronenberg's career before it even got started. Nonetheless, the film received generally favourable reviews and became a commercial success, rare for a Canadian film. Cronenberg began to emerge as a major talent. Over the years, he made a string of famous movies such as The Fly *and* A History of Violence *that brought him fame as a world-class director. He continued to make the majority of his films in Canada but usually for American studios and with international stars. Some years later, working at the studio, I shuttled between the Paramount lot and a suite at the Chateau Marmont. The legendary ambiance failed to make up for the lack of a restaurant or room service. Subsequent trips generally meant not as much fun as that first one but mostly a lot of hard work. My early love affair with Los Angeles bloomed into a full-blown passion but I never did move there; Toronto roots proved just too deep. Roger Corman continued producing exploitation films but the critics stopped taking him so seriously. He never discovered another Scorsese. Lorne Michaels went on to produce the epochal Saturday Night Live. Moses Znaimer pioneered the era of MTV-style television around the world. Gwen Welles died too young.*

GLENN GOULD AT FORTY-FIVE

You couldn't imagine a more perfect Glenn Gould day in Toronto: a dull afternoon in November, grey and cold. It's about four o'clock at Yonge and St. Clair and corporate Machiavellis are thinking about knocking off for the day. They peer out of their high-rise windows onto St. Clair, turning sallow faces gratefully toward a meagre ray of late-afternoon sunlight. In an apartment across the street, Gould goes to the window and yanks the curtain shut, making sure that not even one ray will penetrate his private world. Glenn Gould is not fond of sunlight. When he is forced to leave his apartment during daylight hours, he wears dark glasses. In general, though, he does most of his living, like some kind of subterranean creature, at night. He often works until dawn, and when the sun comes up, stays awake just long enough to catch the headlines on television's *Today* show. Then, when most people are beginning their daytime lives, he sleeps. Now, in the late afternoon, he's getting ready to begin his own version of what a day should be. He's put on a few pounds lately. But his weight has never been a constant, fluctuating as it does with his health and mood. At forty-five, Gould is still a striking man, despite his pianist's tendency toward round shoulders. He has deep-set eyes and Slavic cheekbones; these days his hair is quite thin and he has a luxuriant pair of sideburns. The St. Clair apartment must have had a certain elegance in 1960 when he moved in, but now the furniture is the worse for wear because of his habit of putting his feet up on anything in sight. One gathers the impression that back in 1960, when he moved in, he ordered up a load of furniture on the phone, men were dispatched to move it in, and that took care of that for a lifetime. Similarly, with his clothes: Glenn Gould simply does not care about these things. When he is obliged to perform in front of cameras he puts on a suit that he could have picked up during his 1957 tour of the Soviet Union. He still wears lace-up shoes, damn decent oxfords, with ankle socks leaving a nice bit of pale flesh showing. Gould has remained a bachelor and has maintained certain donnish characteristics outside of dress. He has the visual presence of a professor of Sinology, say, or the world's foremost expert on arachnids.

Gould also maintains a private studio at the Inn on the Park hotel, on the northeast outskirts, and he knows that the recording equipment he has amassed there would do credit to most of the CBC's installations. Few know of its existence. The secret studio features such fastidious objects as a complete Studer eight-track board with twenty Dolbys lined up in front of it. He floats between his studio and the apartment in a large American car, often with his personal, low-slung piano stool, insured to the hilt, stashed in the back seat. Like the piano stool, the front seat has been thoroughly customized to his personal specifications. Gould likes to play the piano at headlong tempos and he likes to drive fast. Critics have chastised him for his tempos and traffic cops have done the same about his driving.

The television has been on since he got out of bed. The maestro watches a lot of daytime television – talk shows, soaps. Eventually, he switches off the set and goes to the piano. He's rehearsing a work by the American composer Carl Ruggles for a taping of *Musicamera*. When Gould plays, his face is transformed into a sightless mask, with the pallor one associates with trance states. The music is a typical Gould choice, a work by a composer few except the specialists know about. It's characteristic of Gould to take an obscure piece of music and reveal it to be radiant and important. He has been doing this since age twenty-two, when he went to New York and recorded his famous *Goldberg Variations* for Columbia Records and made a smash hit of what was then regarded as a relatively unknown piece of music. Bach's *Goldberg Variations* is a standard item in the catalogue now, but back then Gould's feat was tantamount to a first-time film director grabbing big box office from an adaptation of the *Eclogues* of Virgil.

Later, Gould turns away from the piano to his next favourite instrument, the telephone. Gould never answers his phone; there's a watchdog answering service keeping permanent guard. The number is, naturally, unlisted. Today, though, he has granted a rare interview, with yet another of the emissaries of public curiosity. Glenn Gould does not grant in-person interviews. There are writers in Paris, in Berlin, in London, in New York, ready to depart for Toronto at a moment's notice. They are all gently but firmly turned back by Gould before they even head for the airport. Since his retirement from the concert stage in 1964, Gould has become all but invisible, cherishing the details of his Garbo existence. But interviewers are so dull, forever asking the same questions, always trying to get a gossipy edge on his private life. Why did you give up concerts, Mr. Gould? Why do you hum on your records? He has a new recording, uncompromisingly highbrow, coming out – Hindemith's original draft of *Das Marienleben* (the life of Mary based on the cycle of poems by Rilke). Gould considers Hindemith's often-recorded later version uninspiring – and he's eager to talk about that; it's a subject to some purpose. But as to the rest, about his life in this apartment on St. Clair Avenue, and all the other chatty details, he is determined that we will never, never find out.

By the time Glenn Gould called me that evening I had given up on him. After all, I had been trying to get in touch for weeks. I knew other writers, plenty of them, who had tried for this story and had come up flat. Even Leonard Cohen, my editor told me, had, some years ago, planned a piece on Gould, even spent a day with him, then bowed out of the assignment. Many lesser souls had come up against insoluble problems. I was determined not to be denied. I remembered that the late Nicholas Tomalin, at his zenith as Britain's leading investigative reporter, was once asked on a television program what, in his opinion, was the first quality a journalist must possess. Without hesitation, he answered: "Ratlike cunning." In the course of tracking down Glenn Gould, I would be forced to lean a great deal on our magnificent rodent heritage. I knew that the direct, brutal approach was out of the question. It had been tried before and it had failed. Using all my ratlike powers of persuasion, I managed to extract Gould's address from a magazine editor who had dealt with him in the past.

I sat down and wrote Gould a serious-minded letter. I was hoping for at least a telephone call, at which time I would try to lure him out into the open. Meanwhile, I waited for Gould to answer my letter. And I waited. After a couple of weeks had gone by with no word from Gould, I prevailed upon my magazine editor friend for his telephone number and left messages with Gould's service – two a day. Still nothing. I bombarded the guy with letters. Finally, I got a response. Late on Sunday afternoon, the phone rang.

"Norman Snider, please," said a pleasant baritone voice on the end of the line. "This is Glenn Gould speaking."

Yes, Gould said, he had received my letters. He was sorry for not phoning sooner. No, he would not venture out to meet me, but he would consent to an interview. How would I like to do it right now?

"Uhhh," I stammered, "maybe you could give me a couple days to do a little . . . research? If that's possible?"

Well, Gould said, he had to go to New York. In two weeks, he'd give me a call and see what he could do. When I hung up the phone, I was jubilant. Now all I had to do was familiarize myself with four centuries, about seventy recordings, a dozen of his radio programs, and I would be ready.

Both Glenn Gould and I were first taught piano by our mothers. There the similarity ends. I sometimes think that the world can be divided into two groups: those who practise when their mothers tell them and those who don't. Those in the first category become concert pianists, newspaper editors, social workers, movie reviewers, teachers, judges and policemen; the others become doomed writers. Gould was playing Beethoven by age eight, an age that found me reluctantly at the piano with an envious ear cocked to the sound of the other kids playing ball hockey out on the street. My father had been a symphony musician when young and my mother taught piano with some conviction. It was music that had brought my parents together. As young people they had worshipped Rubinstein, Casals and Schnabel in the manner that another generation would adore the Beatles and Bob Dylan. On the weekends, amateur string quartets would play at our house. Whether I wanted it or not, I received the benefits of a musical education. For my parents and their friends, Glenn Gould was the wunderkind, the local boy made good. My mother had seen him astound the Kiwanis Festival, debut at the age of fourteen with the Toronto Symphony, then go on to establish an international reputation.

The young genius was one of the Canadian cultural heroes to emerge in the 1950s. Although the music Gould played was austere, severe, abstract "Bauhaus Bach," the Gould persona was of sufficient theatrical extravagance to please the most romantic expectations. The movies themselves, with Dirk Bogarde as Franz Liszt, could not create such a persona.

A Gould recital, according to contemporary accounts, would begin with a lean, young man loping in from the wings in an unpressed set of tails that hung about him as loosely as an overcoat. Gould would throw the audience a perfunctory bow, which they could barely detect among the nodding, bobbing anarchy of his physical movements. He would then proceed to plant himself on a low, folding chair, his long arms almost dangling to the floor. Interminable moments would go by and nothing would happen. "What's going on? Has he forgotten the music? Has the poor boy descended into catatonia?" Then Gould would leave off communing with his inner depths and lean into the piano. The thunder of a two-fisted fortissimo would have been the conventional way of cutting through the fog of mystification the audience found itself in, something out of Rachmaninoff or Tchaikovsky. But Gould was no more likely to appease convention than he would be inclined to start pumping out "Great Balls of Fire." His concerts would begin with the purest, sweetest, most chaste piece of Elizabethan pre-baroque – a Byrd pavane, or something by his favourite composer, Orlando Gibbons. Gould would conduct himself with one hand, while the other would state the theme. With both hands on the keyboard, his jaw, inches from the piano, would serve as baton; and of course, there would be his most characteristic mannerism, his signature – his sing-along mumble which would accompany each performance. Gould was simply an astonishing, dramatic performer.

At this time, I was trudging mournfully every Saturday to the old Royal Conservatory of Music, which stood at the southwest corner of College and University, to be duly instructed in the joys of the violin. Today, I can't play a note, but I do remember that building. For me, the building was classical music.

Built just before the turn of the century, it was as musty as old sheet music. As for the students, I remember short, intense, dark girls, who usually wore their black hair long, down to the waist, and walked on thick ankles – girls who wanted nothing so desperately as they wanted to be concert artists. They would practice the piano or the violin or the cello twelve hours a day, but they were not quite good enough. Then, they would practice fourteen, then sixteen hours, and presently something would snap and you wouldn't see Janet or Erica or Ellen for a while and you'd know that the shrinks had been brought in. And after too many tears they would come to accept the sad fact they would never step on the stage of Carnegie Hall like Glenn Gould, who claimed, damn it, to almost never practice.

What was even more galling, Gould regarded the whole world of the concert performer – the applause, the adulation, the travel, all the glamour, everything my fellow students desired with every fiber of their being – with enormous distaste. He had phobias about planes, about air conditioning, about drafty halls. He wore fingerless mittens and mufflers in all weather. He popped pills and seemed to subsist on a diet of Arrowroot biscuits and Poland water. Then, in 1964, Gould retired from the concert stage and the legendary, quirky persona vanished from the celebrity rolls. Gould had surgically excised the figure of romance from public view. Never had that adage about the singularity of the gifted been so apt.

I now encountered the recorded output of Glenn Gould. It was enormous. Over the span of his twenty-two years with Columbia, Gould has issued a flood of recordings, at a pace of two or three a year: an astounding total of sixty-four releases. One way or another, I amassed as many of the records as I could find and submerged myself. I would sit in front of the speakers, the volume of the sound system set at the max. It was a theory of mine, one of many, that recorded sound should approximate actual volume, that a grand piano should sound at the same level of volume that it would if it were in the room with you. As I listened, it now became clear to me that, technically, Gould could do anything he wanted. The most superficial listening would demonstrate that Gould had the clearest and warmest piano tones, an extreme delicacy of touch, and a technical articulation that was comparable to the dexterity of the greatest athletes. To me, however, this was not of primary interest. As I sat and listened, with all the massed concentration I could summon, musical dictionaries at hand, analytic works on the composers at the ready, I came to the realization that Gould possessed a unique artistic vision, a brilliant conceptual viewpoint – all in all, an incredible display of analytic clarity. In literary terms, it was as if a great critic of his generation, an F.R. Leavis or a Lionel Trilling, gifted with the speaking voice and dramatic presence of a Richard Burton, had recorded the better part of English poetry, revealing the works to be something quite other than what they are usually thought to be.

Gould, in his recording of the Mozart *Piano Sonatas No. 6* and *7*, pounded out the stabbing, jagged spikiness of the music that lurks just underneath the stately rococo elegance. Conversely, amidst the thunder and drama of a Beethoven concerto, Gould would make clear that underneath there exists a perfectly balanced classicism of structure. Gould had a restorative approach: rather than impose an interpretation from without, he chose to reveal the music as written and let it shine with its own inner light.

If there were revelations, there were also mysteries.

Over the years, the recordings with orchestra became a rarity. The bulk of the Gould catalogue consists of recordings for solo piano. His tastes are almost entirely non-Latin. He's recorded most of Bach's piano music, plenty of Beethoven and Mozart. He's chosen few French impressionists, few Russian works. Music is important to Gould more for its structural than sensory appeal. One has the sense of a mental landscape spare as an arctic waste, a profound solitude.

If American charismatic qualities can be seen in extrovert gregariousness, the style of great Canadian artists like Glenn Gould is by comparison much more introverted and isolated. I wanted to ask Gould if he saw something peculiarly Canadian in his own sense of isolation.

In the meantime, I began to talk with some of the people who knew him, who had worked with him, like Andrew Kazdin who has been Gould's producer for Columbia Records on more than forty of his releases. For six years Kazdin had come up from New York to record Gould at Eaton Auditorium.

I had a conversation on the phone with Kazdin in New York. According to Kazdin, Gould is thorough, co-operative and indefatigable. Not a difficult man to work with at all. There is, however, an inviolable, ironclad rule barring visitors. There was Gould, Kazdin, the engineer, a piano tuner, the recording equipment, the music and a very empty Eaton Auditorium.

"I think his reason for the no-visitors rule," Kazdin said, "is that even if one person is present, then, in some sense, the performance becomes a concert. If Glenn is aware that even one person is listening, I think he's so conscious of that person that he feels it will change his approach in some way."

"If that's the case," I said, "does he care if anybody listens to the records at all?"

"Oh, yes," he said. "He's very interested in the statistics. I know that he's constantly interested in the sales figures and does extensive analysis of his royalty reports when they come in twice a year. He knows what's selling in what part of the world and he'll call me to tell me that such-and-such a record was not supposed to be such a good seller but really it's doing quite well in such-and-such a place. Our opinion corporately about Gould is that anything he's interested in, he'll put himself behind, and it's bound to be interesting to his audience."

If Andrew Kazdin was forthcoming, none of the others I spoke to were particularly so. Gould keeps close track of the specks of information he discloses to friends about himself and thus is able to trace any treacherous leaks, should they pop up in print. Then, there were those people who had the reputation of being close to Gould, who, when questioned, said, yes, they talked on the phone to him for hours at a time but had only met him once or twice, to listen to some tapes. They were all acutely aware that to betray this secretive man's confidence was to forfeit his friendship and thus were exceedingly wary as to what they would disclose to a journalist.

But, bit by bit, a picture did begin to emerge. There was the story of how Gould, leaving a recording studio in New York one Christmas Eve, was wished a hearty holiday by a doorman and given a comradely whack on the back. Gould claimed this cheery gesture did terrible things to his shoulder and immediately began to explore the possibilities of suing for damages. It was obvious that he was not a man to relish close physical contact. I began to sense that the things he was hiding from public view were not that shattering – details about his health perhaps, matters that would not shock anyone nowadays but meant a lot to the man. One had the sense of a paranoid Gould being terribly concerned that he not be recognized by importunate fans, yet there being very few souls around who had any idea at all what he looked like now!

As I read his magazine articles, listened to his radio programs, audited his appearances on *Musicamera*, it became clear to me that Glenn Gould, a lifelong bachelor, conceivably did little else but work. He was the media man as Trappist monk. In addition to his recording career he had a full panoply of occupations, each of which would suffice for a full-time job for any lesser mortal. He had performed and arranged the soundtrack music for the film *Slaughterhouse Five*, based on the Kurt Vonnegut book; he had made four films about music and technology for French television, programs for German television. For a week in August, the listeners of CBC Radio were royally entertained by Gould in a new role – that of disc jockey. Naturally, he was brilliant, an accomplished, polished professional. If the CBC wanted to ensure the presence of an audience riveted to their radios every afternoon, it could do much worse than give Gould a full-time slot.

I had now finished my research. Now all I had to do was wait for Gould to call. I waited a few days – nothing. I phoned and left a message. I left more messages. Still nothing. I began to fear that Gould was backing out so I left a whole flood of messages. Then I got a call from a guy who called himself Ray Roberts but sounded a lot like Glenn Gould. He told me Gould was still in New York but would phone when he returned. I was then left wondering whether there was a man called Ray Roberts who was Gould's assistant or whether Gould, using one of the verbal disguises for which he was famous, had phoned in the form of one of his alter egos. Gould has invented for his radio programs a whole gallery of comic impersonations ranging from Theodore Slutz, a kind of fuzzed-out Brando impression, to Professor Karlheinz Heinkel. Was Ray Roberts one of these creatures or a real breathing person?

There then followed a week where I did nothing but wait for Glenn Gould to call. I turned down social invitations, passed up parties, the lot. Then, I really began to get obsessed. Gould's tastes in music were beginning to become my own. I developed a liking for the music of Richard Strauss cranked at deafening volume. One night, fixated on Gould, the house echoing with the Valkyrie strains of Strauss' *Festliches Praeludium*, the speakers thundering out the organ fanfares, I saw Adolf Hitler biting off Goering's head in a German beer hall.

It was shortly after that terrible night that I decided I could not spend my life waiting for Glenn Gould. So I accepted another assignment, a profile of Nicky Furlano, the lightweight fighter. Then something like sanity began to return. One night I was getting ready to go to bed early, since I was jogging with Furlano at six the next morning. It was then the phone rang. Glenn Gould was ready to be interviewed.

The voice on the phone is rapid, cultivated, precise, with the occasional hint of tycoon. There are remarkably few glottal hesitations, few of the "uhs" and "ahs" that mark most telephone conversations. But then Gould is a master of the instrument, a virtuoso. Most of us merely use the phone as a convenience. Gould, aware of its potential for creative expression, its use as one-on-one radio, has a commanding aural presence and his performance that night was articulate, formal, unashamedly pedantic, the sentences all perfectly grammatical. Just back of his formality, though, lurks an infectious good humour, manic laughter as dry and crackling as the rustle of crickets. Gould may have sounded solipsistic, even wildly eccentric to others. But his tone suggested that his way was the only reasonable way, the only sane way to proceed.

I attached the little black rubber microphone to the receiver and flipped on the tape machine. I asked him how he viewed his younger self, the romantic young man of the concert halls of 25 years ago.

"I can't connect with myself in the '50s," said Gould. "I think that persona was a media concoction. I never set out to have that effect. Out of sheer laziness I may not have bothered to contradict it. I don't feel guilty about it because I don't feel much responsibility for it. I can't connect with myself in the '50s if only because the kind of life one leads when trodding the boards is one that I can't even imagine now." He laughs. "In fact, I barely could imagine it then. So I connect with that particular distaste I felt for touring but with little else. It's very difficult for me to imagine how I got through those years. Somehow, I did. I really think that for all the personal discomforts that for me go into that way of life, the main objection is a moral one. I just don't think one is really ever able to concentrate on the musical object while sitting in a concert hall, and if you encourage people to do that, what you encourage them to do is to respond in a collective fashion that is anti-musical, it's anti-art in some way. Beyond that, without judging the motives of all concerned, an awful lot of people go to any public display for pretty awful reasons: somewhat in the hope that catastrophe lies just around the corner. And that's part of the moral objection I was talking about. I certainly do stand behind all the things I've said in somewhat more violent language. I'm feeling mellow tonight and not up to any abrasive quotes, but I haven't changed my feelings at all about the general – to put it in its mildest terms – unpleasantness about playing in public.

"When you retired," I said, "you made a series of pronouncements to the effect that the concert hall was well on the way to extinction. Now it seems that concerts are everywhere, flourishing as never before."

"That particular prediction of mine doesn't seem to be working out too well," Gould said. "I'm happy for those working in the concert-management field because I don't begrudge them their living. I broke Horowitz's retirement record last year, I can't go back now. Above all, it's simply a question of competing with your own recordings. Once I sensed what you could do with the electronic media, it seemed so utterly ridiculous to compete with that. And thereafter I simply lost interest in what I was doing. By the end I was just going through the motions."

It was my feeling that, since his retirement in 1964, Gould had made a profound change in the very identity of performers of serious music. I saw the difference as similar to that between the stage actor and the movie actor. A stage actor performs texts in their entirety for an audience, the movie actor does bits and pieces for the camera. The concert pianist was of necessity limited to a narrow repertoire that he could count on to satisfy the paying customer. Although he was best known for his recordings of Bach, performing exclusively for "analytic dissection by microphone" allowed him to range freely from the pre-baroque to modernists like Schoenberg and Hindemith.

Before Gould, the recording of serious music was treated in the following manner: the recording artist would tape several performances of the piece of music in question; the best take was chosen and issued. Gould would do seven or eight takes and edit and splice together from them what he considered the ideal performance. If necessary, he would record short passages or "inserts" and splice them in until he was completely satisfied. The astonishing thing, however, was that the result sounded entirely spontaneous; you had the impression that you were overhearing the man sit down at the piano at a whim, not in the studio at all, and play for his own private amusement and gratification. There was a time when it seemed that this was a technique all performers of serious music would come to use. This was standard practice in other forms of music. I asked Gould why, so far, it had remained an approach unique to himself.

"It's an issue," he said, "on which I disagree strongly with most of my colleagues. I think there's still the strange mystical notion that there is something magical about the long, self-sustaining line that once set in motion must never end. This is nonsense. The record is real to the extent that it is a collection or montage of your best thoughts at a given time in your life. It is not real by virtue of the fact that you did it in one fell swoop. Who cares? I used to think it was purely and simply a generation gap, that Sir Adrian Boult didn't think as I did because he was in his eighties. Now it seems that there's a whole new generation much younger than I who have gone back that way."

"Why have you recorded so few concertos of late? Most of the records seem to be for solo piano. Is it a problem of finding congenial conductors or is that there are economic problems in recording orchestras?"

"In recent years," Gould said, "apart from one project – which is the Bach concertos, just to say we've done it – there aren't really any concertos that I want to do because basically I don't like concertos. I don't even approve of concertos morally. I don't like the whole, competitive 'Let me decorate this phrase more elegantly than you can' aspect of the concerto. So, apart from the Beethoven concertos, which for obvious reasons interest just about everybody, and such oddities as the Schoenberg, it's perfectly true that I've recorded very few concertos. One of the reasons I've been so slow to finish the Bach thing is that I'd prefer to work with the strings of the Philharmonic or something of that sort. But I would not do any more concertos whether or not I had more frequent access to studios in New York. I think, on the whole, I've had awfully good relations with a lot of really quite remarkable conductors. There have been a couple of mistakenly publicized incidents that were supposed to have been quarrels and weren't, that sort of thing. The problem with the orchestra is economic in that, I find, over the years, I've become an awful lot more meticulous than when I started out. Things that I let go in 1960 would not find their way onto a finished tape now. Beginning in the early 1960s I started to do all my own editing and that really did make a difference; because with the orchestra, no matter how much you want to do, economically you can only have them in the studio for a limited number of hours; thereafter, you're pretty much at the end of what you've managed to put down. If you're lucky, you might get two or three basic takes, whereas for a solo session I might get nine or ten. The actual ratio of finished product per hour of studio time is just so much greater with the orchestra, but I don't find it very much fun."

I thought I'd raise the ante, turn the conversation toward more personal topics, however gently. I remembered the sense of isolation I got from his work. So I asked Gould if that impression came in any way from living in Toronto.

"I like to think," he said, "that if I had happened to live in Leningrad I'd have developed the same way. I mention Leningrad only because I happen to like that city very much; it's a very quiet and relaxing place. But as for Toronto, I don't have any particular feeling for the city because I'm not a city person at all. But I guess to the extent that one has to pick a place to live, Toronto is not as objectionable as many other cities I can think of because its cityness is less apparent and I like that very much. There are certain cities that would obviously get on my nerves. I can't imagine happily living in New York or Los Angeles, but I don't think I would be any more in contact with colleagues there than I am with colleagues here. I don't think that would change. I think I might be depressed all the time because I find cities that are acutely aware of their cityness depressing places to be. In fact, this may be looking at things through rose-coloured glasses, but my memories of Toronto in the '40s are much more pleasant than my observations of Toronto today. And I think this is because Toronto to some extent has become a self-conscious, citified scape. I can't say that it bothers me because I don't have any particular part in it. But I think if I did, it would. I think the main thing is to keep away from any collegual influence. That seems to me to be the object of the game. Keep away from anyone who wants to talk to you about the process of what you're doing, whatever it might be. Not that they do it necessarily in an antagonistic sense or a deliberately destructive sense, but I think it ends up, in point of fact, having a less than advantageous result. What I'm saying is, given my concern for that particular kind of influence, it would have been possible for me to feel quite nicely isolated in Leningrad or Wichita or whatever and probably in Los Angeles or New York too, except that I'd be depressed because I couldn't stand what I had to look at. I think your question was addressed to the fact that there is some kind of benign indifference to what you do here. Maybe so. That would be a plus as far as I'm concerned."

Gould gave up playing in Toronto four years before he gave up the concert stage entirely. Rather than be flattered, he used to look upon earnest local concertgoers with horror when they came up to him in the street.

"It really wasn't pleasant," he said. "My reluctance to give interviews in Canada at all is a direct result of those years. I now can wander into any place at all and not be recognized, which is marvellous. And that would not have been true when I was giving concerts locally. And it's not a question of blaming the Toronto scape for that: it would have happened wherever one happened to be, if one didn't have a better sense of how to control the media than I did at the time."

"Would you say then," I said, "that the artist is doomed to be a highly specialized, alienated and isolated figure, permanently cloistered from the rest of humanity?"

"I certainly find it difficult," Gould said, "to operate in any circumstance where I couldn't feel isolated. Happiness for me relates in direct proportion to the creative isolation I sense. But I don't know that that has anything to do per se with the musician or artist except that that life lends itself to being more isolated. But I certainly don't think it's a doom to which one submits."

"Are you lonely?" I asked.

The answer quick and crisp.

"No," he said, "certainly not."

"Then, I have a final question. Do you in fact have a corporeal existence? Or are you a wraith, a spirit of the wires?"

There followed that crackling phantom laugh.

"Why don't we leave that hanging in the air," said the voice on the phone, "and that's yours to decide."

A few weeks after our conversation, Glenn Gould's recording of the piano music of Jean Sibelius appeared, recorded from four different microphone ranks – "shot from four different camera angles" – as Gould put it. The music was haunting: the experimental recording technique leading the piano to sound as if it were calling from snow-capped mountain to mountain, a disembodied northern voice echoing across vast spaces in magnificent isolation.

THE NEW CLASS

Basil has a job in television, although recently he's been thinking of getting out. For the last several years, he has lived, without benefit of clergy, with Josephine. Last year they managed to scrape up a down payment for an old house off Carlton Street. They've knocked down a few interior walls and given the place a coat of white paint but further renovations are going to have to wait. Basil drives a Honda Civic and voted NDP in the last election. He watches the Leafs on Saturday night and then hangs on to watch *Saturday Night Live*. While he has no use for Punk rock, he adores Etta James and anything by Elvis Costello. The last time he was in a church was when he was a child but he is thinking of going back into analysis. Although he doesn't do cocaine anymore, since the prices got so "outrageous," he'll pay almost anything for top-drawer grass, that good Maui-Wowie, and of course, he likes nothing better than a bottle of good wine. Basil isn't all that discontent with his life; everyone who knows him finds him cheerful and co-operative. He is reliable at work and thoughtful at home. Yet, there are those who consider Basil the most baleful of oppressors, sort of the Attila *de nos jours*. More than the Soviets, more than inflation, Basil poses a threat to civilization as we know it because he is a member of the New Class.

The concept of the New Class is a bit of pseudo-sociology that has been promulgated by writers in neo-conservative publications like *The Public Interest* and *Commentary* and dutifully echoed in Canada by the Dark Ladies of Canadian conservatism, Barbara Amiel of *Macleans* and Marie-Josée Drouin of the Hudson Institute. The concept of the New Class originated with disaffected Eastern European communists like the Yugoslavian, Milovan Djilas, who asserted that, although landlords and businessmen were expropriated in the name of the workers, the chief beneficiaries of communism were those professional revolutionaries, party members, and bureaucrats who became society's new masters.

In the East European communist context this analysis seems accurate enough. But when neo-cons attempt to transpose it into a Western one it becomes flat nonsense. Sometimes they extend the pseudo-class to include anyone with a university education: academics, journalists, doctors, lawyers, teachers and social workers – what used to be known as the intelligentsia. Anyone, that is, whose position in society is a result of his or her personal expertise and knowledge, rather than a consequence of their wealth and property. Other times, it means merely those professors and journalists who write in an ideological way about the society. It has never been clear whether scientists and engineers belong to the category.

At any rate, it is the contention of the neo-cons that, like the middle class before them, the New Class has a distinct culture – an "adversary culture" – derived from modernist art and literature characterized by the affirmation of the individual against the constraints of social authority, contempt for convention, insatiable thirst for experience, experimental hedonism, and alienation from everything that constitutes the ordinary in life – the family, the neighbourhood, the routine job. Worse, through its vise-like grip on the media, the new class is contaminating the rest of society with these "new values." It is the further contention of the neo-cons that the political expression of the New Class is democratic socialism. According to this argument, the New Class votes monolithically for the NDP and PQ in Canada and Quebec, the Labour party in Great Britain, and the Democrats in the U.S. because these parties represent the direct expression of its material interests – which is to increase the public sector. That is, increases in state education, social welfare, nationalized industry mean not more benefits for the underprivileged but more jobs, prestige, influence – raw power – for the New Class.

It is clear that the concept of the New Class is a polemical device masquerading as a scientific category. According to this analysis, a doctor who works within the confines of OHIP is a member of the New Class. If he drops out and moves to Phoenix, what class does he belong to? If a Ph.D. candidate gives up hope of ever finding a job teaching Spenser and instead devotes his life to the market by writing copy for Campbell's Chunky Soup, has he ceased to belong to the New Class? Furthermore, how can the class interests of federal bureaucrats and journalists be identical when they are in fact engaged in day-by-day combat?

Nonetheless, what neo-cons gain by this fiction is the opportunity to paint themselves as the voices of brave, lonely dissent against a backdrop of monolithic opposition, daring to stand shoulder-to-shoulder with the oil companies and the banks, facing the wrath of a tyrannical intelligentsia as they courageously defend God, Motherhood, and Decency in the face of insuperable odds. It would be possible to regard all this talk of a New Class as so much amusing paranoid fantasy if it didn't have an element of danger about it.

First, there is the prospect of a return to bland conformity. Then, there's the danger of a return to the anti-intellectual atmosphere of the McCarthy-ite 1950s. If the neo-cons succeed in portraying the educated as constituting a threat to the morality of society, then the door is open to a fine host of horrors, from loyalty oaths to increased censorship to the curtailing of funds for education. The characteristic stamp of the intelligentsia in a democratic society has always been the critical analysis of public life. The variety of ethnicities and lifestyles that diverge from the conformist norm is evidence of a vigorously free society, and not, as the neo-cons would have it, of one in crisis and decline.

NO WAY, MARIE-JOSÉE

It always happens when Marie-Josée Drouin walks into a room. Heads swivel, eyes light up, paunches are sucked in – the full range of slightly comic male behaviour in the presence of a beautiful woman. All this eye-bulging and tie-straightening would come as no surprise if the lady were some showbiz heart-stopper, but what we have this day at Ryerson Polytechnical Institute is a practitioner of the dismal science – economics – and a neo-conservative one at that.

Courtesy of the Ford Motor Company, which has sponsored a series of lectures on the subject, Marie-Josée Drouin is holding forth in that leaden jargon of s-curves, depth adjustments and negative indicators that out of the mouth of a less magnetic personage could bore an audience to tears.

Nobody here, though, is taking their eyes off her. They're hanging on every neo-con breath – zero productivity growth. The influence of the New Class – as though it were revealed truth. Drouin is gorgeous in the most understated way. Dark hair drops from her head in two raven's wings that frame a sorrowing Madonna's face and full bee-stung lips. She is as slim and graceful as any Balmain model and wears grey from head to foot. Entirely cool, controlled and correct, she carries an aura around her of telephone calls to Washington, full-length mink coats and Concorde flights to Brussels. The scent that comes off her in discreet waves is the perfume of power.

Marie-Josée Drouin is a twenty-nine-year-old director of the Hudson Institute, profiled in *Chatelaine* as a career woman's dream, profiled in the *Financial Post* as a think-tank intellectual. She first came to public consciousness in a somewhat scandalous way in June, 1976, when Supply and Services Minister Jean-Pierre Goyer claimed she was his common-law wife to qualify her for an Air Canada pass for a free flight to Mexico. Later that year there were questions in the House when the opposition claimed Goyer's influence was responsible for Canadian National Railways putting $25,000 into a Hudson Institute study on the future of Canada.

In action, she is arresting, a woman with the appeal of Catherine Deneuve and the beliefs of a Milton Friedman. Recently, she was in New York City for a session of something called The Corporate Environment Program, put on by the Hudson Institute at the Harvard Club. There, at the heart of the Establishment, in the mahogany-panelled Biddle Room, row upon row of corporate honchos sit at long tables in the dim orange glow of ancient lighting fixtures to listen to the prognostications of Herman Genghis Khan. Hugely obese in a rabbinical beard, Khan rambles on in accents of a Brooklyn cab driver, with the timing of a Catskills comic, about prospects of global economic development. Futurology, these days, is old hat. As McLuhan once remarked, the future isn't what it used to be. What Kahn does now is called policy research.

He's at the dais lashing at paranoids and hysterics who doubt the unique virtue and destiny of the multinational corporation. The corporations are all there in the audience in their blue three-piece suits – Exxon, Timex, the Mitsui Trading Co., IBM, General Electric, the Banques Bruxelles Lambert and the rest – and they've all shelled out $18,000 a year to participate in the Corporate Environment Program, for the privilege of having Fat Herman, the man who coined the word megadeaths, the man who was the original of Dr. Strangelove in Stanley Kubrick's film, blow a little smoke up their pipes.

Why, one might ask, do all these gents listen so intently to Mr. Kahn? Isn't prediction just for the weirdos who believe in astrology? Well, not if you've put it all on the line, the house in Westchester or Belgravia or the Sèizieme, and your kids are in good schools, and you wear $400 suits, and it all rests on you're knowing exactly what the Corporate Environment is all about.

Kahn is asked to do an economic study for the Government of Algeria – it doesn't matter that it's socialist. He tells the Algerians they shouldn't sulk at home so much but get out in the world and meet people, such as the Japanese who are Herman's friends. And he personally escorts the top Algerians to meet the top Japanese and the two nations increase trading. So when Herman talks, the representatives of corporation land are more than willing to listen.

And what a relief to have someone who's articulate, someone with reasonable intellectual credentials, on your side. None of those radic-lib professors, none of those gimlet-eyed newspaper columnists or those pinko labour types.

Khan bathes them in reassurance: all Communist countries have huge economic problems, the Soviets are fraught with anxiety, Eye-ran is going to be stable, the Ayatollah will have the oil flowing in three months. *He knows!* With a nervous snuffling laugh, he takes on the environmentalists – the health and safety fascists who couldn't care less if you fornicate in public but won't let you burn coal. He counsels the assembled corporate gents on the odds on investing in China (no better than 3 to 1) and the best place to build a factory (Mississippi and Alabama, little unionization, low wage rates). Music to corporate ears.

Marie-Josée Drouin is listening a trifle impatiently to Mr. Kahn's talk; he's a little too rambling and repetitive for her taste. She gets up and leaves the room, finds a phone, calls Montreal and dictates a few corrections in the weekly column on economics she writes for *La Presse*.

Marie-Josée Drouin was raised in Ottawa, one of seven children. Until the age of fifteen, when she entered university, she attended a convent school in Ottawa. While at university it wasn't hard for her to avoid the manic currents of separatism and feminism and the counterculture that were coursing through colleges in those years. When she was growing up, she wanted to be a dentist. While others organized demonstrations, she organized career seminars.

For one of these seminars, she persuaded Claude Frenette, vice-president of Power Corporation and fundraiser for the Quebec Liberals, to appear. After persistent reminders, she further persuaded him to hire her as a financial analyst – at the age of twenty. From the Power Corporation, she returned to

Ottawa, where she simultaneously studied for her Master's degree in economics and worked as a special assistant to Solicitor-General Jean-Pierre Goyer. In 1973 she attended a Hudson Institute seminar and, after a two-hour talk with Kahn, was hired to work on the economic study of Algeria. After working on various Hudson projects, she was made director of Hudson, Canada.

When the day's session at the Harvard Club ends, Marie-Josée Drouin walks back to her hotel, stopping off to buy stockings at Bergdorf-Goodman. She looks wistfully at pastel anklets in lime green and iridescent orange; Mr. Kahn does not appreciate flamboyance in dress and was not amused when Marie-Josée Drouin appeared last year with her hair done in tight Afro curls.

"What colour?" asks the saleswoman.

"Neutral," replies Marie-Josée Drouin.

The next day, before the assembled corporate hosts, she talks on the economic future of Canada. Although she has written a book titled *Canada Has a Future*, full of Hudson optimism, this morning the outlook is pretty dismal. In a small voice that somehow reminds one of a television weathergirl, she informs the assembled Lords of Exxon, Bank of America et al. that economically speaking, as far as the prospects for growth are concerned, Canada is a stiff, a turkey, the sick man of North America. Quebec has the highest minimum wage in the world; next to Italy, Canada has the worst strike record; there's a reluctance to invest because of uncertain regulation policies, high taxes and too much government intervention.

What's more, those of you who are thinking of funding the opposition party will not get too much relief even if there is a change in government, she says, since the positions of the two parties are not all that different as regards capital investment. Furthermore, the demon of the limits to growth movement has yet to be exorcised. Canadians are too comfortable, too concerned with the quality of life so, realistically speaking, even if the Tories are elected, forget it, chaps. The outlook is still bleak.

After the speech, she is cornered by a Canadian journalist.

"Listen," he says, "do you really think Canadians are that hostile to business?"

"I didn't say hostile," she says. "What I tried to get across was that there was no need for them to become pro-business all of a sudden. I don't think the Conservatives could change the economic system. No matter how much people complain about unemployment insurance, the Tories wouldn't be able to do much about it, because they haven't got the public support."

"Do you really think the American public is more pro-business?"

"Well," Marie-Josée Drouin tells him, "there's less of an ideological stance in Canada that opposes government intervention. You have national railways and national airlines, things that are unthinkable in the U.S. for ideological reasons. So even though there's this so-called neo-conservative trend and the feeling that the economy has to get moving again, it's not necessarily a pro-business trend. No matter which party wins, even if it is the Conservatives, they will be limited by Canadian attitudes toward business."

There are observers who believe Marie-Josée Drouin will end up in the Cabinet one day. First, though, the Canadian mood will have to catch up to hers, the pressures of the world economy will have to force us to drop inconvenient notions of a liberal society, and we will have made the choice to opt for the Hudson Institute's vision of a boundless plutocracy.

BRAWLING FOR PEACE

I was drinking brandy squash in the officers' mess in the Wolsely Barracks in Nicosia, on the island of Cyprus, when they asked me the question. I was thinking just what a colonial sort of drink brandy squash was, like something you'd sip on the northwest frontier of India in the 19th century. But then the mess itself was straight out of Rudyard Kipling. During the time of the Ottoman Empire, the building had been the house of a high Turkish official; the ceiling fans were making a valiant but failing effort against the 100-degree heat. On the walls hung regimental paraphernalia, pictures of regimental sergeant majors of yesteryear and artists' impressions of the great battles of the 1st Battalion of the Princess Patricia's Canadian Light Infantry.

The question was asked by a young lieutenant from Montreal named Mike Morneault. Blond and tanned from his four months on the island, Morneault looked like a cross between Jack Armstrong, all-American boy, and a Nazi tank commander. "Well, Norm," he said, "are you pro-military or anti-military?"

Now there was a question. The bar was teeming with Swedish officers and Austrians who spoke English with an uncanny American accent, and huge Australian police from

UNCIVPOL. While I considered, conversation around the bar ceased. Captain L.W. Hackle smoothed his luxurious moustache and Lieutenant Vaillancourt tugged at his. They were all awaiting a reply.

Unlike previous generations, mine has had no experience of war and next to none of military life. Moreover, the attitude of the Vietnam generation toward armies of any nation is entirely negative. Our martial fantasies, as endemic to adolescence as acne, had been of the French Resistance variety, the band of partisans in the hills fighting for freedom. After a decade, however, I was becoming bored and irritated with smug and stereotyped attitudes toward the military. I now believed that Canada undervalued its soldiers and what they did for the country.

"Well," I replied diplomatically, "I like to keep an open mind." I turned to the Swedish lieutenant standing on my right. Swedes liked hockey. I said, "That Borje Salming was a hell of a defenceman, eh?" I was evading the question and everybody in the mess knew it. As subsequent events were to prove, it was just as well.

Cyprus is only 150 miles from the continent of Africa. In the summer the sun beats down with inhuman ferocity. The air is dry and scented with lemon, mimosa and olive. A faint breeze stirs the leaves of the palm trees. Unlike Canada, the island has been anything but a peaceable kingdom. Since the 14th century BC it has been colonized by Myceneans, Ionians, Phoenicians and Persians; captured by the Egyptians; annexed by the Romans; taken by the English; conquered by the Turks; then controlled by the British again before gaining its independence in 1960. Large-scale fighting first broke out between Turkish and Greek Cypriots in 1964, and it was then that the United Nations intervened. In the years since, Cyprus has welcomed troops from Sweden, Denmark, Finland, Austria and Canada – UNFCYP, the United Nations Force in Cyprus.

The notion of a UN peacekeeping force was conceived by Lester Pearson in 1956, and since then – besides NATO and NORAD commitments – peacekeeping around the world has been the most important Canadian military activity. Acting as referee was, finally, an odd occupation for fighting men and it was accompanied by a smugness on the part of Canadians who never have to face the threat of an external enemy. Canadian troops have been going to Cyprus for more than fourteen years, and some of the officers and men of the 1st PPCLI are on the island for the third or fourth time. Since the Turkish invasion of Cyprus in 1974, the 515 Canadians have operated in the capital, Nicosia, right in the middle, where the Greek and Turkish armies face each other.

The farthest point east along the eight miles of ceasefire line patrolled by the Canadians is called Omorphita. The battleground looks like a cross between the siege of the Alamo and the trench warfare of WWI. The positions are fortified by rusty oil barrels wired together and filled with sand. In the buffer zone there are boobytrapped houses surrounded by mines, the letters UN painted on the walls in blue. A brisk desert wind blows the red crescent of the Turks and the blue cross of the Greeks as the two sides peer at each other through their gunports.

Between the lines of Greeks and Turks at Omorphita is a UN observation post. It's manned 24-hours-a-day by the soldiers of A Company of the Princess Pats. It's not the Norwegians or Fijians or the Dutch or other NATO troops who do the hard task of keeping Turk and Greek from slaughtering one another but Canadian soldiers. Equipped only with rifles and radios, they stand out here eight-hours-a-day maintaining the ceasefire. Teddy Andrews is on duty this afternoon. Andrews is a taciturn Cree Indian in his twenties from Vost, Alberta. I had been out on the line with Mike Morneault and his section NCO, Sgt. Barry Blake, a grizzled veteran. Morneault nodded at Andrews and said to me, "Ask him any questions you want."

"Well," I ventured tentatively, "how do you like Cyprus?" If Blake fit the standard picture of the grizzled sergeant, I was slipping nicely into the role of the fatuous correspondent.

"To tell you the truth," said Andrews, "I don't."

"What don't you like about it?"

"It's too hot."

I tried again: "What do you do if the Turks and the Greeks start making trouble?"

"I tell them to stop."

"In what language?"

Andrews looked to his Sarge for help.

"In Turk," said Blake obligingly, "you say *dur*. In Greek you say *stomata*."

Blake went on to explain that if privates like Andrews can't stop an incident on the line, it's up to the senior non-commissioned officer on duty to step in. Most incidents are stopped at the NCO level. If not, there is usually a protest from one side or the other and the duty officer must investigate, as in any police action. The duty officer finds out who started the incident, contacts the side that made the protest, and explains who's at fault; usually it's both sides. He then asks the officer responsible to get a grip on his men.

This particular afternoon everything on the line is quiet. There are no shots in the area, no vehicle movement for Andrews to report back to the converted beauty parlour that serves as A Company headquarters at the Ledra Palace Hotel in Nicosia. The heat is keeping the two sides, except for the off sentry, inside their bunkers. At night, when it gets cooler, they tend to come out and exchange pleasantries about one another's sisters and sexual preferences. They heave rocks and point weapons. There have been 114 shooting reports since the PPCLI came to Cyprus in March, and as many as four incidents in a 24-hour period.

Blake and Morneault and I left Observation Post Omorphita and entered the old section of Nicosia, winding through the narrow streets in a white UN jeep with a blue flag flying. The surrounding houses are ancient stucco and sandstone, of a mellow ochre shade unique to the Levant. Here, too, the Turks and Greeks are separate but at extremely close quarters, only a few yards from each other. On the roof of an abandoned apartment building between the two sides is OP Maple. A Canadian soldier at the observation post had been stabbed by an unknown assailant, and the men on duty were obliged to lock themselves inside.

It was payday, and when I got to OP Maple Lieutenant Ed Vaillancourt was there with his NCO, Corporal Holst, collecting a debt. The relationship between the officers and men of the 1st PPCLI veers back and forth between the formally military and the wildly democratic. Vaillancourt, a burly, barrel-chested fellow, indicates the two soldiers on duty at the OP and says to me, "Feel free to ask these two nits, uh, people, anything you like."

Corporal Holst is wearing a tattoo that says "Never Again."

"Never again what?" I ask.

"Cyprus," he replies with sturdy wit. "Never again."

"It's his third time here," offers Vaillancourt. "He was here in '74. He's our war-torn veteran. He's seen it all."

"What happened to you in '74?" I ask.

"I don't want to get into it, y'know. Once I start, you'll never shut me up."

"I got lots of time."

"Let me tell you, I bear the scars."

"What did happen in '74?"

"Just war," Corporal Holst says. "Just boring, everyday war."

"There was a lot of blood."

"It's smelly, too. That napalm, sir, it's a bitch. Y'know the smell of burned flesh and all? If there were Greek people trapped when the Turks advanced we took them behind the Greek lines. Nothing very much, y'know. Just saved their lives."

"He's a modest hero," says Vaillancourt.

"Just an everyday superstar, sir," says Holst.

OP Maple is equipped with an escape route in case serious fighting breaks out. The Canadians carry only one magazine of ammo for their submachine guns or their .45s, and the magazine is carried in the shirt pocket of their combat fatigues so that neither Turk nor Greek will view it as a provocation. In front of OP Maple there remains the chaos of combat, all the deserted apartments with their trashed interiors, yellowing family albums, abandoned toys, kitchen utensils left in haste – poignant souvenirs of war's disruption of ordinary lives. On all sides Cyprus is strewn with reminders of recent violence. Yet the Cypriots have returned to a kind of bizarre normalcy. In the old city there are workshops that still do business, and families still live mere yards from the battle zone. Cooking smells float over the sandbagged entrenchments while the funky sounds of Santana and Pink Floyd waft out of the Canadian soldiers' cassette players at OP Maple over the ancient city.

After nightfall the air in Nicosia is heavy and thick. Bars and cafés are open until dawn, and soldiers of half-a-dozen nations swarm in the streets. Inside the walls of the old city, the whores sit on plastic chairs, towels wrapped around their legs, whispering at the passersby. Regaena Street is one of the world's great red-light districts. Because it's payday, joints like Sam's UN Bar and the Star Bar are jammed with soldiers from the Princess Pats.

Inside the Blue Beret Bar the atmosphere is as close as the air in a coffin. On the jukebox, Johnny Cash is singing about other wars and other heroes. A Swedish soldier is passed out at one table, mouth open like a beached whale. Behind the counter a huge grandmama serves the local Keo beer, guaranteed to land you with an instant case of what the Princess Pats call "Gyppo gut."

Working the bar are the whiskey dollies, guaranteed to separate a man from his money quicker than piranhas can tear flesh from bone. At the bar, at the tables, in a back booth, they sit necking with soldiers of the Princess Pats. Every so often, one of the men stirs himself, as if waking from a trance, and dashes into the street.

At the bar I ran into a gap-toothed private from the Maritimes. He was wearing the off-duty uniform of the Canadian Forces, which resembles an elevator operator's uniform. Instead of the Vietnam-style jungle boots the Canadians wear with their combat fatigues, he was wearing Hush Puppies. On his head was his blue beret, locally known as a don't-shoot-me hat. I asked what he knew about the ladies of the night out on the street. Before I could say anything he pushed forward one of his whiskey dollies. "Here you are," he said. "This little lady will take care of you."

The girl's name was Helen but then every girl on Regaena Street was called Helen. She was nineteen and dressed in some kind of wild military chic outfit open to the navel. She was all over me like a jellyfish. In another moment I was in a back booth, buying whiskeys. Another dolly suddenly perched on my knee. My money began to swirl away in a haze of cheap beer and low lust. Then a beefy red face peered into the booth. It was Corporal Singer, a driver I'd met that afternoon.

"You all right there, buddy?" Canadian soldiers look after their own.

"Well, I said, "could you pry these two bloodsuckers off me?"

Like bikers, soldiers know two kinds of women – old ladies and hogs. Singer yanked one whiskey dolly off my knee and propelled her out of the booth. I disentangled myself from Helen. Behind the counter grandmama was stashing my money into the family cash register.

I sat down with a group of Princess Pats.

"Listen," a corporal said to me, "we've got a saying here: 'Fighting for peace is like screwing for virginity.'" I reached for my notebook. Another soldier shouted drunkenly from the bar, "Don't let him write that down." He staggered across the room. My press pass was back at my hotel. Things were looking ugly until Singer vouched for me. The corporal bought me a beer. "The only reason the Turks and Greeks aren't fighting," he said, "is because we're here."

I took a final walk before turning in. Brits, Greeks, Canucks: the MPs were busy up and down Regaena Street that night. By now I was in a high, self-congratulatory mood. So far the soldiers of the Princess Pats had shown themselves to be open and cheerful and hard-bitten. Nothing could be that wrong with an army in which officers thanked enlisted men for saluting them.

Never make your mind up too soon.

A couple of days later I was talking to a man on the beach. He wore a bathing suit. The sun shone and the Mediterranean sparkled and I was holding forth in a playful sort of way about how the Canadian forces would soon be like the Swedes.

Having never seen actual combat for generations, Canadians would join the army in the same spirit one joined the forestry department or the fisheries. The man was deeply tanned and muscled, tough and wiry.

"By the way," I said, "what is it you do with PPCLI?"

"I'm the regimental sergeant major," he said with emphasis.

Inwardly, I started kicking myself as a bigmouth.

Regimental sergeant majors aren't known for a highly developed sense of humor and this guy sure didn't know when he was being put on. That evening, I was sitting in the officers' mess getting ready to go out on reconnaissance patrol when the major in charge of 'A' Company took me aside. Before I was going any further on this story, he said, he was going to have a word with me. The major's name was Jurek, and if the mess was out of Kipling, Major Jurek, an ex-Toronto Transit Commission employee, was straight out of Joseph Heller and *Catch-22.* It seems the RSM had been on the phone to the CO. They were troubled by some of the questions I'd been asking his men. They were concerned I might be getting the wrong impression. Furthermore, the major wasn't too happy that I was running around the island unsupervised. Other journalists were content to go on organized tours. And what was this about the Swedes?

I backtracked and tap danced. I became suddenly deferential, trying to ensure that my stay on Cyprus was not cut short. Inwardly, I seethed. The military mind was revealing its detestation and distrust of anything or anybody it couldn't control.

Well, Norm, are you pro-military or anti-military?

I was still seething when I went out with the boys on reconnaissance patrol. Reconnaissance is usually done in armoured personnel carriers, but the Turks were upset by the very sight of the rumbling giants so the patrol is now done in two jeeps. As we drove along the old green line – the line of UN posts set up before the 1974 invasion (known by the Turks, in a wonderful example of Orwellian doublespeak, as the Turkish Peacekeeping Expedition) – we could see soldiers of the Princess Pats happily jogging, getting in their five miles, just as if they were back home in Calgary.

This insouciance seems part of the Canadian military style. OP Lizard is a UN checkpoint between the UN protected area around the disused Nicosia airport and the Turkish side. Here, Canadians and Turks stand within five yards of one another across the road in darkness. While Turkish officers and officials mostly speak English and are civilized enough to talk to you about Jean-Paul Sartre, the average Turkish soldier is a peasant from the Anatolian plain and has roughly the sentient capacity of a tree. When we got to OP Lizard three Turks were standing across the road, their hair cut 1/16 of an inch from their scalps, German G-3 rifles slung across their chests.

The Turks are grim. They stare across at us, dead-eyed as snakes, muttering to themselves. They do not have cassette recorders or TV in the barracks or movies at night. There is still corporal punishment in the Turkish army. Sentries have been shot for falling asleep on duty. Turkish officers do not thank their men for saluting.

After the patrol, Pvt. Williams and I go for a beer in the privates' club in the Ledra Palace Hotel, once the epitome of elegance in Nicosia. Now it is ringed with sandbags and barbed wire. From its windows checkpoints of both sides are visible. This Saturday night the club was awash in broken glass. While Williams and I talk, MPs drag a drunk soldier up to his room to sleep it off. Pvt. Harley, a soldier who had totalled a Greek civilian in a brawl the night before, is about to be returned to Canada for his sins. Harley is lurching around the place, demolishing furniture, ready to rumble.

Pvt. Williams feels underappreciated by Canadians. He knocks back a beer, shoves another cassette into his ever-present recorder, and says, "I listen to the same music as any longhair hippie punk, but he thinks he can call me a pig and it's all OK." The theme was not limited to enlisted men. A couple of days earlier a young RMC graduate, Capt. Jim Penman, complained about the lack of status of the Canadian officer class compared to his British or American equivalent. "In Britain," he said, "officers are thought of in the same way as engineers or any other member of the professional class. In Canada, they think you're some kind of oddity."

In the end, I came to the conclusion that the Princess Pats, despite the occasional obtuse officer and thuggish soldier, were doing a conscientious, professional job in circumstances that were tedious at best and dangerous at worst.

Since the observation posts are manned 24-hours-a-day, the Ledra Palace is always jumping, a strange timeless sensation. The place was still perking with activity at three in the morning while I got ready to make the drive from Nicosia to the airport. Just as I reached the gate where my taxi was waiting, a group of Princess Pats came staggering back from town. One of them regarded me with a wry eye. He looked about sixteen.

"Are you that reporter?"

"Yeah."

"You're going back?"

"Yeah."

"Well, don't you give them no bullshit. You write it like it is."

I got into the cab. The driver did 80 all the way to the airport in the dark.

AD NOUVEAU MEETS ART NOUVEAU

On a grey morning, under the darkest veil of secrecy, Oscar Wilde was in a recording studio on Adelaide Street with his sidekick Andy Warhol, recording a music track for a beer commercial.

Let's try that one again.

One morning not so long ago, the creative spirits of the Divine Oscar and the Pallid Prince of Pop were hovering ectoplasmically about a crowded recording studio, curiously incarnated in the earthly forms of Gary Prouk, an advertising executive, and his associate, Andre Morkel. Together they were making a pitch for an account promoting the virtues of light beer.

Prouk does, in fact, bear a resemblance to his idol, perhaps as portrayed in the later phases of decadence. Successively a tough Polish street kid from the east end, a high-school quarterback, a Beat poet and an *enfant terrible* of New York advertising, Prouk now looks like a cross between the Roman Emperor Nero and a jolly monk. He loves to eat and drink. He is tall, heavily built, a walking admonition against the perils of living too well. There are dark circles under Prouk's eyes, his complexion is of that hothouse hue, indoor olive, his thinning hair is combed forward like some sybarite out of *I, Caligula*, and his tailoring sports a Mayfair accent-flapping vents, shooting cuffs, Turnbull & Asser stripes, and a silvery elegant tie that reminds me of merchant banking or the diplomatic corps. On Prouk's desk at Scali, McCabe, Sloves is a sign given to him by those copywriters and art directors whose work he oversees. On one side it reads "Dr. Jekyll," on the other "Mr. Hyde," a testament to his mercurial temperament. This morning, however, is a good one for Prouk. "Terrific," he keeps saying, "that's great."

Morkel, a bearded South African, even though he has a picture of Warhol in his office, far from looking languid, resembles nothing so much as the U-boat commander of stereotype imagination: crow's feet around the eyes, hair trim and greying. As for secrecy, the atmosphere is rather like a nuke base on Sakhalin Island. Prouk desires to practise his black art and sullen craft on behalf of Blue Light beer and he is putting the final touches to a proposed commercial that will hopefully knock the socks off the boys at Labatt's.

Since the different brands of beer aren't all that different in taste, advertising is a matter of life or death for the breweries. Consequently, the advertising budget for Blue Light is worth some 3.5 million, large dollars. Because there is no paranoia quite like that of a big corporation about to launch a new product, Prouk's entire enterprise is under wraps, code-named, with NASA-like inflection, "Project Gemini." There's a handwritten sign taped to the studio door that says, "Closed Session." Some guy walks into the studio and tells Prouk that the J. Walter

Thompson agency, Scali's competition for the Blue Light account, is just down the hall – recording its version. "My God," says Prouk, "the CIA and the KGB just showed up at the same Holiday Inn."

The previous night, some mad rockers were ripping it up in the studio; there is a faint, sulfurous whiff of vomit wafting up from the floor. This morning, Prouk's session is being supervised by Syd Kessler, King of the Jingles. Kessler is a big man with a bushy beard and a swelling gut. In his track suit, possessed of a rabbinical air of authority, he is behind the wheel of this particular craft. Like Kessler, many of his assistants are walking around in warm-up suits. Prouk and Morkel are keen, ironic observers of style, or its lack. They are wondering when the track meet starts.

The music being recorded this morning is for a proposed commercial that features a baseball game between Bad-News-Bears-style ballplayers hard up against a team of corporate clones: a group of gritty individualists pushed to the grim wall of life by a gang of android conformists. The amount of research, sheer introspection and applied sociology that goes into a humble beer spot is nothing short of breathtaking, given that the form itself is as ritualized and ossified as Japanese Noh theatre.

The buttons Prouk wants to push in this commercial are located inside the skulls of that age group in their 30s who remember the wild old days of their dewy youth, and now in the Big Squeeze of maturity, feel their precious sense of self to be under siege. In this TV ad, the gritty, ragtag bunch of ball-players come back from the very jaws of defeat and put the plastic men to rout. "You don't quit," goes the slogan, "and neither does your beer."

Recording a jingle resembles factory work. First of all, Kessler and a couple of keyboard players work out a synthesizer and piano riff, reminiscent of the theme from *Chariots of Fire*, replete with all the majesty suited to the introduction of a new brand of beer. Then, section by section, other musicians file in, sight-read the music, and leave: string players, white-haired and professorial, who've spent years toiling over Bach and Brahms and now derive the heart of their income from jingles; saxophone players who started out to be the new Charlie Parker; and the rhythm section, studio rockers with their 50s vintage outfits and Bahamian tax shelters. Each section files into the studio and dispassionately plays its part. "Thank you strings," Kessler roars. "Thank you and goodbye."

A new discovery of Kessler's, a young Jamaican singer named Aubrey Mann, comes in to do the vocal. Mann, eager and dapper in a mustard-yellow jacket and suede strides zippered at the ankles, has mostly sung reggae music. He's a slight, shy fellow, but when he sings, a huge, powerful black voice just explodes out of his mouth:

When something deep down . . . When everything fits
Won't let you quit . . . Here it comes
Here it comes . . . This is it
This is it . . . Labatt's Blue Light
That one special moment . . . Its taste doesn't quit

"Un-fucking believable," says Prouk.

"Deluxe," says Morkel.

There's just one problem. Mann's phrasing and diction are pure Kingston and the boys in the booth want him to articulate like Johnny Mathis.

"More *legato*," says a guy in the booth.

"How do you tell Bob Marley 'more *legato*?'" Prouk wonders.

After two more tries, Mann finally takes the islands out of his voice to their collective satisfaction.

"Bye-bye, Aubrey," Kessler says. "That was wonderful."

An announcer, Jim Morris, comes in to lay a narration track in a voice so full of gristle, so gravelly, so goddamn tough that you can barely survive its sheer masculinity. The whole production shines forth, and the morning's work is completed. Synthesizers, brass, strings, bells, chimes, and the enormous soulful power of Aubrey Mann punch through a male choir that would not shame the Red Army Chorus in a cosmic fanfare, a musical tribute to the great Celtic God of Beer.

Since the late '40s, Madison Avenue and advertising have replaced Wall Street and financial speculation as the chief villains of capitalism. In *The Hidden Persuaders* and countless other books, advertising has been portrayed as an evil force that strips free will from its victims as a harvesting machine shucks so many ears of ripe corn, forcing consumers to buy a mess of shoddy goods for which they have no conceivable need.

On the other hand, there are those commentators on the social consequences of advertising such as Erving Goffman who view it as one of the Humanities, a popular art form akin to the comic strip or the top ten tunes. Going further, the historian, Daniel Boorstin, regards mass consumption as the great democratizing force in America. For Boorstin, democracy is a set of institutions that aim to make everything available to everybody. Advertising, then, is the herald of that democracy.

Whether trumpeting angel or devil's handmaiden, Gary Prouk came into the advertising business, wanting to be the Polish Leonard Cohen. He'd been influenced strongly by his reading, not only by the Beats, but by the English and French Symbolist and Decadent poets: Baudelaire, Mallarmé, Rimbaud, Verlaine, Wilde, Swinburne, Dowson, Thompson. The whole *fin de siècle* period, its arts and artifacts, began to be an obsession. In addition, he haunted Playter's Hall at Danforth and Broadview, a dance palace that was in those days the only spot you could hear the electric city blues of Muddy Waters, Howlin' Wolf and company. He wrote his own poetry, read it at such coffee houses as the old Bohemian Embassy on St. Nicholas Street for five dollars a set, and supplemented this meagre income with shooting pool.

At any other time in the history of advertising, the ethnic roots, the coffee-house background, would have been enough to keep Prouk out of the ad biz, which, heretofore, had been a very preppie, WASPy biz. Advertising, however, is remarkable in this respect: it can take any aesthetic movement, no matter how avant-garde, smooth away the rough edges and use it to sell soda pop. As that arch promoter Allen Ginsberg realized, it is but a small jump from the Beat Generation to the Pepsi Generation.

To stay alive, Prouk got a job writing copy at MacLaren Advertising at thirty-five bucks a week. He was soon in a rented room in the old Lord Simcoe Hotel writing day and night – a brash copywriting star at the age of twenty-two. With his rapidly increasing earnings, he was cultivating his Wildean sensibilities: collecting rare glass, first editions, wine, all the paraphernalia of the dedicated young fop of the 1890s.

First in Toronto, then in New York, Prouk worked for Doyle Dane Bernbach, an international agency that was the irreverent, innovative ad firm of the times. (There was a Madison Avenue joke that went as follows: Somebody phones J. Walter Thompson and asks what time it is. "What time do you want it to be?" goes the reply. He phones up Doyle Dane Bernbach and asks the same question. "None of your fucking business" is the answer. Put it this way – what the Beatles were to pop music, William Bernbach was to advertising. Bernbach was no preppie but a Jewish guy from the Bronx. Prouk became a student of Bernbach's and years later, he still repeats his maxims the way a priest quotes Aquinas.

In the 1950s, advertising theory was dominated by the leading proponent of the hard sell, Rosser Reeves, and what he termed the Unique Selling Proposition. According to this doctrine, advertising should show a specific benefit to a customer, one that the competition does not provide. Targeted to a lowest-common-denominator audience, this advertising sought to differentiate a brand from its competitors. These were the great years of the hard-edged pitchmen who looked like Ronald Reagan (and sometimes were Ronald Reagan) hectoring the TV audience about Secret Ingredients! Whiter than White! Greater Horsepower!! Large numbers of the public cordially detested the hard sell and the USP. It was insistent, dull, insulting, and seemed in a direct line from advertising's patent medicine and magic truss days. Bernbach discovered an incredible, revolutionary concept in advertising: honesty. He advocated an objective appraisal of a client's product, its advantages and disadvantages. This became known as the Creative Revolution. Bernbach's biggest triumph, some say the advertising coup of the century, occurred when he took a small, cheap, slow, uncomfortable car designed by the Nazis called the Volkswagen and, by means of self-deprecating Jewish humour, turned it into a staple of American life. Bernbach distrusted research, believed in creativity and intuition, and brought all the full resources of film and drama into advertising. Where Rosser Reeves was content to tell the audience something again and again, Bernbach involved them in the ongoing dramatization of a product. Thus was born the soft sell.

After a couple of years in New York, Prouk came back to Toronto. Bernbach believed in copywriter and art director teams creating advertising, instead of the traditional two-step process; first the copy, then the art. Back home, with Andre Morkel, he made the series of ads for which he is best known: Cadbury's chocolate. Where the Rosser Reeves style of advertising liked to make bombastic statements about a product, Bernbach asked a question. The question Prouk considered regarding Caramilk was: "How does Cadbury get the caramel inside the Caramilk bar?"

That question, in essence, was the making of Gary Prouk. It became the basis of some of the wittiest advertising ever done in Canada. There was the TV ad in which Mona Lisa (played by a nice young Jewish girl) poses while a bearded Leonardo rambles on about how the damned caramel might possibly get inside the bar. Mona nibbles away at the delicious candy and smiles that delightful, enigmatic smile. Leonardo looks across his studio, does a double take, and bellows, "Mona – hold it. *Magnifico*!" The result, which was still on the air years later, was the first Canadian commercial elected to the international television advertising hall of fame.

Next, there was the invention of a new chocolate bar category – *thick*. At a certain point, the candy bar business was in the doldrums. Customers with a sweet tooth were getting less chocolate of an increasingly lousy quality for their money. Cadbury decided to design a new bar. The word *thick*, the research discovered, pushed some heavy buttons. To the slavering consumers of candy bars *thick* did not mean "stupid," it meant "a good eat." It denoted, believe it or not, "a good mouth feel."

Through a series of punning, Monty Pythonesque animated TV ads and billboards, *thick* began to appeal to upmarket, young adults (aka yuppies). There was Thickelangelo, Beethoven's Thicks Symphony. With *thick*, Prouk had made gooey kid stuff – candy bars – attractive to the culturati who were tuned into the fine arts the ads parodied. More important, many millions of dollars' worth of chocolate was sold. So much so that other chocolate manufacturers were compelled to put out thick bars of their own.

Gary Prouk had changed the history of candy bars in our time.

In the meantime, he had moved on from Doyle Dane Bernbach. He had been lured away by an Englishman named Richard Kelly who had worked in the advertising business in London and New York. Kelly had been hired to establish the Toronto office of Scali, McCabe, Sloves. With a recession rampaging through the economy, witty creativity alone was no longer adequate. There was less money in ad budgets. In a society suffering from terminal information overload, it became tougher and tougher to punch a message through to the public, no matter how droll.

A man named Jack Trout wrote an article for *Industrial Marketing* called "Positioning Is the Game People Play in Today's Me-Too Marketplace." Positioning became the ad game buzzword of the era. The biographer Ted Morgan, in a magazine profile of Scali, McCabe, Sloves, likened positioning to finding a seat on a crowded bus. A company took a look at the marketplace, saw what vacancy was there and built a campaign to establish its product in the vacancy. Done properly, no competitor could budge it from its seat. *Sports Illustrated* positioned itself with *Time* and *Newsweek* as a third newsmagazine and its circulation shot up. In the age of daily hair-washing, Johnson & Johnson took its baby shampoo into the adult market and turned it into a $20,000,000 business. The agency created by Sam Scali, an art director, Ed McCabe, a copywriter, and Marvin Sloves, an account executive, took positioning one large step further, in the context of the cutthroat business ambiance of the age. There were only so many seats on the bus. If you wanted one you had to pick somebody up off his and kick his ass into the traffic. Scali, McCabe believed that every client had an enemy, that it was Coke against Pepsi, Honda against General Motors, Savarin against Maxwell House.

Up in Canada, the agency's first international office got off to a poor start. Prouk, Kelly, and the third partner, Pegi Gross, were not doing so well. For the first fifteen months after they were hired, the three of them, plus a secretary, were the only employees. Their first account was a pizza franchise based in Scoudouc, New Brunswick. Soon, a sense of desperation was beginning to be felt around the fledgling agency. Then Nabob coffee entered their lives. Based in Vancouver, Nabob had hoped to revolutionize the entire coffee market across Canada with a new vacuum pack. But Nabob had not only failed to increase sales on the East Coast, it had also slipped on the West.

Prouk and Morkel devised an ad featuring an actor whose manner bore a similarity to that of suave, roguish James Coburn. In the commercial, the guy holds a metal-edged, vacuum-packed paper container of Nabob coffee which, with droll self-amusement, he uses to smash the competition – Chase & Sanborn, Blue Ribbon and Maxwell House – into a shredded mess, spewing their grounds across a table.

This was the hardest-edged comparative ad ever to appear in the country and it worked. Nabob went from 7 to 22 percent of the Ontario coffee market and 23 percent nation-wide. Prouk's agency was touted as the hot new shop. Major corporate accounts made their way to Scali. Cadbury, Ralston Purina, Thomas J. Lipton, all came over to the agency and it went from zero billings to $12,000,000 in six months. The romance of capitalism where thirty seconds of airtime and a few thoughtful words can unlock fortunes!

A few weeks after the recording session for Blue Light, Gary Prouk, looking more than ever like an easily amused emperor penguin, was showing a guest around his remarkable digs on Avenue Road, which he shares with an attractive woman named Carol. Prouk's crib is one of the more extraordinary condo apartments in the city. You get into an elevator in the building's lobby, ascend, doors slide open, and suddenly you're back at the turn of the century. It's London and the flat of Oscar Wilde at the peak of his theatrical and social success. There are Tiffany lamps (no singles-bar knockoffs but the real thing), Lalique and Quezal glass, an entire collection of lamps and glassware of the *fin de siècle*, an orgy of Art Nouveau, *chinoiserie* and incredible pieces of glass in sunset colours of blue and orange that Prouk has collected over the years. The room is filled with the characteristic flora of the period, the iris and the lily, bunched in extravagant profusion; there are miniature palm trees growing out of a large dragon-emblazoned jar. The entire flat is painted Chinese lacquer red, trimmed in black and gold. There are black screens, and a Matisse serigraph Prouk won years ago in a poker game. Off the main room is a library that houses a collection of books, letters and manuscripts many a major library has been angling after: first editions of Wilde, Thompson and Dowson; letters from Lady Wilde to her dear son; letters from Wilde's twentieth-century disciple, Evelyn Waugh, written from his club; and the framed originals of turn-of-the-century Parisian music hall ads. The effect is somewhere between a Chinese brothel and a museum.

The next day Prouk is forced to emerge from his Art Nouveau paradise and deal with the suits. Prouk is in his office at Scali, McCabe when an account supervisor pokes her head in the door. She's been slogging through a meeting with a product manager and a market researcher from a large corporation. They are balking at a research proposal the agency has submitted as background for a new batch of commercials.

"What I need," says the account supervisor to Prouk, "is for you to come in and explain things with a two-by-four."

Prouk makes his way out of his office to the boardroom. The suits, Ron and Harry, wait for Prouk there. Ron is a strangely prophetic-looking researcher with grey hair and beard. Harry, the product manager, is another transplanted Brit, a real corporate jungle fighter.

There may be those who think that the councils of corporationland are teeming with pragmatists, all fixated on the bottom line. In truth, this meeting sounds like a colloquy of metaphysicians, such is the hairsplitting taking place, all in the pseudoscientific jargon of market research. The corporation guys want to project hard, rational figures about the specific benefits of their brand. The ad guys are saying commercials aren't about statistics, they're about emotions. It's the old battle: hard sell versus soft sell.

In his younger days, Prouk may well have uttered a few well-chosen expletives and stalked from the room. These days, he doesn't have the inclination for such confrontations. Instead, he tells worldly wise parables from the great world of Madison Avenue: "Many years ago at Doyle Dane Bernbach in New York they launched a booze named Chivas Regal. Nobody will tell you why they buy Chivas Regal, but I suspect the reason they do it is because they think if they order it in a bar somebody will say, 'Hey, that guy's rich.' As far as I know, it has nothing to do with quantitative measurement and they're still using the same campaign twenty-five years later and it still works. And quite frankly, there are certain buttons that we're trying to press that you won't find in any focus group."

None of this impresses the boys from the corporation. But then, a product manager is the ultimate corporate bureaucrat. He wakes up in the morning and realizes he owes his whole life to this thing, his product. And the whole universe revolves around that. Worse, there are six other product managers in the company and only one of them is going to become a marketing manager, and if you don't do that before you're thirty, your life is over. So when ad agencies talk about changing ads or, God forbid, changing the product itself, major anxiety is aroused in middle managers.

"Listen," says the marketing man, "if you're saying you can't measure quantitatively, then all the research I've ever done doesn't make sense."

"I'll buy that," says Prouk. There's nervous laughter in the room. What the boys from the corporation are concerned about are "action standards"; that is, the little nuggets of information that trigger the consumer and make him say, "I want that."

"The thing is," says Prouk, "I'm going to have to spend a month of my life shooting commercials, so quite frankly, let's get going."

It is meetings like this one that give the ad biz the nickname "ulcer gulch." If all ad men had to deal with were nice rational people with terrific products, life would be a breeze. Instead, there's a lot of heavy juicing because ad guys have to take a lot of shit and just grin and bear it. And there is rapid change and turnover. Prouk was eventually made chairman of Scali. Harry lost his job. J. Walter Thompson got the Blue Light account. But Scali landed the rich plum of Apple, Canada, and its campaign for its home computers with the $10,000,000 ad budget.

As to the larger question of whether advertising is a force for good or evil, that admits no easy answers. As Prouk is the first to point out, the airwaves are still full of much dumb advertising. But at its witty best, advertising does amuse, providing a little colour in our democratic landscape.

Gary Prouk still stays down in the trenches, writing ads. He doesn't want to lose touch with the guts of the biz. He sits in Morkel's office under the baleful eye of St. Andy Warhol, enthusing about a new Caramilk ad. It starts off with a guy in silhouette doing a hush-hush TV interview with a couple of hard-nosed reporters.

"Let me get this straight, Mr. X," one of them says. "Are you telling us that you've solved the secret of how Cadbury gets the soft, creamy caramel inside the Caramilk bar?"

"Yes, I have," says this very mellifluous voice. When Mr. X speaks, all the lights start dimming and the water glasses start to shake. Then the bar levitates into his hand and unwraps all by itself.

"It's hard to believe," says the woman reporter.

"It's child's play," says Mr. X.

"OK, genius," says the first reporter. "Tell us."

"No," says Mr. X. "You're not ready yet."

"Why should we believe you anyway?" asks the woman, and the man adds, "No one on earth has ever been able to solve it before."

"Who said anything about earth?" replies Mr. X. Then he de-materializes, the candy bar disappears, and up comes the super which reads, "Still one of life's sweet mysteries." Then, it de-materializes too.

End of commercial.

MORLEY CALLAGHAN'S TORONTO *NOIR*

It was an electrifying time for writing. Morley Callaghan was a rising twenty-seven-year-old novelist with a Paris and New York reputation and an instinct for the provocative. He had dealt with incest (*An Autumn Penitent*), lesbianism (*No Man's Meat*), and gang warfare (*Strange Fugitive*). In 1930, he published, in New York and Toronto, his second novel, *It's Never Over*. Callaghan's darkest book, it is one of the most original of his stories, an extraordinary meditation on sexuality, on possession as an abscess of the spirit, and violence.

This bleak yet exhilarating tale demonstrates that Callaghan stands with the William Faulkner of *Sanctuary* or that "poet of the tabloid murder," James M. Cain, whose *The Postman Always Rings Twice* Callaghan's novel anticipates by more than a decade.

Callaghan, however, did not miss a tabloid career writing for *Thrilling Detective*: he is no perpetrator of sex and murder pulp fiction; the killing and execution he depicts in *It's Never Over* take place off-stage, at the beginning of the story and the sex he describes is not Faulkner's corncob rape or Cain's "jungle lust," though, in the context of the morality of the times, the candid sensuality of his characters is definitely illicit and has the gravest social consequences. Moreover, the connection he makes between sex and violence places Morley Callaghan in the company of the hard-boiled bunch that Edmund Wilson called "The Boys in the Back Room." Ring Lardner, Cain, John O'Hara, Hemingway, James T. Farrell. Like Callaghan, this crew of writers who emerged in the late 1920s and early 1930s, with one or two exceptions, came from the world of journalism. Their stories came out of combat reporting, the sports world, show biz, and the crime beat.

Newspaper reporters were the day labourers of the intellectual world and proud of it. They shared H.L. Mencken's hostility to cant, piety, and pietistic institutions. They were more than likely to be found in the back rooms of nightclubs and saloons and police stations as they explored the less polite precincts of the culture. Iconoclastic, they did not see themselves as stenographers to the established orders of society.

The novels of this school often emerged from a vanishing staple of newspaper writing, known as "the human interest story," stories fuelled by a sense of injustice, outrage at the undeserved fate suffered by an embattled individual. For Morley Callaghan, the ruggedest of individuals himself, a political liberal, and an anarchist in spirit, the individual and the individual's soul were of singular importance in God's creation.

Toronto in the 1920s. The violence of the Great War is a recent and searing memory. Fred Thompson, a high-school friend of the protagonist, John Hughes, is found guilty of murder and is hanged at the Don Jail while a sullen but not unruly crowd mills outside. Thompson, once a high-minded young man, disillusioned by the war in the trenches, had devoted himself to drink, to partying. Quick to anger, he had killed a policeman who had slugged him in a speakeasy raid, smashing him on the head with a chair.

Where a writer like Cain detailed the beginnings of a relationship that ended up in the electric chair, Callaghan depicts the ruinous moral and psychological effects the murder and subsequent execution have on Hughes, on Fred's sister Isabelle, and on his fiancée Lillian. John Hughes, an aspiring oratorio singer and something of an intellectual who reads Mencken's *American Mercury*, drops Isabelle out of cowardice and snobbery, and starts sleeping with Lillian.

(Callaghan expertly depicts this event in a fresh and quite startlingly matter-of-fact fashion. Hughes announces to Lillian that he wants to "love" her. In the parlance of the time, he means he wants to have sex. She wants to have sex, too, and immediately rents an apartment on the outskirts of the city where neither of them are known and they begin to meet there and make love. Just like that. No moral trepidation. Just the desire to be out of the public eye so that they can be who they want to be, do what they want to do.)

Isabelle, sister to the hanged man, believing herself ostracized from polite Toronto society, instead of retreating to a convent, transforms herself into an apostle of evil and turns her sexuality to destructive ends. After bedding down other men, she seeks out Hughes at his rooming house, imposes herself on him, and succeeds – as she seems to want to – in both costing him his room in a respectable house and his job as a basso soloist in a church choir. More and more Isabelle seems in the grip of the imp of the perverse. She informs Lillian of what's happened and Hughes loses her too. Isabelle and Lillian set up an informal cult of two, feeding on the memory of the dead Fred. (Callaghan implies that the relationship is also lesbian.) Believing that Isabelle is bent on destroying both himself and Lillian, Hughes loses control of himself and goes right to the brink of murder but the Toronto weather beats him to it. As her psychic wound, the obsession with the hanging of her brother, has festered, so too has she began to waste away physically, becoming more vulnerable to the natural elements. She dies of pneumonia, a kind of wintering away of the spirit, instead.

Callaghan's attitude is unflinching. "A hanging draws everybody into it," he writes. "It takes hold of some stronger than others. Some are sentimental and some are hard, but they're all crucified in their own way."

Read in a new century, *It's Never Over* – for all its focus on obsession and on the hanging spirit at the heart of the city – exudes period charm. The men wear hard derby hats and winged collars; they carry gold watches in their vest pockets. Professional baseball is played on Toronto Island. Single men room with families. Young couples canoe for enjoyment in the pure waters of Lake Ontario close to a dance hall by the Scarborough Bluffs. There aren't many automobiles: the book's characters either take the streetcar or walk. Folks don't lock their doors at night. Some local landmarks remain: Hart House, St. James Cathedral, the Bloor Viaduct. But Callaghan doesn't overdo the local colour in a breast-beating, nationalistic fashion; he just describes what the characters see around them as they move through their lives. His small city on a lake is completely specific yet somehow universal because, as Edmund Wilson writes, what the characters see is "made most effectively to merge with the uncomfortable personal relations, the insoluble emotional problems, the stifled guilt that at last takes possession in the dark lie of an insane fixation."

If Callaghan's stance is unflinching, his prose is not. In a delicately lyrical style, Callaghan distills a potent brand of nostalgic local description. In the era before malls, the characters walk through slush as it melts on the sidewalks in front of the department stores at Queen and Yonge; moonlight glints on the roofs of the garages in the East End, and a cold wind is always blowing up from the lake.

And it's more than the weather that's chilling.

Toronto is a place rife with intolerance. Here is a chill composure among the people, in their eyes, the way they walk. Little Belfast, a city strained with a palpable tension between Catholic and Orange Lodge Protestants. Hypocrisy is inlaid in the climate. Errington, the Protestant landlord who throws the Catholic Hughes out of his house because of his sexual delinquency is, in a stroke of delicious irony, a dogmatic socialist, a loudmouth "progressive." His belief in a better world doesn't prevent him from making it his business to get in touch with Hughes' Protestant employers and getting him fired. Callaghan calls Errington "really a hard Puritan"; that is to say, a total piece of shit.

Oh, those Presbyterian blues.

The cruel side of social condescension is a theme that informs Callaghan's fiction from *It's Never Over* to *Such Is My Beloved, The Loved and the Lost, The Many Coloured Coat* and *A Time for Judas.* For all the expansive and outward feel of his work, *It's Never Over* is totally in tune with Northrop Frye who wrote that Canada is a garrison society; that is, the local gentry are forever looking for a reason to throw the unworthy out of the fort and into the cold. It's a concern Callaghan shares with that other "Irish" writer, John O'Hara. His garrison stories of social disgrace were set amongst the country club cliques of small-town Pennsylvania. Callaghan wrote of the humiliations of the aspiring middle class of Toronto and English-speaking Montreal. Though both novelists' characters are more at risk of social or financial ruin than of violent death, death is likely to follow on the heels of social rejection. In O'Hara's novel, *Appointment in Samarra,* the alcoholic auto-dealer Julian English is a suicide by carbon monoxide. In *It's Never Over,* Isabelle Thompson dies of pneumonia brought on by the self-neglect caused by social ostracism. It is no accident, given their minority status, that this sense of shame and social rejection is felt by Irish-Catholic writers on either side of the border.

Callaghan is never more convincing than in just these scenes of humiliation. In O'Hara, the character is likely to be thrown out of a bar; in Callaghan, he or she is liable to be thrown out of their job. But Callaghan's characters, as Max Perkins said to him in a letter, "are true, and interesting not as representatives of certain classes, but as individuals." Callaghan is by far the superior psychologist. He's better able than O'Hara to portray the dark states of mind of his outcasts as they tramp the winter streets. Callaghan approaches the great Russian, Dostoevsky, in his sense of the drama of possession, for Isabelle is possessed by and is pursuing what Jean-Paul Sartre would later describe as a phantom that is an all too real parasite, a parasite within, "like a rat within a rat" that feeds on her anguish and her weariness until it kills her.

Callaghan's originality is increased by his depiction of the way possession as parasitical social shame moves in the precise fashion of a sexually transmitted disease from the promiscuous Isabelle to John to Lillian. The trio is connected by their bodies, their very flesh in the morbid progress of possession as it traps them in the shadow of death. This is sustained insight of a very high order.

All the same, these characters caught up in such high drama are quiet sinners. John Hughes is a grown-up choirboy, so high-minded he won't stoop to singing popular songs. Rather than dump Isabelle and go on his jolly way, he is forever tied to her by guilt and shame and the ghost-like memory of her hanged brother. Hughes succumbs to her vamp-like charms protestingly, reluctantly. The sexual act that ruins his life is all over in seconds; he doesn't even enjoy himself that much. And when Hughes sleeps with Lillian, at Isabelle's behest, she keeps her fists tightly clenched throughout. In this world, even the damned are inhibited.

Nonetheless, it is just this connection that Callaghan makes between sex and death that creates exhilaration. After all, it is this emotional juncture that unleashed the dark energies of European romanticism from Laclos to Wilde. What's striking is to see the Toronto novelist portraying dangerous, fatal liaisons against the Scots Presbyterian backdrop of the 1920s.

The minor characters impress as well. Father Mason, the whiskey priest who walks Fred Thompson to the gallows would do the same for many another doomed prisoner in Callaghan's succeeding novels. In *It's Never Over*, he talks John Hughes out of murdering Isabelle. (Another novelist might have thought of bringing the story full circle by letting Hughes whack the girl and end up in the death-row cell formerly inhabited by his friend.) Paul Ross is another victim of both the war and Isabelle's charms. Abandoning his architectural studies, he travels small-town Ontario selling magazines door-to-door on the strength of his tales of the horrors of the trenches, which he has reduced to a Fuller Brush Man's sales talk. Unlike John Hughes, he can take his pleasure of Isabelle and then just keep on partying.

Callaghan doesn't moralize about such behaviour. As far as he's concerned, Fred Thompson's mortal sin resides solely in his turning his back on his belief in himself as a unique individual as a result of his experience of the mass slaughter of the war. His death and his sister's are a direct result of his abandoning his own self-respect. The only other character who proposes a similar denigration of the individual is the Communist John Hughes encounters in a seedy rooming house after he's been thrown out by the respectable Eddington. Hughes is infuriated when the guy enunciates his theory of the paramount importantance of the masses over any individual existence. One senses that Callaghan shares his rage. It is the collective opinion of respectable Toronto that has destroyed Hughes' life.

As for Callaghan's resemblances to and parallels with writers like Cain, Farrell, and O'Hara, it's possible to push too far. As a writer, he was his own man almost to the point of solipsism. His characters are far more reflective and genteel than Cain's or Farrell's, and not as grand and socially glib as O'Hara's. John Hughes is no Studs Lonigan and he is passive compared to the general run of *noir* protagonists, yet he compels our interest.

The sensibility of the novel is essentially Christian and forgiving. Not only does Callaghan not condemn Hughes and Isabelle for their sexual transgressions, he depicts them with an extraordinary compassion. For the embattled individual, Callaghan has nothing but sympathy. He is permanently on the side of the lone soul, even if the lone soul is damned and condemned by all of society. Callaghan offers Isabelle as a kind of inverted martyr; Father Mason is the only man in the city who understands this but his Church has no satisfactory response; his only recourse is drink.

In the last words of the novel, the cityscape and the emotional landscape merge in an exceptional bit of writing as Callaghan uses the Toronto climate to symbolize the final distance between his characters: *"They were at the corner where the car stopped. The wind was blowing and Lillian was holding her hat with one hand and her coat with the other. A car was coming and they went to speak, but the wind carried the words away. It was such a cold wind it was more important Lillian should not miss the car than they should go on talking."*

Callaghan's novel is a book with a relevance that is not only peculiarly contemporary but of perennial value. All ages and all generations must deal with death and tragedy, whether as a result of war or terrorism or the garden-variety disaster that visits all of us at one time or another. The sentimentality of the Victorians has been replaced by a therapeutic sentimentality that asks for "closure." Morley Callaghan's novel refutes this Wal-Mart optimism, this forlorn hope that one can "move on" from a devastating, tragic event such as a brother's hanging and emerge from it innocent once again. There are some things in life so awful that they stay with you forever. It's Callaghan's belief that the only remedy is a kind of unflinching hope that faces up honestly to despondency and even despair. Time moves on but, in the heart, the hanging is never over.

THE ANGRY JOURNEY OF TREVOR BERBICK

On Saturday evening, just days before he is to fight Larry Holmes, Trevor Berbick sits demolishing a mammoth steak in the Caffé Roma in Caesars Palace, Las Vegas, talking to some white dude wearing a grey sharkskin Italian-cut suit and looking out over the railing into the penny arcade gloom of the hotel casino. The guy wants to talk about the fight. Trevor's mind is elsewhere: he's girl watching, hunting for female company.

"Hiii-eee," he coos to a passing morsel, in the tone one ordinarily reserves for an eight-year-old of doubtful mental capacity. "Hel-loo." The morsel, a thirty-ish keno runner wearing some Vegas costume designer's idea of a Roman toga conceived of in terms of a miniskirt, high heels, an uplift bodice extravagantly filled, and a bullet-proof expression, sails on, tray in hand, as if he doesn't exist. This doesn't faze the big fighter. He watches her disappear. The muscles in his neck ripple as he turns. Berbick is enormously strong.

"Look at that, man," he says in a soft Jamaican lilt that not only puts exotic stress on the syllables of some words and does eccentric things to the vowels of others, but also bears the mark of five or so years in Halifax, Nova Scotia. "She don't want me to talk to her."

"I thought you weren't supposed to think about that sort of thing before a fight," says the dude. Conventional wisdom has decreed that fighters conduct themselves like Buddhist monks while they train for a fight.

"I was just lookin'," Berbick says. "I gotta lotta ways, different ways of doin' things. When I fought John Tate, I had a girl with me. Lotta people thought I was messin' up but it works. I'm used to bein' around a lotta women. My parents got a grocery store and bar in Jamaica, Port Antonio. Lotta women, especially on the weekend. I'm used to bein' around a lotta women."

Another casino cupcake passes by. "Hel-loo," purrs Berbick again, with the same lack of result. "Whoo," he says, between bites of steak and baked potato, "she a fashion show. You married?"

"Yeah."

"Good luck, buddy. My girlfriend, she a lawyer, she beautiful. My girlfriend, she come down here, all eyes turn. I'm not gonna get married, boy. I tell her, 'Let's keep it the way it is for awhile.' They change, boy. They bite too."

Just then, one of Larry Holmes' sparring partners, Marvin Stimson, ambles hugely by, sporting the red, white and blue warm-up suit and baseball hat with the LH monogram which the entire Holmes entourage seems to wear. Ever since Berbick has come to Las Vegas, the Holmes camp has been razzing him without mercy and Stimson is not about to let up.

"Hooo," he says, on catching sight of Berbick. "Hooo." Scary things, he implies, await Berbick at the hands of Larry Holmes.

"Hiya, Marvin," says Berbick.

"Don't eat too much, buddy," says Stimson, before he strolls on to the tables, managing in one sentence to subtly mock both Berbick's prodigious appetite and his down-east style of addressing the world at large as "buddy."

"I won't, man," replies Berbick. Then, following Stimson's departing back, he reflects, "They all wear them shirts." Instead of a track suit, Berbick looms inside a lightweight beige number, white shirt and neat tie. At twenty-nine, he has the wondering air of a country boy come to the city for the first time. This was Berbick's first fight in Las Vegas or any other big town and it was for the heavyweight championship of the world and he doesn't even have a stars-and-stripes outfit.

"I don't need that," he says, nodding at Stimson's flash tracksuit. Then, his mind wanders to the shabby treatment he feels he's getting from the Toronto media.

"I think I be gettin' better coverage by now, y'know. But I don't worry about it no more. I be doin' good without it."

"That's alright," says the guy. "Beat Holmes and the whole goddamn world has to call you champ."

"I like watchin' them girls, boy," says Berbick, in a complete non sequitur. "Hah, some of them got funny shapes." Another keno runner catches his attention on her way to the casino. "Hi," says Berbick in the same little-boy tone. "Hi." Then, he reconsiders. When he remembers, Berbick is a born-again Christian. "Oh, my Lord, I shouldn't be doin' this, today's Sunday." Then he relents: "I'm only sayin' 'hi' anyway." Suddenly, Berbick's mood veers sharply downward.

"I don't feel right," he says.

"What's wrong?" the guy asks.

"I don't like the food here," says Berbick, turning whiny and paranoid. He suspects his food may be tampered with. "I don't know what I'm eatin'. I should have my own doctor here. It's natural for me to be around a lotta women. I feel a lot better. I don't like bein' around men. Around women, I'm so relaxed, I go to sleep."

Despite Berbick's massive size, there's something spoiled and babyish about him, as if he has indeed gone through life pampered with mother love. "It's probably a state of mind," he reflects. "I'm gonna see the hotel doctor. I'll probably be fine when I run tomorrow. That's when I can tell what's goin' on."

Berbick finishes his meal and announces that he's going to get a rubdown. "I see you tomorrow, buddy," he tells the guy with the Italian tailoring. Just then, one more Las Vegas lamb chop floats by on the blood-red carpeting. "Hi-eee," says Berbick. "Hi-ee."

He turns to the guy in the Italian suit and says, "Whoo! Some of them white girls sure look fine. Las Vegas, I never forget it."

Before Trevor Berbick came along, there hadn't been any Canadian heavyweight boxers worth considering since the time George Chuvalo had taken on all the top fighters of his day – Muhammad Ali, Joe Frazier, Jerry Quarry, George Foreman – in a seeming effort to prove just how much punishment a man could take and never leave his feet. Clyde Gray had made many a gallant attempt at the welterweight championship, Nicky

Furlano had looked promising for a while, Gaetan Hart, after the death of Cleveland Denny and the battering of Ralph Racine, looked like he might be of world calibre until he ran into the jazzy virtuosity of Aaron Pryor. Nonetheless, all these fighters inhabited the lower weight divisions and all the glamour of boxing lies in the heavyweight division. Occasionally, Chuvalo, now an amiable, portly gent in middle age, has been lured out of retirement to dispose of such gaudily named but otherwise undistinguished canvasbacks as Pretty Boy Felstein and Earl "Cowboy" McLeay. By and large, boxing in Canada has been in the doldrums. The sport thrived in Halifax, Edmonton and Winnipeg, where local fans came out to support local fighters of modest reputation. But in Toronto and Montreal and Vancouver, the big crowds that could fill arenas will only come out for a fighter of the dimensions of a George Chuvalo or a Muhammad Ali. It is a situation that Berbick hoped to change. In moments of bravado he likes to claim that when he wins the world title, Canadian kids will drop their hockey sticks and get in the ring.

Berbick grew up in relatively comfortable circumstances in Port Antonio, a resort town, and sometimes he liked to say that he started fighting to protect himself from his older sister. In Jamaica, children grow up playing baseball without a bat, using their fist to connect, and Berbick's sister learned how to punch. She was a big girl and used to beat up guys much bigger than herself. One right hand and bang, *good night*. Berbick had to learn to defend himself. Family roughhousing aside, Berbick didn't box at all when he was growing up in Jamaica. But after a stint on a cruise ship out of Miami, he found himself working as the civilian maitre d' in a canteen at the U.S. naval station at Guantanamo Bay. Berbick had more energy than he knew what to with so he decided to work some of it off learning karate. At the relatively late age of twenty-three, he began to box, and after a few weeks in the ring he felt he could get up there and compete and win.

He entered a competition at Guantanamo. The first marine he faced, he knocked flat – and the second, and the third. Berbick said to himself, "Boy, I'm gonna make it to the Olympics." So he returned to Jamaica when they were holding trials for the Olympic boxing team and he qualified. Berbick entered the pre-Olympics, the Pan American Games, the Central American Games, won a few, lost a few, even scored some medals. In the 1976 Montreal Olympics, Berbick lost in the semifinal to a Romanian, the finalist against the great Cuban heavyweight Teofilo Stevenson. It killed his dream of winning the gold medal but since it was gone, he thought, no sense to cry about it.

So Berbick formulated a shrewd strategy. He felt, given the low level of competition in Canada, it would be easier to gain a reputation there than in the United States, win the Canadian title, and then nobody could deny him a shot at a world title fight. Berbick had come to Canada in order to train for the Olympics and for a time had trained with the Canadian Olympic team in Halifax. The city was on the water, like Port

Antonio. It was small and Berbick felt at home there. At first, he was managing himself, then there were a couple of misfires. The Canadian National Amateur Boxing coach introduced him to Don Kerr, a Halifax lawyer specializing in marine law, a one-time boxer himself and a lifelong fan. Kerr agreed to manage him. Berbick quickly began knocking out an unimpressive group of Canadian heavyweights: Horst Geisler, Ron Rouselle, Chuck Findlay. There were efforts to lure the estimable George Chuvalo out of retirement to fight Berbick but either the purse wasn't big enough or Chuvalo was sufficiently prudent not to take on a fighter better than 15 years his junior.

Although Berbick eventually won the Canadian title against Earl McLeay on May 22, 1979, he did not inspire undying love across the country. First of all, he was a Jamaican who fought out of Halifax; all the star-making machinery was in Toronto. Even in Halifax, Berbick had his detractors. He had proven himself to be inconsistent. Berbick was one boxer who fought on his emotions: if he was up, he was dynamite. If he was down, he was stale soda. For instance, Bernardo Mercado, a Colombian Berbick had defeated as an amateur, knocked him out in Halifax in the first round. Rod Kerr, Don Kerr's son, when confronted with that loss, likes to say, "Oh, Trevor could have won that fight if he'd been in the mood."

Then there was a curious combination of circumstances, peculiar to the world of boxing. A match against big Leroy Caldwell, from New Orleans, was all arranged, but then had to be cancelled at the last moment because Berbick had developed a cold in his throat. Then there began to arise a nasty suspicion that his cold was a blind, that Berbick was, in fact, terrified of Caldwell and had ducked the fight. As has often happened with Berbick, this played to his advantage in a curious fashion. The promoter, Bob Arum, was looking for an unranked chump to fight the leading heavyweight contender, John Tate, in a prelim at the Duran-Leonard welterweight title bout at the Olympic Stadium in Montreal. Everybody who counted in the boxing world would be there. It was thought that Trevor Berbick might be a no-risk opponent for Tate, who at that stage in his career badly needed a win.

Here Berbick encountered the crawling mess of snakes who constitute politics in boxing.

There were two major promoters in the world of big-time boxing in the U.S., Bob Arum and the legendary Don King. Arum had his champion in the World Boxing Association, Mike Weaver, and King had his champion, Larry Holmes. Top contenders tended to belong to the stable of one promoter or the other. John Tate was a Bob Arum fighter. Suffice to say that in Montreal, after nine rounds of absorbing Tate's best punches, Berbick caught his opponent with a heavy right to the jaw. It was as if he had hit Tate with a sledgehammer. At that point, Tate decided that he had suffered enough, turned his back on Berbick and attempted to seek refuge in his corner. Berbick raced across the ring after him and hit Tate two thunderous shots to the back of his head that sent the guy down, pole-axed. Just a straight, stiff-legged, 90-degree drop and crash. While a bloody Tate was writhing in near-convulsions on the canvas, Berbick was consummating business relations with

Don King. "You and me, Trevor!" shouted King from ringside. "You and me!" And with a tune-up in Jamaica here, a rematch with Rouselle there, here was Trevor Berbick in Las Vegas, the first Canadian, albeit a naturalized one, to fight for the heavyweight championship since Chuvalo took on Ali in 1966.

During the week before the fight, the man apparently the insurmountable object in the way of Trevor Berbick's aspirations, Larry Holmes, worked out in the Caesars Palace Sports Pavilion. In times past, the heavyweight championship of the world was staged in famous stadiums that bore all the mythological resonance of Madison Square Garden. You thought of vast, roaring crowds, the Great White Way, movie stars and socialites in attendance, the very quintessence of the big time. Instead, the Caesars Palace Sports Pavilion, out beyond the hotel swimming pool and the tennis courts, looks like the North York Centennial Centre Arena. It is a tin hangar of modest size, with bleacher seats on four sides, a ring in the centre, and klieg lights everywhere. The Sports Palace Pavilion is not so much an arena as a television studio; in the modern era of boxing, television, with its vast potential audience, is where the big loot hides. American network television, for one reason or another – mostly because of the impression that Berbick wasn't going to last much past the introductions – had taken a pass in favor of HBO. Irving Ungerman, Berbick's agent, had even been unable to sell Canadian rights to CTV. In the Sports Palace Pavilion studio, there was a huge Stars and Stripes on the wall, a vast Mexican flag, but no red and white Maple Leaf to be seen anywhere. On the door of a closet-sized dressing room, there was a surprisingly small, hand-pencilled sign that stated in wavery characters, "Larry Holmes, World Champion."

Nonetheless, whenever Holmes emerged from the dressing room in trunks, T-shirt, warm-up pants and terry-cloth robe, his manner was truly regal. He moved with the soft, powerful grace of a big cat; yet his head was not at all leonine but curiously small in proportion to the rest of his body. I was reminded of a king cobra or a mighty boa constrictor. Berbick called him a pinhead. When Holmes spotted the fair-sized crowd that assembled to watch him train – all the leisure suits and Instamatics of Tourist America – Holmes acknowledged their spontaneous applause with a majestic twinkle of the eyes. He appeared to be enormously enjoying all the attention that came with the championship.

Holmes' workouts moved with the precision of a barracks-square drill and the flamboyance of a carnival sideshow. The part of emcee was played by one of Holmes' trainers, a pale, watery-eyed man in his late fifties, Bill Prezant. With mike in hand, he kept a running commentary on the proceedings. Prezant was given to carny superlatives. Every ancient in sight, even if seventy years old, was a "fine young man." Every palooka sparring partner was a "champion of tomorrow." It was a vaudeville sideshow.

Looking on were a dozen reporters and photographers, a film crew from ZDF, German television, all Nietzschean moustaches and Teutonic thoroughness, recording Holmes' every gesture, his every twitch, as background for a documentary on Don King. Every day, Holmes' routine was unvarying. He warmed up, loping around the ring, shadowboxing, hands held low, his extraordinarily long arms flicking out rights and lefts. Then, consulting with his new trainer and chief tactician, the debonair, venerable Eddie Futch, he rehearsed strategy. "How about here?" he would say to Futch, moving in from the ropes to the centre of the ring and throwing a flurry of punches. The ring had its various tactical areas and it was a likely Holmes strategy for Berbick to dominate the ropes and with the long jab circle him to the inside where Holmes would close with the poor sap and administer the *coup de grace*. In effect, he was choosing Berbick's killing ground.

After the strategy sessions, Holmes donned his yellow, red and black headgear and boxed three rounds with his sparring partners. Although Holmes is a considerable champion and a virtuoso undefeated fighter, knocking out his last eight opponents, a formidable ghost haunts him: the memory of Muhammad Ali in his prime.

Although Holmes had resoundingly defeated the aging Ali the previous fall, his debt to him was visible in every move he made. Ali was the trickster of boxing, the master of many stances, moods and styles. Both a boxer and a puncher, Holmes had formed his style out of Ali's middle period, when Muhammad had given up the dancing and the Ali Shuffle, but still forced opponents to come to him, holding them off with the jab, racking up points with his left. If Ali had his early, middle, and late periods, Holmes was the boxer as pure technician, refining his style to methodical perfection.

Although Holmes was a formidable presence in the ring, he couldn't hope to compare to Ali as a media persona. This was his tragedy. After he had put on an astounding display on the light bag, danced on the jump rope as if he were the reincarnation of Bojangles Robinson, Holmes' brother and manager, Jake, would whip out a table and a chair would be dispatched underneath the champ. Then he would begin to address the crowd. Unceasingly. Before Ali, fighters didn't talk much. After Ali, they talked forever, without having more than a mumbling word to say. Ali had a relevance to the larger world beyond boxing. Holmes' after-workout raps, delivered in an unintended parody of Ali's whispery, hypnotic cadences, were one long whine of self-pity. "Everyone tryin' to reduce me down," he complained. He went on at cruel length, about how hard he was working, how many opponents he had knocked out in a row, how he was going to knock Berbick out but how everybody would forget him as soon as he lost the championship. It was an entire therapy session of protest, barely redeemed by humour. There were the homilies about motivation, determination and the setting of goals. His sparring partners and the tourists laughed at Holmes' jokes. The media remained resolutely unimpressed. "I hope I'm not boring you," he told them, just before launching into another ten minutes of speechifying, oppressive in the desert heat.

If the current era is the great television age of boxing, Holmes demonstrated his utter lack of flair for the medium on

Wednesday afternoon. After the workout, he was to make a commercial for a local black adoption agency. Holmes tried take after take, pathetically unable to remember his lines. It began to look as if he'd be there until midnight, unable to do one usable take. Then Don King stepped in. King, with his fright-wig hairdo, his prison record, his gold watch, his Cohiba cigar, his fustian rhetoric, his air of being the first black W.C. Fields, is nothing if not a showman. King removed the script from Holmes' hands as if it were a contract from Bob Arum. "Forget about that," he boomed. "Tell them how you feel, use your own words." Soon, the commercial was finished. "I don't know why they try to deal around me," muttered King.

Larry Holmes is not a media performer. He is a very good fighter. "I don't predict rounds," he told a reporter one day in his dressing room. "I don't make no statements about politics. I don't make up rhymes. I cain't do that. All I do is knock people out." During Ali's time, the heavyweight championship had taken on a new symbolic importance. It had reverted to a trivial athletic distinction.

The workouts of Trevor Berbick were a very different affair. The tourists had vanished; most of the press had gone, except for a sprinkling of Canadians. There were no documentary crews, nobody filming commercials, there was no ringside barker. The girlfriends of Berbick's sparring partners sat in the bleachers, his trainer and manager worked his corner, and Berbick conducted a small series of wars inside the ring. He would chase his two sparring partners, Jesse Prieto and Charlie Singleton, a Latino and a black American, across the ring, catch them on the ropes and just whale away. "C'mon, c'mon," he would say, gesturing with his gloves as if they were in a street fight instead of a professional training session. Holmes is a buddy to the men he has trained with. Berbick tends to go through sparring partners. He has broken the ribs of one fighter and now there are some hard feelings developing between him and Charlie Singleton, a fast, skinny light heavyweight. Once, as Berbick caught Singleton and started mauling him with mighty, crushing blows, causing the ring ropes to vibrate madly, Singleton mumbled bitterly to him, "I ain't the one you got to worry about, sucker." To Holmes, Berbick looked slow and awkward, raw and untutored. Just a slugger.

Lee Black, Berbick's trainer, has worked hard to correct some of the fighter's flaws; he had worked on some of the fighter's problems with his balance. And Berbick can take a punch. The wise guys at ringside are not impressed. Berbick quickly loses his concentration, they say, he lurched, leaped across the ring. He can be made to lose his temper too easily. Holmes will have little trouble with him. "Christ," said one of the wits at ringside, "this is the biggest turkey Irving Ungerman ever sold."

Despite all Berbick's apparent unsophistication, his unpredictable moods, there is a solid core of a fellow who knows very well what he's about. On Tuesday morning he is in his hotel room, watching tapes of Holmes' toughest fight, his 15-round decision over Ken Norton in the spring of 1978, at the same time as he orders up . . . *a little something to eat.* A gigantic meal.

"Yeah," he says into the telephone, "can I have some blueberry pancakes? What would I get with it, mashed potatoes?

Baked? Yeah, soup, how about some French onion? What kinda fish you got? And some salad, right? And some apple juice, okay, and a pot of tea? . . . Perfect."

"That's your breakfast?" asks a hanger-on.

"That's not breakfast," says Berbick, "that's just somethin' to do. Boxin's a borin' life."

The huge meal arrives and Berbick sets it down in front of the television monitor. He swarms all over the food at the same time as he punches in unison with Ken Norton, using his fingers to rip at his fish, wiping them off carelessly on the hotel tablecloth, leaving a long, greasy stain.

"Let's see about this turkey, Larry Holmes," he says, attempting to work up some animosity towards his opponent. "I'm tired of seein' this turkey around. I'm tired of all his talkin'."

As Norton bores in effectively on Holmes with his own awkward style, Berbick grunts in approval, rooting him on. "Hmmmm-hmmmmm, uhmmmm. Don't give that long boy too much room." Then, when the camera catches Holmes glowering at Norton, Berbick says disdainfully, "Look at Larry tryin' to act bad. Look at that pinhead. I'll kick his butt. I wanna be mean. I'm gonna be mean with this guy. Catch him round the rib there. I'm gonna break somethin'." When Norton connects on Holmes with a flurry of punches, Berbick gives a high-pitched squeal of delight. "Uh-huh," he says, "uh-huh. Norton was a good fighter then. Missed a lot, but he hit him. Holmes won, but he got beat up. See, Norton got him fightin' flat foot, standin' there." As Holmes starts to take decisive control of the fight, Berbick begins to lose interest. His snack finished, Norton no longer pressing Holmes, Berbick's attention wanders. Then, suddenly without warning, he just falls asleep, like a child, wham, out cold in front of the television, coppin' *zzzs*, an elemental soul if there ever was one. Silently, discreetly, the hangers-on, the jogging partners, switch off the set and leave Trevor Berbick to his dreams.

On Wednesday, at the pre-fight press conference, Trevor is up there on the dais in the Spanish Steps restaurant with Holmes, the prelim fighters, all the trainers and managers, the Nevada commissioner of boxing, and he's still eating, just got his head down and forking it in. But Berbick is not the focus of attention here. Nor, for that matter, is Larry Holmes. It's the Don King Show. At the moment, there's an aroma of scandal around King and boxing that's so ripe it's Gorgonzola. Combined with the general shady atmosphere of Vegas, its mob links, its Teamster links, all the itinerant squads of hookers ensconced in the Caesars Palace bar and showing some leg on the strip, it makes for am ambiance so corrupt it's thrilling.

While there is nothing about it in the Las Vegas papers, according to the *San Francisco Chronicle*, the Machiavellian King, a convicted killer, is being investigated for alleged kickbacks, under-the-table payments for the fighters under his control, and for illegal contracts with his fighters. Holmes' former manager, Richie Giachetti, has quit, in favour of Jacob Holmes, the champion's brother. The rumour around Caesars Palace is that Giachetti is only a front man for King, that he crumbled under the pressure of the FBI investigation. There are also rumours that the management of Caesars Palace was unhappy with the scandal, that in order to keep their gambling license they cannot deal with an indicted figure and that the entire King-dom was in jeopardy. A boxing promoter named Harold Smith has been revealed to be, in reality, a man called Ross Fields and, more important, a con man of heroic dimensions. Whatever changes have come to boxing, it is in many respects the Damon Runyon world it has always been.

King's is by far the largest personality around. He does not seem in the least flustered. Just brazens the whole deal out. Laughing enormously, Bloody Mary in one hand, foot-long cigar in the other, he tap dances for the press. With an absolutely straight face, he assures them of his snowy innocence. "I'll be absolutely straight with you," he assures a reporter. "Everybody gets away with everything but they scrutinize my every move. Every time you see a picture of Harold Smith, you see a picture of Don King. This is totally unfair and unwarranted and this is how the media rules."

Thus disposing of his most recent scandal, King turns to the fight at hand. He introduces the fighters and managers in a style so flowery, so jammed with outrageously mixed metaphors, a style halfway between chitlin-circuit emcee and Baptist preacher, in short, a style so inflated by bluster that while you can help admire the pure bravado of it, you don't believe a word King says. It was a style that has the effect of deadly serious play.

As he introduces the prelim fighters, he's like the ringmaster of a circus, trying to urge the animals to perform. "You gonna knock him out?" he demands. "What round? You tell him what you tol' me, y'hear?" The prelim boys fail to rise to the magnitude of the occasion. Ill at ease in the limelight, they twist their hands and say things like, "Naw. I don't predict nothin'. I do my talkin' in the ring." Thus proving that they will remain prelim boys. When Trevor Berbick is introduced, he stands up in his beige suit and neat tie as if he was in church back in small-town Jamaica and says in a saccharine tone of voice, "Ladies and gentlemen, it's a privilege to be here today, to be in Las Vegas." King knows humility and sweet gratitude won't sell any tickets. "Tell 'em what you gonna do, Trevor!" he shouts, "You ain't takin' no backseat." Berbick does his meagre best to be confrontational. He turns to Holmes, who is doing is Bad Dude act, sitting sullen and silent in a blue velvet jump-suit. "Hey, Larry, you kind of down today, buddy?" he asks. "Guess you not sayin' too much today, gonna let me have the show." The sullen Bad Dude routine may convey menace on the street but it doesn't give the cameras much to work with. And I get the feeling that Berbick would actually prefer that Holmes liked him. He turns to the assembled gentlemen of the sporting press. "I guess you all interested in what the fight goin' to be. Last four or five fights, Larry have proven himself to be a great fighter. I think I'm a pretty good fighter myself. I think it's gonna be a pretty good show. Tell the people to come to see the great fight." All things considered, the pre-fight show has been judged a flop.

Disgusted by such lame stuff, a burly black reporter suddenly demands of Berbick, "You really think you gonna win this fight?" Berbick pretends to get mad: "You think a fighter get paid to lay down, something like that? A fighter train, he fight to win, doesn't he? Even if a fighter don't think he gonna win, he gonna tell you that?"

"I didn't ask you that," persists the reporter, " I asked you if you thought you were going to win."

"No," growls Holmes in a low voice. "He ain't gonna win."

"See," says Berbick, delighted. "I got him up. I know how to get him up."

"Enough of this foolishness," says the reporter, "I asked you a question. Do you think you can win?"

"I'm gonna fight to win," says Berbick.

"There's no way," says Holmes.

"I prove to you when I get in the ring. You gonna be in for a rumble, buddy."

Holmes smiles hugely.

"Look at him smile! He smile!" says Berbick. "You all be there now. It be a good show."

If Trevor Berbick has a strutting confidence in himself, there were few others in Las Vegas who share it. Although the odds against him are 50 to 1, no casino on the strip is taking bets on the bout. The best a willing gambler can do is to get 11-10 odds that both fighters will be standing after eight rounds.

On the morning of the fight, Trevor Berbick's name, along with the champion's, is on the big eight-storey neon sign in front of the casino, underneath that of Diana Ross, who is performing there. Berbick himself is sitting in his white suit and neat tie at his old stand in the Caffé Roma. Somewhere along the line he has acquired a sporty ivory cane and the beginnings of an entourage. "Hey," he tells the guy in the Italian suit, "I almost took away Sugar Ray Leonard's girlfriend last night." Just then Berbick spots Sugar Ray himself, looking smooth and self-contained, sitting with the identical lady, who is not his girlfriend but his wife. "Heyyy," says Berbick, going over to Leonard's table. "Heyyy," he tells the lady in question, "tell him what happened." Berbick crouches down at the side of Sugar Ray's table and whispers what happened. Sugar Ray does not bat an eye, does not betray any visible sign of interest.

When Berbick goes into the ring to fight that evening, he has the nervous look of the sacrificial lamb. As with the Tate fight, the talk around the casino is that he is messing up. There are stories about late-night activities at the gambling tables, stories about Berbick going out to church at three in the afternoon and stopping off on the way for a glutton's feast of Chinese food. But, as the fight starts, with every peach-coloured leisure suit, urban cowboy, platinum blonde, gambler, pimp, and lamster in attendance, Berbick starts in proving that whatever else is going to happen, he is determined to provide some entertainment.

In the first round, Berbick drops his gloves and says, "C,mon, c'mon," inviting Holmes to hit him, to brawl. Yet, when Holmes does try to take advantage of the invitation, Berbick neatly dodges with quick, clever sideways movements of his head. Berbick's slowness is deceptive; he's much quicker than is apparent. "C'mon," he insists to Holmes, "try to hit me.

C'mon out here, I ain't no Ali." Unlike most straight-ahead punchers, Berbick can move. When the opponent counter-punches, he's gone. In the next second, he's moving in.

When the bell sounds at the end of the first round, Berbick says something vile to Holmes. In return, Holmes pushes his chest with both hands and Berbick comes swarming after him in the corner, mayhem in mind. As the referee, Mills Lane, tries to get between them, Holmes falls to the canvas. Berbick's handlers rush across the ring to take him back to his corner, calm him down, and try to give the bout the semblance of a professional match.

From there, the fight takes on a pattern. Berbick bores in on Holmes in the manner of Ken Norton, staying in a crouch. Holmes scores at will with the long jab, attempting to set up Berbick for that heavy shot with his right hand. Yet, Berbick's reflexes save him from serious damage again and again. In the fourth round, toward the end, Berbick forces Holmes back into his own corner and the two fighters stand there, exchanging blows, both landing solidly. But neither goes down. Berbick keeps trying to get Holmes to brawl with him. There's little chance; Holmes is a master of self-control. As the fight wears on and Berbick shows no sign of going down, the crowd begins to move over to the underdog. "Ber-bick! Ber-bick! Ber-bick!" they chant. At the end of the seventh round, Berbick again backs Holmes into a corner and they trade heavy blows. In the tenth, Holmes comes out of his corner looking determined, like a workman who has delayed too long on a job, and proceeds to throw his entire arsenal at Berbick. But Berbick ducks, crouches, moves away, and once again weathers the storm. At the end of the round, Berbick shoots Holmes a big, friendly smile as if to say, "See, I told you I can fight." Holmes just glowers, pushes Berbick against the chest, sneering in contempt.

"You got to hand it to that Berbich," says an elderly black gentleman in the crowd, mispronouncing the fighter's name. "He's tough. He's taken everything Holmes has thought of throwing at him." In the late rounds, Holmes begins to dance heavily in the manner of Ali. Berbick's retaliatory tactic is to launch himself bodily into a clinch, as if he wanted to wrestle Holmes to the ground. While Berbick looks fresh, Holmes is beginning to tire. One way or another, to the surprise of all concerned, with his enormous stamina, Trevor Berbick is making the undefeated Larry Holmes look like an ineffective fighter. At the end of the fourteenth, Holmes throws Berbick a big wink and says, "You fightin' a hell of a fight, boy." In the end, unfortunately for Berbick, Holmes' jab has prevailed. The judges announce a unanimous decision for Holmes, 150-135, 146-139,146-140, on a 10-point must system.

In the dressing room afterward, Holmes is tired. Berbick is the strongest man he has ever fought, as well as the most awkward. "I tried to knock him out, but he refused to go." For his part, Berbick must be the happiest man ever to lose a championship fight. When he sees that Holmes is wearing an HBO boxing cap, he demands one for himself, and sets it atop his large head.

When one of the reporters tells Berbick of Holmes' comment about his awkwardness, Berbick replies, "What's awkward? Awkward is when a fighter can't hit you with his punches, he calls you awkward." Berbick's deal with Don King has guaranteed him several more fights, whatever has happened tonight. But Berbick, better than anyone, knows that these other fights might have been slow in coming had he not shown so well against Holmes.

Berbick, elated, turns to King and howls, "Another chance, Don! Give me another chance!"

"You got it, kid," King rumbles magnanimously.

"I feel young. I feel strong. I be back," says Berbick. "I want to fight more in Vegas. I belong to the universe and I deserve to be a world contender."

He leaves the pressroom, shaking hands with all comers, including the security guard, standing watch over the door.

"Thank you," he says sweetly, "thank you for having me in Las Vegas."

Later on that night in the casino, a gambler named Joe Hicks is watching Berbick make his way through the place to the post-fight party. Hicks, in his Stetson hat, his lime-green suit, two-tone lime-green patent shoes, big cigar and bluff manner, gives every impression he was about to audition for Sportin' Life in *Porgy and Bess.*

"Yeah," he says mysteriously to a couple of reporters, ready to flee Las Vegas on the red-eye. "Yeah, made $10,000 on the fight." He looks at the departing back of Trevor Berbick and shakes his head. "Done everything wrong," said Joe Hicks. "Come out right."

Postscript 2007

Never capturing the public imagination, Trevor Berbick abandoned Canada and moved to Florida. In 1982, he became the last man to fight Muhammad Ali, sending the greatest of all time into retirement. Berbick was briefly heavyweight world champion in 1986 before being obliterated in the first round by Mike Tyson. Unchecked appetites eventually got the better of Berbick. He was arrested several times before being sent to jail in 1992 for the rape of his children's babysitter. He was deported from the United States to Canada and later settled in Jamaica, where his nephew allegedly murdered him near his hometown of Port Antonio in November of 2006. He is forgotten in Canada but remembered in Jamaica as a hero.

HENRY MILLER

I remember the first time I saw a copy of *The Tropic of Cancer*. It was a Grove paperback with a blue cover that somebody's father had smuggled into the country and it glowed with that wicked light particular to the forbidden. In those long-ago days, Henry Miller's chief reputation was as a pornographer; it was as a tyro enthusiast of the erotic that I approached his work. Those famous sexy passages that the politically correct continue to deplore did not disappoint but there was a lot more in old Henry to consider. After all, there were three books that constituted obligatory reading for the male adolescent of literary bent. They were Kerouac's *On the Road*, Hemingway's *The Sun Also Rises*, and *The Tropic of Cancer*. Therein you learned how to begin your life as a man.

When Miller died in 1980, he was finally recognized, in the most belated of ways, as a major modern writer, the eulogies running along the lines of "He Made the World Safe for Dirty Books." Miller was much more than an apostle of literary freedom. He was the first incarnation of Contemporary Man, as we've grown to know him and sort of love him. As such, he served well as a young man's guide on to how to live. Henry Miller, as he revealed himself in his novels, was a pioneer on so many cultural fronts, it's impossible to name them all. Years before the culture of narcissism, what fascinated Henry Miller, above all, was one Henry V. Miller. World Wars, Depressions came and went; they didn't interest Henry much. He was the despair of wife and mother, friend and stranger; he didn't care at all. He was supremely happy in the satisfactions of self-contemplation. The way it looked to him, every woman he met wanted to make love to him; every man wished to float him a loan. As he recalled it, everybody wanted him for a friend, even though he often informed his friends of hard truths about themselves, devoted as he was to telling it like it is.

In *The Tropic of Capricorn*, Henry recalled his days of hiring and firing in what is now called, nauseatingly, "the Department of Human Resources." Henry V. Miller was not your model manager and he bagged the whole thing just as soon he could find a woman willing to support him, laying bare the absurdities of working for a big corporation, the remorseless savagery and suffering that lies just under the surface of respectable, gainful employment. Miller was the precursor of those ungrateful wretches that right-wingers love to prate about: fiddling unemployment, laying up on welfare, screwing the system for all its worth.

Then again, decades before the era of New Age religion, Miller was an avid enthusiast of astrology and the other half-baked Eastern philosophies that made their way to California after World War II, along with Miller himself. While a writer like Hemingway insisted that the darkness of life was something you tried to dominate, moment to moment, with as much disciplined grace under pressure as possible, Henry, with no fear of chaos, with a feel for the comic in erotic affairs, was going with the flow, happy as a clam. So at ease with the body, not surprisingly, he was a partisan of the environment (aka nature) half a century before David Suzuki.

In one literary sense, Miller was our granddaddy. Before other memoirists and monologists, Henry was pioneering the confessional genre, laying out for perusal, at extraordinary length, his life and times. It was he who was responsible for a stylistic liberation, and neither Tom Wolfe nor Hunter S. Thompson nor even Saul Bellow could have written as colloquially and freely if it hadn't been for Miller. Then, too, he was the first of the hard-boiled heroes. Even though Raymond Chandler and James M. Cain first popularized writing out of the side of the mouth, they still retained certain traditional notions of gentlemanly nobility. Miller revelled in his own swinishness, his lack of conscience, his monumental amusement at the approbation of others. Yet somehow, he stayed in the mind as loveable.

Even though Miller was a supreme narcissist, he was never a snob; rather he was the spirit of egalitarianism personified. In Miller there was never any thirst for the limelight; successful people bored him silly. He was content with the company of blatant failures. Self-taught, self-educated, Miller was the mug as man in the street *par excellence*. He never lost his unadulterated Brooklyn accent: he was all Deses, Dems and Doses to the end, a dead-end kid as literary immortal.

The point is, Miller, at a time of ennui among the downstruck, was an incomparable, promiscuous celebrant of life.

Always hungry for love in any nook, hungry for sex in any corner, hungry for food, hungry for conversation and friendship, hungry for art. Often without much money, without "best-selling" success, without academic approval, he always thrived, "merry and bright." Henry Miller published 60 books and lived to be eighty-eight, looked after til the end by young ladies who were given to taking off their clothes. The old bastard knew something.

STEPHEN VIZINCZEY

The story of the young man making his career in the great metropolitan world is pre-eminently the theme of the nineteenth-century European novel. An author, who wished to define his time and place, would concern himself a good deal with the world of business. Balzac, for instance, was obsessed with money. In his novels, you know exactly how much everything costs. In *Lost Illusions*, the expenses that Lucien Chardon incurs trying to establish himself as a dandy in Paris contributes substantially to his ruin. Balzac computes it all to the last centime – so much for lodgings, so much for the tailor, so much for the carriage. It must have been Balzac's profound concern for cold cash and how it affects human lives that attracted Karl Marx to his work.

The interest in filthy lucre, made and lost, continued through Zola to Theodore Dreiser. (*The Financier* tells you everything you don't want to know about the streetcar business in Chicago.) This concern for the workings of cash largely disappeared in the novels of Hemingway and Fitzgerald who were more like James and Wharton in their focus on the leisure life of their characters. Their typical protagonist, for whom the rich are simply rich, never concerns himself with the mechanics of making a living. In a typical modern novel, the protagonist is either a victim of the economic machine as in *The Grapes of Wrath* or Studs Lonigan or on a professor's salary like Herzog or Lucky Jim and their many offspring. For *On the Road*'s Sal Paradise, money and all its sordid works is something he is ardently fleeing, and, like Ginsberg, howling "Moloch! Moloch!" as he goes.

Coinage has once again come to interest us all. For the most part, it has been left to journalists to document the antics of corporate business and its inexorable companion, the law. Such journalistic chroniclers, ever aware of the hypersensitive and litigious nature of the brutes they are writing about, have been careful not to antagonize businessmen, that is, not until those selfsame businessmen are actually indicted.

I am the last man to turn up my nose toward greed. It is, in many ways, similar to that other primal human desire, lust. In both endeavours, I wish all of humankind the multifold joys of satisfaction. What I refuse to take seriously is the sanctimonious aura in which business cloaks its activities. There is little that is holy about making a buck: but business likes to suggest that its activities lie supine somewhere between social work and philanthropy. If the entrepreneur is not a villain, neither is he a saint. But if journalists are often intimidated by the power of big money, novelists need not be.

Stephen Vizinczey is a Hungarian exile, whose mastery of the English language has been compared to that of Joseph Conrad and Vladimir Nabokov. Vizinczey's novel, *An Innocent Millionaire,* represents a return to the material themes of his favourite authors, Balzac and Stendhal. Mark Niven, a young, ambitious son of expatriate American parents, pursues a dream derided by more sensible folks – finding a sunken Spanish treasure ship in the Caribbean. The underwater predators he battles on the reefs while diving for the booty are meek as lambs compared to the gallery owners, lawyers, thugs, and taxmen he encounters once he's made his fortune.

With hard-bitten worldly insight, Vizinczey describes his hero's futile lawsuits against the rip-off artists who succeed in cheating him. Shrewdly, he contends that anybody who tells you that life is a jungle, fully intends to eat you.

As D.H. Lawrence is to sex, Vizinczey is to money. Both are experts on what it is like to take a good screwing. Anybody who's had business dealings of any sort will have met a respectable-seeming crook like Valentine the art dealer, whose nice-guy demeanor hides larcenous intentions. As for Bernie Wattman, he's the sort of lawyer you dread hiring: at once predatory towards his client and incompetent with the opposition.

If, as a novelist, Vizinczey is a nineteenth-century man (unlike a traditionalist like Robertson Davies), he is anything but a Victorian. He dislikes Dickens and Thackeray on the grounds of their sexual and social hypocrisy; Dickens' characters are too cheerfully content with their station; and Thackeray depicts Becky Sharp as wicked because of her determination to rise in the world.

In his collection of essays and reviews, *Truth and Lies in Literature,* Vizinczey even finds Flaubert lacking because he sees Emma Bovary's attempt to escape a loveless marriage as vulgar.

He insists that "There are two basic kinds of literature. One helps you to understand, and the other helps you forget; the first helps you to be a free person and a free citizen, the other helps people manipulate you. One is like astronomy, the other is like astrology."

Even though a literary conservative, Vizinczey is paradoxical in that he has the burning soul of an insurrectionist. His heroes, especially Stendhal, had a sensibility that was a direct consequence of the French Revolution and the Napoleonic era that followed. In many ways, theirs was an era resembling our own as it settles down to a quieter existence after the social revolutions of the 1960s.

Vizinczey, whose life has been forever marked by his experiences in the Hungarian uprising of 1956, has a large spirit, an enormous heart and a relentless sense of freedom, refreshing qualities in an era of narrow-minded conservatism. "The trouble about the truth about anything," he maintains in one essay, "is that it tends to be offensive, either because it's bad news or because it's confusingly different from received notions . . . or because it punctures a successful pretence."

It is to Vizinczey's great credit that he invokes the glories of Western culture as fighting on behalf of the free individual, rather than the powers-that-be, as do conservative writers such as Allan Bloom, who seem to regard the works of Mozart and Tolstoy as so many bulwarks against sexual chaos and the collapse of civilization. The big corporations, as so many crotchety traditionalists claim, do not stand on guard for the values of western civilization – they are far more likely to be found, with the lords of trashy mass communication, amongst the enemies of art. Vizinczey has done us all an incalculable service by pointing out with passion and lucidity that our cultural inheritance is not repressive and restrictive, as many would have us believe, but liberating, rebellious and yes, joyful.

THE 66 PERCENT SOLUTION

Our technicians of the soul, the psychoanalysts, tell us depression is introverted hate. Murderous impulses turn in on themselves, curdle the mood, and sit upon the spirit with all the weight of poured concrete. You don't have to be Freud to detect the depression that comes off the delegates to the general meeting of the Progressive Conservative Party of Canada as they hurry out of the freezing cold into the Winnipeg Convention Centre on a Wednesday afternoon late in January. Unimproved by the tootling of a ragged trio of musicians playing sourly out of tune, their low spirits float all through the lobby and up the escalators like steam from a sewer.

Who can blame them? Instead of lolling on a beach in the Bahamas or Florida soaking up some rays, they're in Winnipeg where the news on television keeps the citizenry informed on the frostbite factor – from that point where it's comfortable to ski to the one where exposed skin will freeze in less than a minute. Yes, here they are, condemned to three or four days in melancholy Winnipeg, unpretentious, homely Winnipeg, a small, flat place that never boomed, never bust, decrepit at the core.

The Winnipeg Convention Centre is a vast oblong cathedral in concrete that concedes little to aesthetic needs. The bottom floor is divided into a warren of small meeting rooms where the party men and women are to gather; the second floor, conforming to the current multi-use architectural dogma, sports a cinema, a mini-mall with a bookstore, florist, travel agency, two restaurants and a gift shop, and two big rooms on the top floor named with all the poetry of a telephone listing: Hall A and Hall B. Hall A, which will serve as the convention floor, is currently closed to journalists who are bridling at being shut out. The effect of having two huge halls on the top floor gives the building an upside-down feeling, like a steamship with its engines and cargo above and bridge below. Since nobody is in a hurry to venture into frostbite country, the convention hall gives a sense of being hermetically sealed, outward bound, on a bizarre voyage of its own.

Looking down at the arriving delegates searching in the lobby for their luggage, you are confronted by a sea of blue pinstripes. Under their fawn camel-hair jobs or 1920s raccoon coats, two male Tories out of three wear a blue suit. It is, after all, the perfect closet in which to hide. Jews, Orientals, homosexuals appear in their blue suits and announce to the world: "I am for order, decorum and piety, I am for the promise of Tory free enterprise in which anybody wearing such a suit can become management." The blue suit's message: "I was born to give orders."

Several weeks before, I had lunched with a man known to be "too bright for the Tory party." He had worked for Stanfield, written speeches for Joe Clark and Bill Davis, differed with them both, and now was out of politics. He was indeed an intelligent gent, with a shrewd sense of the disabling afflictions of his party. "Disraeli once said," he told me over pasta in one of Toronto's glossier bistros, "that the Conservative Party was an organized hypocrisy. In Canada, it's a disorganized hypocrisy." On the plane out to Winnipeg, a delegate from Eglinton-Lawrence, the riding within whose stolid confines I grew up, offered a further definition. "A Tory," he said, "is a man who knows what he doesn't want, but doesn't know how to go about getting it."

Here in Winnipeg, there is an underlying feeling that if weren't for Joe Clark's poor political judgment, instead of palely languishing out of power, the Tories would be in boisterous good health, rolling in the clover of perks, patronage and power, vigorously throwing the bums off welfare, privatizing every Crown corporation, and generally saving the world from socialism. Though nothing is more important to the Tory mindset than loyalty, obedience to authority, nothing trumps respect for the boss faster than disappointment. They may treasure loyalty but they are here to determine their chief's fitness to lead. There are, of course, no overt demonstrations against Clark, but late at night in my hotel two pieces of paper arrive within moments of each other. The first is a card depicting a red, high-heeled slipper and promising "Attractive Female Companions for Discriminating Gents, Free Transportation Provided," and the other is a flyer for the pro-leadership forces: "71 percent of Canadians want a PC Leadership Convention." Tory delegates, it seems, were feeling an itch to depose their leader just as they were itching to fool around on the wife. Being a cauldron of conflicting emotions, little wonder the Tory delegate's depressed.

What a strange creature is Charles Joseph Clark. On Thursday morning, he makes his entrance into Hall A. Wearing a blue suit with a subtle wine-red stripe, awkward as a stork on stilts, he's accompanied by the modern panoply of power – television cameras, boom mikes, and exploding flashbulbs, men and women who are all brashness and elbows. While many Tories are afflicted with a bad case of jowls, that swelling ham of meat under the chin, Clark is all jowls. They quiver wildly as he nods and shakes hands and nods again. His eyes are disproportionately small, his ears disproportionately large. A network of small veins threatens to turn into the full red mottle of apoplexy. His chest is puffed like a pouter pigeon's; after all, he's proud to be world-famous in Canada. Every time he goes to Cornwall or Moncton, the locals are thrilled to meet him. Nonetheless, those who think Clark is a wattled wimp and pushover are wrong. He exudes authority. No, Joe Clark is Prince of Wimps, King of Mugwumps.

Maureen McTeer is a surprise. Where seven years of celebrity have merely puffed up her husband, they have made her striking, her dark hair shiny and her violet eyes glittering. Conservative women come in three varieties. First, is the old-style Rosedale Tory who looks as if she was once head girl at Havergal College and serves on the boards of Children's Aid and the Humane Society. Her style is *sensible*: cashmere sweaters, plaid skirts, unadorned and slightly dowdy, as if high fashion were the preoccupation of the feckless and irresponsible.

The second sees her political activity as a useful adjunct to her career. She often wears a strange blue or red outfit, which resembles an airline stewardess's uniform. It is the female equivalent to the blue suit. She joins investment clubs and takes courses on How to Manage Men on the Job.

In contrast, the third type, of which Maureen McTeer is a premier example, radiates the ultra-groomed look of powerful Ottawa or Washington: Holt Renfrew and Bonwit Teller on the hoof, but not hip enough for Bloomingdale's, let alone Fiorucci. If Joe Clark walked into a room in New York City, he would need an introduction and an explanation before anybody paid him the least attention. His wife could turn heads at most places. Seen together, they make a curious couple.

Hall A is jammed with the party delegates squirming in molded plastic red, yellow and blue seats. Up on the six-foot-high platform there is a backdrop depicting the nation in Tory blue. On each side of this map of Canada there is a an Eskimo, Ukrainians folk dancing, blue collar workers, fishermen – all the minorities conspicuous by their absence in Hall A.

Up front there's a band wearing straw hats and blue-striped vests that wouldn't be out of place at a Polish wedding in Kapuskasing, playing every type of music from polkas to Dixieland, the Ike Kelneck Band. The girl singer, a juicy little thing in poured-on jeans, pounding a tambourine, the only bit of overt sex visible for miles. She sings: *"Parties make the world go round, so let's have a party."*

Arrayed around the room are the massed forces of the media: CBC, French and English, radio and television, CTV,

CITY-TV from Toronto. *Le Devoir* to the *Globe and Mail* to the *Herald*, the *Chronicle*, the *Spectator*, the *Whig-Standard*, the various *Suns*, and the *Windsor Star*. There is a celebrity convoy that contains Allan Fotheringham, Barbara Amiel and Mordecai Richler. There's Dalton Camp, *éminence gris*, who greased the demise of John Diefenbaker and recently described the Tory right wing as "a cashew coalition of nuts and extremists."

Before the meeting starts, the supporters of Peter Elzinga, a candidate for the party's presidency and an ardent proponent of a return to the noose, make what passes for a demonstration on behalf of their man. Wearing cowboy hats and carrying placards, they shuffle around, grim, diffident, embarrassed, waiting for the cameras to take notice. They look terribly uncomfortable, these polite yahoos, like Depression farmers posing for a snapshot. After all, it was big-city weirdos who made such public exhibitions of themselves with placards, nuclear disarmers, striking unionists, women against pornography, never Tories.

The meeting starts with all due ceremony. Conservatives practice ritual. Everybody sings along to the national anthem. Except there's one problem: the verse presents a host of conflicting variations – somebody keeps changing the words to the damn thing! Disharmony is the effect, appropriate to what's to come. Then, a parson with a bleating nasal voice begs God to bring down "the spirit of wisdom upon our leaders." The Deity must have gone deaf for the next speaker is Peter Blaikie the outgoing president of the party.

Blaikie is tall, with dark, beetling eyebrows, and wants it known right away that as far as he is concerned, there is no talk about the division in his party, it is "gratuitous rubbish" invented by the media. He denounces the pundits by name, Gwyn, Winsor and Fotheringham, and then – letting it be known to the confusion of all that he is "positively neutral" amidst disputes – he condemns the press as a pack of hanging vultures.

"Oh, yes," my Tory insider had said back in Toronto, "there's one other thing about Conservatives, they hate the media." There is no mystery about that. The Tories believe in order and decorum, and the media were a carnival sideshow that, so far from believing in privacy and self-restraint and shoving the unseemly under the carpet, insisted every time on hauling the bleeding guts of the party onto the table and sorting through the entrails for omens. As much as the Tories hate the media, the media are not impressed. Through Blaikie's diatribe, Fotheringham ostentatiously reads from a pile of newspapers, periodically checking his watch, then announces, "It's 20 minutes now." A few seconds before Blaikie ends, Fotheringham says, "They're going to give him a standing ovation now." As if on cue, the hall leaps to its feet, applauding.

Now it's Clark's turn. When every other kid his age was idolizing somebody like Elvis Presley, Joe Clark was idolizing John Diefenbaker. He tucks his chin deep into his jowls, strikes a grave, self-important, grandfatherly tone. Yet he is a young man. In his speech, he says that his own party has "an unparalleled opportunity to elect a national government that will quite fundamentally and quite literally change the course of Canadian history. They are weak," he says, "we are strong. Where they are weakening, we are strengthening." Then, Clark makes a remarkable slip of the tongue. "The eighteenth of February this year begins the fourth year in office of the Trudeau government. It is the last year of Pierre Trudeau's life . . . " Pause. Stutter. "Political life." Heavens! Is this the return of the repressed! With a vengeance! I'd read that Clark detests the man who has been kicking sand in his face for seven years, but now it appears that at some level of his psyche he actually wishes him dead!

The corridors outside the hall are lined with large colour posters of Clark looking statesmanlike. The ubiquity of these posters throughout the convention centre becomes oppressive, almost totalitarian. Of all the Tory politicians he is the one personality officially recognized. Nobody else is to give a major speech. Peter Worthington, a persistent critic of Clark's, stands in the corridor, next to his ally, Elmer Mackay. "This, officially, isn't a leadership convention, but it is," he's saying. At this point, Worthington is a journalist on the way to becoming a politician. "They can pretend what they like," he continues, "but there's only one issue, leadership."

"Isn't that hypocritical?" somebody asks.

"Of course it is," he replies, green eyes flashing in anger. "It's ludicrous. But this is a very strange party."

Mackay maintains, even though they are opposed to Clark, they're all Conservatives together and there's no ill will. A delegate beside him, elderly, with a white crew cut, his coat festooned with buttons, disagrees. "Anybody who isn't for Joe Clark is on the side of the Liberals," he shouts. The woman beside him yells, "We're here to elect Joe Clark!" No, she realizes, they're not here to elect Joe Clark, they're here to . . . what?

Later, in the mall, I run into Peter Blaikie. I ask him whether he thinks the leadership issue has been concocted by the press.

"What I say," he asserts, "is that the discussion is taking place privately, that what the thinking people are doing privately does not lead to the kind of sensationalism we have heard."

"Don't you think you're trying to sweep it all into a closet?"

Blaikie is losing patience. He really dislikes reporters. "We're not sweeping anything into a closet. People are going to vote tomorrow night. Whatever is the result of that vote, we'll live with. But that is something completely different from the sense that's being created that everybody in the party is practically on a street corner on a soapbox. That's just not the case."

"But if leadership isn't an issue, why are you here?"

"You're not listening," he explodes. "Not to one word I say! Of course it's an issue. I'm saying it's a private issue. People are making a private decision and that's how it should be."

"Aren't politics public, not private?"

"It'll be public tomorrow night."

Walking away from Blaikie, it occurs to me that Conservatives are like a certain kind of WASP family where the daughter is going crazy upstairs alone in her bedroom, the son is getting ready to elope with the Jamaican maid, mother is drowning her sorrows in gin, but not a word is said at the dinner table, on the front porch all is calm. One day father takes a shotgun to them all and the neighbours say, "They were such a quiet, private family."

That afternoon, across the street in the Manitoba suite of the Charter House Hotel, the overt anti-Clark forces are in full distemper, getting ready to make a move. As well as being a political party, the Conservatives are a lifelong social club, and there are several long-time members who have been maneuvered off the roster of delegates by the Clark organization. Some are in this room, all from the extreme right of the party, and they're festering with an ugly rancour. They're bigots and lunkheads and have the unlikely effect of making you sympathize with Joe Clark. The sergeant-at-arms has mean close-set eyes and the look of a private-school bully. A delegate from Etobicoke-Lakeshore twirls his mustachios, a silent-movie villain. He's wearing a button: "Socialism is just a phase you're going through." There is even a reporter from William F. Buckley's *National Review*. John Gamble, a right-wing MP from Toronto, is wearing a fur-trimmed coat, a fur hat, and yes, a pinstriped suit. He gives a speech that relies heavily on the accumulated wisdom of cab drivers he has met. Not one cab driver likes Joe Clark.

Another conspirator gets up and says that things are going their way. "The change is amazing," he says. "The change from yesterday to today is amazing. They've come to this convention thinking Joe Clark is safe, and they've started to talk to people and they see he's in deep trouble. Our base vote is 40 percent, it's rock hard and so we're at 50 percent." He sits down to cheers and applause.

A westerner goes into a full, choleric denunciation, a raging tirade: "Dalton Camp is a Judas goat, another thing, a Black Angel, and unchristian. We have to get rid of that man. We have to get him off the media, we have to get rid of him, we have to get rid of Eddie Goodman and all those Red Tories, and then we'll have the westerner a bit better."

John Morrison, one of the chief instigators of the anti-Clark movement, a jowly, "freelance public relations man," does not like Camp's comments either. Swathed in a heavy parka, Morrison has an unpleasant red moustache and a florid complexion. When Camp's name is mentioned, he gets so angry he looks as if he's going to hit somebody. "We are the mainstream party. We are going to prove that Friday night. If Dalton Camp doesn't like it, he can join another party or go back to the Liberals where he came from." There is little of the traditional Tory belief in keeping things bottled up in this room: the rage and frustration are out in the open, here, for all to see.

"Shouldn't we have some kind of march?" asks a young Tory. Enraged as they are, the anti-Clark forces know their party. They have to organize some hypocrisy.

On the convention floor, a London delegate is in disagreement with a reporter. Vic Graat, an oily-haired man in the ubiquitous blue pinstriped suit, with an unpleasant rosebud mouth, believes Pierre Trudeau is a communist. In all seriousness.

"Fidel Castro wouldn't think so."

"Three Crown corporations were taken over by the government," he shouts incoherently. "No reason. Just because they were the government. That's communism, no question."

"That's indiscreet," allows Peter Millar, who is standing by, "but it's true."

"Petrocan!" hollers Graat. "That's communism! I go to your bank account and take it. What's that?"

The reporter shrugs, dreaming of summer porches.

"It's communism!"

Graat is another Tory who doesn't like the media. He's mad too. "These guys don't want to hear the truth!" he shouts. "They just want to hear garbage!"

Wandering off to the press lounge I run into a grizzled delegate from Quebec, who has the appearance of a mortician from Chicoutimi. "I'm with Joe," he tells me. "If Joe gets out, I get out. I've had enough of this bullshit." The guy is exercised over the recent Jerusalem incident where Clark opined that he would make Jerusalem, not Tel Aviv, the capital of Israel. Why did Joe get involved? "Arabs and Jews," he says. "That's like Lucifer and Satan. Let them kill each other!"

The delegates I have met like Graat, have been right-wingers, small businessmen, farmers – the *petite bourgeoisie*, originally from the east but settled in the west – bristling with resentment at the high-taxing politicians, the idlers on welfare, the city slickers and trendies, intellectuals, and all the rest.

On Thursday morning, in the coffee shop of the Marlborough Inn, I met up with the left wing of Canadian conservatism. I met the son of E.P. Taylor, the country's greatest tycoon. I met Charles Taylor, son of E.P. and author of *Radical Tories: The Conservative Tradition in Canada.*

We are in an age of conservatism, ideologically speaking, but while we have had the testimony of innumerable Jewish ex-Trotskyists who invented the terms of American neo-conservatism in New York and Chicago, there had been very little written in the Canadian context. Although Taylor scorned the nostalgia for Empire that has characterized previous generations of anglophilic Canadian Tories, his book is suffused with a nostalgia for Victorian roots. Taylor professed a brand of conservative thought best characterized as Aesthetic Toryism, that intellectual turn wherein Robert Stanfield is compared to a wonderful piece of Canadiana furniture, wherein Stephen Leacock reminds one of old Ontario summer homes with graceful porches and balconies. There is a calmness, even an attractive rectitude to this approximation of an aristocratic creed, complete with Red Tory notions about social decency and responsibilities to the poor. It is a squire-like vision, anti-American, anti-urban, anti-cosmopolitan.

Charles Taylor is tall, pale, wears severe-looking spectacles, has thinning fair hair. You can see him as a character out of Henry James, half-connoisseur, half-plutocrat. As a Canadian conservative, his attitude to the Progressive Conservative Party is very much *de haut en bas*. He feels Clark is going too far to the right. "Some of his speeches recently," he tells me, "sound like pure Reagan. He has no concept of what the country is about and what the traditions are. Now that may be pure politics on his part because of the poor position he's been in for the past three years. But I think that's true of the party as a whole; they're not aware of their past."

I ask him if the party is moving further to the right. "They deny it," he says. "They say that the Liberals have gone so far to the left, that they're trying to bring it back to the centre. Selling off crown corporations is not part of Conservative tradition or policy. I think they're deceiving themselves and trying to deceive us. They're trying to be ideologues. Which a Conservative never is. The public will never elect a right-wing Conservative Party. The public as a whole don't approach matters ideologically, they're not particularly for or against public enterprise; they just like things that work. A good example is that the public is for Petrocan but against the Post Office. Petrocan works; the Post Office doesn't."

At this convention, there is a distinct absence of policy discussion. This is a reflection of the personality of Joe Clark. He is obsessed with the practical machinery of politics – organization and structure – at the expense of content. This is reflected in an audiovisual workshop entitled "Campaigning to Win." An elaborate, heavy-handed presentation that is right out of a company sales convention. It is paint-by-numbers politics for canvassers, full of demographic analysis, opinion research breakdown analysis, opinion research breakdown of votes into six categories from hard support to hard against.

Clark and his organization resemble the casino owners of Las Vegas in that they are constantly striving to arrange the house odds in their favour. Friday morning, there has been a huge rumpus over the admission of Quebec delegates to a session of PC youth. Party bureaucrats have not given them the correct starting time, and they have arrived at the meeting to find the doors already closed. The suspicion in Clark's camp, of course, is that these delegates are pro-Mulroney and now they are trying to exclude them from the meeting on a technicality. Then, Brian Mulroney arrives. Where Clark is no chin, all jowls, Mulroney is handsome, slick, all chin, no jowls and all charm, all the time. His task is to overthrow Clark without being seen doing it.

Early in the afternoon, the Premier of Ontario, Bill Davis, arrives at the convention. Carrying his unlit pipe close to his chest like a tiny sceptre, bathed in television light, he makes a regal progress up the escalator to Hall B, where a reception is being held in honour of the premiers. Like his fellow provincial potentate, Davis radiates a sense of self-satisfied power. A leader of the opposition, his manner implies, is not cut from the same cloth as himself. Yes, he would accept the prime minister's starring role if somebody else in the party would go through the nastiness of winning power. But move to Ottawa and eat shit at the hands of Lord Dracula and his boys? Actually get down in the gutter of a federal election campaign? That was beneath his dignity. According to my Tory insider, Joe Clark had the following point in his favour: compared to the others, to Davis or Lougheed, he was the hungriest. He wanted the job the most, and was willing to eat any amount of dirt to keep it.

In the afternoon, the mood gets increasingly virulent. There are rumours of scuffles among the women delegates. Goaded beyond endurance, the pro-Clark forces are beginning to lose their cool. On the mall, John Fraser, the MP for Vancouver South, erupts. "Listen," he says with considerable heat, "I'm sick and tired of this right-wing bullshit! Every time John Morrison gets up and craps on our party and our leader, I lose votes in Vancouver South. And if you guys think we have all those seats forever, you're crazy. I fought for that goddamn seat. I took it away from people who said that we could never take it. When you guys are good enough to win a seat with this right-wing bullshit, then you come and give me a lecture!" There are real jobs at stake at this convention, cold cash. It is getting to be hard, serious business.

Friday night, Hall A is jammed with shouting, stomping delegates, for Clark and against. The chairman of the Tory caucus has revealed to the *Globe and Mail* that the parliamentary Conservatives will be in full revolt if Clark does not do better than 66 percent. The anti-Clark forces mount a considerable demonstration. When Clark's supporters chant, "We want Joe, we want Joe," they add, "Out!" The Ike Kelneck Band plays the Tory fight song: polka music. With the noise of these demonstrations, the event begins to take on the outlines of professional sport. The convention is now going out live on television across the country. The nation is watching. Clark clearly has to give the speech of his life. It matters little, in this age of the sound bite, that political oratory is a declining art. Clark breathes fire against the Liberals, calls for party discipline, but never once speaks personally. Oh, he makes a gesture toward contrition for his mistakes, but he never once strikes an intimate note. His personality as leader comprises the real issue of this convention and he refuses to deal with that fact head on. Instead, he talks euphemistically about "unity" and "getting our act together." His anger is mechanical, unconvincing. More than ever, Joe Clark seems a hollow man, synthetic. "In the name of our country," he concludes, "let's get on with the job," implying that questioning his leadership is, at heart, just goofing off.

The media and Clark's supporters think he's won it. But, down on the second floor, it's a different story. The results are brought to Clark, waiting in the business office of the convention centre. Thirty-five minutes later there's no sign of him. Like Blaikie's vultures, reporters begin to gather at the door. Outside, there are Clark staffers with walkie-talkies. A Clark executive assistant, a woman in the unpreventable blue pinstripe, comes out bearing an expression seen around terminal cancer wards. Tim Ralfe, a Tory close to Clark, notices that the press has spotted the stricken look on her face and rushes over to her. Sharp words are exchanged and the most forced smile in the history of smiling appears on the poor woman's face.

It does not look good for Joe.

"What's going on, Tim?" asks Val Sears of *The Toronto Star*, the Silver Fox of Canadian journalism. "It's costing a million dollars to hold the presses."

"Did I mention that I don't really care?" Ralfe replies.

Minutes drag by. Don Mazankowski and Erik Neilsen, the men closest to Clark in caucus, are brought in for consultation. It's certain – a disaster is brewing for Joe Clark. More time goes by. Politics, like war, consists of waiting. Then Finlay Macdonald, Silver Fox of the Conservatives, emerges from the business office, arm-in-arm with the executive assistant.

"Where's Joe?" asks Sears.

"He's gone," replies MacDonald, Silver Fox to Silver Fox. "For serious, Val." Clark has escaped by some back route.

Upstairs in Hall A, the delegates are clueless as to what's going on. The Ike Kelneck outfit has brought out its bar band repertoire and everybody is boogying to "Proud Mary." Beer in plastic cups is being sold out in the corridor, and they're getting ready to party all night long. There is no sensation quite so eerie as going into a hall in possession of knowledge of which a crowd of 2,500 is ignorant. After some Academy Award-style flourishing of ballots, the results are announced. Out of 2,402 votes Clark has got 1,607, 66.9 percent.

He appears on the platform with a visibly pale Maureen McTeer. At first, it seems as if he's going to brazen it out. After all, he has received a majority. "I asked for a clear mandate," he says. "I received the support of a clear majority of the delegates voting here." Then, all at once, he changes direction. "It is not clear enough to enforce the kind of discipline I need to achieve the kind of unity that this party requires."

Near me, a young Tory leaps in the air and shouts, "We've got a convention!" Hall A is in shock. The television reporters are scrambling to line up reaction. Their smart-money predictions have been hopelessly wrong. The anti-Clark forces are congratulating themselves as he calls for a convention and announces himself as a candidate. "He's gone!" they yell. "We got rid of the jerk!"

Then, just like that, the carefully nourished decorum of the Tories falls apart. The delegates file out of Hall A in silence, stunned, lobotomized. Many of the women are in tears. Their collective depression has taken a turn for the worse. In the corridor leading to the Holiday Inn, another drunken delegate throws himself on my shoulders, all restraint gone. "We screwed ourselves again, eh?" Beside him, his friend moans, "Joe's a born loser."

Back in the hall, John Morrison, the anti-Clark conspirator, radiates a positively post-coital sense of satisfaction, declaring himself well pleased. For most delegates, however, there'll be no party tonight, but a wake. They have once more pledged their loyalty to the leader while voting their resentments.

The next day Joe Clark announces that he will step down as party leader. Then, he changes his mind. After a few days of further squabbling, peace is restored. Clark retains his position as party leader for the moment, but steps down as opposition chief in parliament. Possibly the best moment in his entire life had come in Winnipeg when he had called for a leadership convention. If Joe Clark had often reminded me of an actor badly miscast in his role, he had, at that moment, found a part he could play with conviction: Sydney Carton, mounting the scaffold to the guillotine, doing the decent thing for his party and his nation.

ECHOES OF WOODSTOCK: LOOKING BACK AT THE 1960s

Not so long ago, a guy I know, an old friend, got hold of some peyote buds. It was the damnedest thing. He hadn't done any serious drugs in years, oh, smoked a little grass, definitely, but all those mind warpers of his degenerate youth, the LSD, MDT, TSP, mescalin, psilocybin, that hallucinatory arsenal was a thing of the past. But on that particular night, he was in the mood for some diversion. He managed to clean the peyote buds and then choke them down (no mean feat that, because it's nauseating stuff), but it wasn't too long before he realized he had made a monumental mistake. In the intervening years, he had forgotten just how all-devouring such a trip can be – that rocketing, burning liftoff, then the floor dropping out of one's psyche, the entire inside of the skull fibrillating and shuddering, all the shape-shifting and rainbow-hued cranial fissures. There he was, a prosperous solid citizen, a householder, his wife and kids asleep around him while he sat out 12 hours of soul furor. The peyote, it appeared, was an enormously powerful device when it came to unleashing the torrents of memory. The very psychedelic hurricane of the drug seemed to evoke that far-off decade of the 1960s, and suddenly out of the walls of this bourgeois outpost, like the ghost of Jacob Marley, appeared a cavalcade of figures, both personal and public, some admonishing, some beseeching horribly: the friend who, while tripping, took a leap off the Bloor Street viaduct; Jimi Hendrix and Janis Joplin; and all the other friends with whom he had broken irretrievably. And the various seasons of his young manhood returned, vivid as lightning, to his mind; the summer of '67, and the events of '68, and then the summer of 1969, which had been the summer of Woodstock . . .

In August of 1969 I was twenty-three years old. As Charles Dickens had written about another period of upheaval, it was the best of times, it was the worst of times. When a girl I knew told me about a rock festival in upstate New York, in a place called Woodstock, and invited me to go along, I took a pass. I had just that week arrived home with $8 in my pocket. I had hitchhiked from Amsterdam to Istanbul and back. I had listened to the Rolling Stones in Hyde Park. I had sat at the feet of R.D. Laing. I had run from *les flics* in the streets of Paris in the spring of '68. Another pop festival didn't impress me much. I had been to be-ins, sit-ins, teach-ins, acid tests, jazz, folk, and rock festivals beyond counting. When it was said, in small rooms with Indian cotton hangings on the wall and incense and patchouli oil in the air, that Woodstock was going to be the biggest of them all, it just seemed to me that great numbers of new converts were latching onto something that some of us had been hip to for a long time.

In the early '60s there were those of us, teenagers crazy for music, who used to make the pilgrimage down to Newport for the jazz and folk festivals there, to learn from the veteran hipsters of Greenwich Village and Boston Common how it was really done. In July of '63 I was doing my obligatory summer on Jack Kerouac's road, Greyhounding and hitchhiking across the continent. I read in *Time* magazine how, at the Newport Folk Festival, in front of 46,000 people, a scrawny guy named Bob Dylan joined Peter, Paul, and Mary to sing a song called "Blowin' in the Wind." Dylan was a visionary poet-hero, they said, and he was orchestrating something called a youth revolution.

It's hard to appreciate now just how much influence Dylan had in those years. He came over the radio waves and into our consciousness like telepathy. He fried our minds, addled our brains. I was convinced I was Bob Dylan and spent many adolescent hours in front of the mirror trying to get my hair to curl and frizz in just the proper way, trying to perfect the enigmatic, snarling manner. Bob Dylan used to visit my dreams, and I was absolutely sure that there had never been a poet – Rimbaud, Byron, Eliot, Shakespeare – that was his equal.

In those days we used to look to Dylan's next record not to enjoy his music or appreciate his lyrics but to puzzle out what to do with our lives. I can remember one guy, whose hair was curly enough and who had the same hawk-like profile, listening to "Bringing It All Back Home," zonked, lying on the floor face down into a couple of pillows, and wailing, "He's stolen my face, he's stolen my face." A college friend, Louis, had hitchhiked all the way from Forest Hill to Hibbing, Minnesota, to seek out Dylan's mother and father. A troubled gay, he had spent a decade thrashing on the headshrinker's couch. He figured that if he could just puzzle out the difference in his and Bob Dylan's upbringing, all would come clear. Abe and Beatty Zimmerman weren't all that remarkably different from his own folks back in Toronto. (Her Bobby was one sweet boy, Mrs. Z. assured Lou, not nasty at all.) But there Dylan was, telling society at large to stuff it, and for his pains he was getting his picture in *Time* magazine. You did the same and flunked out of school, got turfed out of the house for smoking dope in the basement, and scraped by washing dishes at the Half Beat Coffee House while essaying the intricacies of folk guitar. The Clarke Institute of Psychiatry (and hospitals like it all over the world) was teeming with those of us who couldn't handle the disparity.

By the summer of '69, after his mysterious motorcycle accident, Dylan dropped out at the top. After the Kennedys, after Chicago, after My Lai, America was coming apart like a rotten cantaloupe, and there were thousands who looked not to any politician to point the way. The pressure on him must have been insupportable. But he was in Woodstock and he was determinedly silent. At bottom, he was just as practical as appliance-salesman Abe Zimmerman. Dylan himself knew he was just a recording artist, not a teen Messiah. Woodstock was an artist's colony, like Provincetown in Massachusetts or Key West in Florida, a kind of Greenwich Village North. When we learned that Dylan had moved there, rumours of the wildest sort began to percolate through those rooms with the Indian hangings and incense. Dylan was addicted to heroin, Dylan was a drag queen, Dylan was a vegetable, Dylan was clinically insane. Some chick who knew some bass player who lived in Woodstock would let us in on the real story. The place began to take on a fabled aura; the charisma of Bob Dylan had transferred itself to Woodstock, and now we were going to make a mass pilgrimage to the mystery. We were sure that he would show himself to the multitudes and speak, and truth would be revealed.

It seems to me now that all the histories of that time are inadequate. Morris Dickstein, in *The Gates of Eden,* emphasizes the politics, Vietnam and the New Left. Tom Wolfe, in *The Electric Kool-Aid Acid Test*, emphasizes drugs and New Age religions. Other writers peg the social changes of the era on the sexual revolution and the revolt against the traditional family. None of these explanations will suffice. What was really going on was that an entire generation, brought up after World War II in the greatest time of prosperity and comfort known to modern man, was going to junk everything, 3,000 years of Western civilization and reinvent it all! God, religion, the family, government, sex, the individual, community, art, everything. Just throw away all that had gone before and start again. Only this time it would be perfect. What I remember best from those years was an inner sense of huge, infinite, limitless, wonderful possibility. To that first question that every generation addresses itself upon coming-of-age, namely, W*hat is life*? we answered, *It's whatever you think it is*.

The Woodstock festival was the point of furthest expansion of those possibilities, the youth movement's furthest flowering, its bravest moment. Woodstock was to the counterculture, as it had been somewhat hopefully dubbed, what Chartres was to Catholicism. (It was also immediately perishable, a pseudo-event, on one level just another rock concert. When it was over, nothing remained at the farmer's field where it took place except litter. Later there was the film, successful in its time, now gathering dust, waiting for the inevitable onslaught of nostalgia.)

Besides being a pilgrimage to Bob Dylan, Woodstock was part of a pastoral movement away from the cities to what we, city-bred, conceived of as rural innocence. "We've got to get ourselves back to the garden," sang Joni Mitchell. Cities were evil; we would abandon them. The world of adults was corrupt; we would refuse to grow up. We would turn our backs on the twentieth century and grow our own in the country. We wore dull, faded, patched clothing and looked like so many dust bowl Okies, since anything new was "plastic." We were all artists, we were all magicians. We would make our own clothes, our own houses, our own rules. The result was amateur in every sense, it was infantile. We were heading for a fall and sooner or later reality would teach us a lesson.

If the audience at Woodstock was thus innocent, the performers were street-smart hipsters, tough, shrewd, arrogant, who made the average ward heeler or numbers runner look naive as a bunny rabbit. The audience that worshipped Bob Dylan was largely unaware that his career was to some extent the creation of a middle-aged ex-nightclub owner from Chicago named Albert Grossman who could have given Jack Ruby lessons. We were ignorant of the mechanics of the industry whose stars we worshipped. The process by which Bob Dylan had become celebrated was no different from the one that had created Shecky Greene. But we believed that there was a magical process whereby, attuned to the right looks and attitudes, you became a star, and that's what we wanted most of all: more than we wanted to reinvent civilization, we wanted to be stars. Even though we assailed the evils of corporate enterprise and capitalism, we were lined up at the offices of every producer in the world, the bigger the record company the better, because to be a rock 'n' roll star, in 1969, was to be a god in shades and fringed buckskin. We gave up careers in painting, literature and theatre, to make the attempt at rock stardom. It wasn't just the idea of riches, unlimited sex and drugs that drew us. Musicians were the sole voice of moral authority. Everyone else was cops. Newspapermen were cops, teachers were cops, doctors were cops, businessmen were cops, parents were cops, intellectuals were cops, soldiers were cops, and cops themselves were pigs.

Only musicians seemed to encourage our lust for the future, so we aped them in everything – manners, clothes, habits, way of life. If they were often only slightly less articulate than Piltdown Man, we would be too. I remember forcibly restraining my natural verbal flow so I could talk that stilted Brandoesque lingo of enigmatic grunts which implied a knowingness that one was far too self-possessed ever to express. There were men, and women too, in whose reticence I had perceived a self-contained wisdom, who I later discovered years later had merely nothing to say. But then we mistrusted language itself. Words lied, were inadequate to thoughts, just as acts betrayed the dream. We didn't read – knowledge was suspect – and, as a result, we were prey to all kinds of pernicious nonsense, including those monstrosities of cult religion that came out of the East like the breath of the plague. Since any form of conventional authority was bad, no one at Woodstock would issue a direct command. Chip Monck, the concert announcer, would make statements like, "It's suggested that you stay away from the brown acid. But it's your own trip." He wouldn't dare make a bald statement like, "Don't take that gunk or you'll spend the next 16 hours of your life grovelling in the lowest circle of hell." So there was total chaos at the festival, incidents like the one in which Abbie Hoffman, accustomed to the ethic of everyone doing his own thing, had the nerve to walk on stage interrupting a set by The Who in order to make some self-aggrandizing political statement. Perhaps the audience was willing to suffer such imposition, as were permissive parents, university presidents and the like. Not so Pete Townshend, The Who's tough, Brit working-class guitarist, who flung the bleedin' cunt off the stage.

Since nothing was true, anything was permitted. In the big cities you passed thousands of men and women in the streets who would treat you like a dangerous lunatic if you spoke a word to them. But at festivals like Woodstock, you could talk to strangers as if you had known them all your life, and it was exhilarating. This was the era best characterized by Wolfe's phrase, "Our eyes met, our lips touched, our bodies embraced, and then we were introduced." At gatherings like Woodstock, people would retire to the long grass, 30 seconds after they had met. While conduct of this stripe might have been the acme of liberation, it did have some unforeseen consequences. A man I know, who enjoyed himself to the hilt at Woodstock, is fond of saying that the sole thing he can now remember about the day is the social disease he acquired there, from which sex he remains uncertain.

As for the music itself, it had become a tradition that new stars were made at such festivals. Jimi Hendrix had come to public consciousness in '67 as Dylan had at Newport. At Woodstock it was Crosby, Stills, Nash and Young, newly formed, who emerged; they would go on to embody the hippie pastoralism that the event so perfectly symbolized. But, seeing the film, I didn't feel as if I had missed anything. By 1969, if you couldn't be backstage at a festival, there was no point in going. Who wanted to immerse himself in a mob of freaks when all the amenities were reserved for those backstage? Out front, the music pounded at you out of mammoth speakers, so thundering loud there was no escape; it filled up every cranny of your being. Backstage, the monitors were pitched at a civilized level. Out front, you would be treated to that strange mixture of arrogance and self-righteousness that the stars reserved for their audiences. You would be forced to listen to Joan Baez talking in that complacent, self-congratulatory martyr's style about her then-husband's imprisonment. Backstage, you could pour another glass of champagne and ignore her.

While Vietnam was all too real to those Americans our age who were being asked to fight there, for young Canadians it was a long way off. The war was either something that went on in the newspapers one didn't read, or part of the exotic culture of the nation to the south. There was something curious about Canadians who became seriously obsessed with Vietnam; they reminded one of those civil rights activists at the University of Toronto whose idea of effective action was to protest the events in Selma, Alabama, by sitting-in at the American consulate on University Avenue. What such gestures communicated, above all, was a Canadian anxiety at being excluded from the drama of American experience.

Still, Woodstock was the time of the peace sign. Looking back, that hand signal is as much a pathetic relic as bell-bottomed hip huggers or granny glasses. But at the time, you would get the two fingers flashed at you wherever you went. And, it could be unsettling. On one transatlantic flight I had made a stopover in Iceland, and sitting in the airport was a large group of American soldiers. The movies had taught me that GIs were a collection of John Waynes, fascist beerbellies in their thirties or older. This bunch was very young, a very scared group of kids my age, and several of them, spotting my long hair, surreptitiously flashed the peace sign like prisoners signalling from behind bars. At Woodstock, Sly Stone made the gesture his own personal *Heil Hitler!* salute, thrilled by his ability to make 300,000 screaming zombies throw up their hands in unison at his command, one more freaky kick, baby, as the multitudes throbbed to the tyrannical, repetitive rhythms of "Higher."

That was the supreme slogan of the time. Higher. Many of us didn't pass a straight moment in ten years. We took LSD every day for months just to see what would come first, Valhalla or permanent brain damage. I recall meeting one of Andy Warhol's entourage when the Exploding Plastic Inevitable came to town. Like some psychedelic commissar, he immediately demanded to know how many times I had taken LSD. Only once or twice I admitted, shamefacedly. (My initial experiences with that powerful drug taught me that it was not dope to be trifled with.) Oh, is that all, the guy sniffed. He had done it 300 times. I wondered what his brain cells looked like. A guy I knew became convinced that he had written all the Beatles songs. He had neglected to write them down and they had stolen them from him via telepathy; the Clarke Institute soon had another steady customer for shock therapy. Others would come back from places like Crete and Ibiza and India with their synapses well-scrambled. Years later, I saw them walking dazedly among the shoppers of rebuilt glitzy Yorkville, wondering where it had all gone.

At Woodstock, though, we still had our illusions. As the highways clogged up and the festival was declared a disaster area, and the choppers, symbol of the Vietnam war, flew in food and medicine, the media realized it was a bona fide event and began to give it full play. Members of the audience became instant celebrities, informing the mistrusted and uncomprehending members of the press just where it was all at. Since the newsmagazines had done covers on the generation gap, reporters felt obliged to ask what we thought of our folks. "My dad's OK," we would reply, "but he just doesn't understand because he's an immigrant, you know, and he came over here to better himself economically and socially, and all that rot."

All that rot.

Of course.

As every other rebellious generation found out, there was a price to be paid for defiance. Just as Wilde and the generation of the 1890s paid, and Fitzgerald and the lost generation paid, and Kerouac and the Beats paid, we began to learn the price of overreaching the conventional limits. People died. Of the performers at Woodstock who didn't have much time left there was Janis Joplin, The Who's drummer Keith Moon, and the one true genius of blitzkrieg rock guitar, Jimi Hendrix. They were celebrities. Among us, their audience, the deaths didn't appear in newspapers, wasn't written about in books. Besides the overdoses, there were bike crashes and car crashes, drug ripoffs and shootouts, and there were those who went to prison for one joint and died there.

I knew them, they were friends.

That was another of the anthems sung at Woodstock. "With a Little Help From My Friends." You couldn't trust your family, you couldn't trust your teachers, you couldn't trust society – you could trust your friends. The lesson that we were soon to learn, perhaps the last of the decade, was that you couldn't always trust your friends either. Your best friend went off with your best girl and well, you know, man, it just happened. No need to get so uptight. In the communal houses, you grew tired of going out to some tedious menial dropout's job to earn money while your friends sat around and blew dope all day. After Woodstock came Altamount and the Hell's Angels, and not too long after that came Charlie Manson, and we came to know that evil wasn't just in our families or in society but in ourselves too – that gap between the celebrities and the fans could get some folks ready to kill.

So we came to feel a revulsion for everything Woodstock stood for. Gradually we made up our quarrel with our families, our society. We began to address the necessity of making ourselves a place in the world rather than changing it for everyone else. We began to make the compromises. There was talk about "careers," a word previously absent from our vocabularies. Soon we were calling anything lazy or undisciplined or foolishly naive "'60s stuff." Those not quick enough to notice that big changes were afoot were left behind, "psychedelic relics." Suddenly, there seemed to be less time. As you became acquainted with your mortality, those long days, weeks, months that once floated by in sweet aimlessness came to be filled with frantic activity.

And yet, just as our fathers' generation bored us with tales of the Depression and D-Day, we will doubtless bore our children with tales of Woodstock and what it was like in the bad old days of the 1960s. It was no golden age, but I find myself missing, if not the '60s, my own twenties. For me, the years between 1965 and 1975 seem like centuries; the years since, like the few same months. As I watch '60s radicals become '80s conservatives, I yearn to feel again that inner sense of possibility. It was a notion of the "Woodstock generation" that life was an adventure, life was a mystery, life was a gamble, and that with Bob Dylan we had promised to go wandering. Even now, years later, there are those, wised-up but unrepentant, who regard it as a promise that, one way or another, we intend to keep right up until the end.

MILES DAVIS

Jazz has had a curious relation to pop music. Only once, during the swing era, has jazz actually been the popular music of the day. Most often, the attitude of jazz to the pop song is an odd combination of the parasitic and the satirical. Jazz is primarily a player's art; true jazz composers like Monk and Ellington have been the exception. Jazz probably would not exist without the pop ballads of George Gershwin, Harold Arlen, and Cole Porter. Of these composers, two were Jews, the other was gay. Gershwin's genius consisted, as did Arlen's, in his ability to infuse the Tin Pan Alley form with the blues sensibility of W.C. Handy and James P. Johnson. As for Porter, his Broadway career languished until, he confessed, he learned to write minor-key melodies, "like a Jew." Jazz, including that of its greatest geniuses such as Charlie Parker and Lester Young, would not have existed if it hadn't been for the chord changes of one pop tune, Gershwin's "I Got Rhythm." At the same time, most likely because of the music's marginal relation to mass culture, the lame sentiments of the pop tunes were deformed and changed beyond recognition. Jazzmen like Sonny Rollins delighted in taking an over-ripe Broadway piece of corn such as "There's No Business Like Show Business," throwing it on the floor and beating it to death, just ripping the song into its component parts and sending it up to an unrecognizable fare-thee-well.

Jazz ran into big problems when popular music changed during the 1960s from the Tin Pan Alley song to rock. Buried in avant-garde obscurities at the time, jazz lost touch with the popular audience. As a result, jazz artists sold fewer and fewer records.

In order to counteract this sad economic fact, the record companies encouraged their jazz artists to combine rock with jazz; the result was a hybrid called jazz fusion. Like the attempt, a few years earlier, to fuse jazz with "classical" music (so called "third stream"), jazz-rock was a curious mix and mostly a failure. Visit record stores and the cut-out bins are flowing with unsold attempts at jazz-rock.

One of two things happened when jazz musicians tried their hands at instrumental music that would appeal to a rock audience. They would go on playing the same style of jazz they always did, only they would use electric instruments. The electric guitars, instead of sounding like Eric Clapton or Robbie Robertson, still played in the polite Charlie Christian tradition. This music had the effect of boring the rock audience and antagonizing the hard-core jazz audience, for whom electric guitars were the devil incarnate. The other alternative was producing a danceable funk sound; this musical strategy generally meant abandoning the improvised soloing that is the prime defining characteristic of jazz.

The first jazz musician who succeeded in finding a style that appealed to the rock audience was Miles Davis. The trumpeter was possibly the greatest bandleader in the history of jazz, including Duke Ellington. Davis carried himself with all the street arrogance of a boxing champ: Sugar Ray Robinson. His cool demeanor entered the American consciousness via white imitators like Jack Nicholson and Clint Eastwood. Although Davis wasn't a particularly accomplished composer, his was a complex, fascinating musical mind. His solution to the classical/jazz dilemma, inspired by the Evans boys, Gil and Bill, was to infuse American bop and ballad forms with advanced European harmonic concepts borrowed from modern composers like Ravel. He knew enough to hire the most interesting young musicians around, throw them together, and give them challenging new directions to pursue. Just as jazz musicians had always done, he made pop music more complex, more challenging. He recognized that an R&B innovator like James Brown was a rhythmic genius. Brown's polyrhythms branched out in a completely new direction from jazz's conventional 4/4 swing, which by now sounded fairly plodding and antique. As in his modal period, Davis reduced the harmonic range of a song to a minimum. Brown's funk was blacker, more percussive, more African than what came before, a series of intricate, interlocking riffs. Every instrument was, for him, a drum. Davis was sensitive to the intellectual complexities of rhythm; he had the audacity to blend funk with the electronica of European composers like Karlheinz Stockhausen and still come with a sound that appealed to the black street. He was also a genius of musical taste: he could always tell those young musicians what to leave out. The results, as Ellington would have put it, were beyond category. Davis' followers in fusion, most of whom like Herbie Hancock and Wayne Shorter, had played in his band, were legion. But Davis, because of bad health brought on by addiction, withdrew into seclusion for much of the 1980s and was silent; he had long ago alienated his older fans.

During that time, the new jazzman on the scene was Wynton Marsalis. He repudiated funk and all its works and made a career of playing Davis' acoustic hard bop style of the late 1960s as if it was classical music and playing Haydn just as well as any symphonic trumpeter. In Marsalis' hands, jazz became entirely a music of the concert hall rather than the night club or dance floor. The newly emerging black middle class liked Marsalis' music; it expressed the respectability they craved. The young black audience was bored by it and turned to the crudities of rap. Marsalis also attracted an older white audience and jazz began to connote various notions of lofty class. Cigarette and luxury auto manufacturers wanted their products associated with jazz. They hoped a little of its stylishness would rub off on their products.

When Davis emerged from his hiatus, it seemed as if fusion had really run its course, a curiosity left over from the previous decade. But Davis did not revert to his original acoustic style, as did other erstwhile fusion players like Freddie Hubbard, provoked by Marsalis' example. He just picked up just where he left off. It made for a strange sight, the younger man, loyal to the old music, formal as a banker in his blue suit, the elder in wild shades and leathers well into his fifties, still wearing black street styles. Davis' music was electric, bristling with synthesizers and studio electronics. The hybrid form works. Marsalis went even farther back into the past to the orchestral style that Davis created with Gil Evans in the 1950s. He performed old favourites like "Stardust" and "When You Wish Upon a Star." He played them so reverently they no longer were pop music or even jazz but a form of nostalgic light classical music. Paradoxically, it was Davis, not Marsalis, who remained true to jazz's authentic spirit.

BRIAN MULRONEY: THE FIXER

The most salient fact about Brian Mulroney is that he is the first prime minister born into the Canadian working class. His career, a testimony to social mobility in this country, is also the story of one individual's eager assimilation of the values of the branch plant class. It is also the story of a socially disadvantaged though passionately ambitious young man on the rise prepared to stroke and appease whatever powers could hasten his advance. For Mulroney, growing up in an isolated town on the north shore of the St. Lawrence in Quebec, any consideration of whether it should have been Canadians or Americans who owned the town's paper mill would have been a luxury. The critical difference between respectability and the miseries of welfare lay in whether or not the mill employed you at all.

At St. Francis Xavier University in Nova Scotia in the 1950s, the campus Conservative club offered a little more opportunity of advancement than did an association with the Liberals. Campus Liberal clubs were universally recognized as the incubators of future cabinet ministers, senior bureaucrats, and lawyers with clout. Thus, the competition within them verged on the brutal. A young outsider interested in the interlocking careers of law and politics had more chance of being noticed among the Tories, who were seldom overburdened with young talent. Neither at St. Francis Xavier nor at law school did Brian Mulroney distinguish himself as a luminous academic mind. Rather, he impressed those around him with his ability to get practical things done in campus politics and ingratiate himself with those of his peers and superiors who counted in terms of climbing the greasy pole. He made himself invaluable, for instance, to John Diefenbaker. Trusting the student politician as an English-speaker, Diefenbaker relied on Mulroney to give him primer lessons on Quebec, territory as foreign to a prime minister from the prairies as the moons of Mars. Similarly, when Mulroney moved on to law school at Laval, he befriended a group of the young Anglo-Quebec gentry, which included Michael Meighen, grandson of a Tory prime minister and afterwards a Toronto lawyer, and Peter White, later Mulroney's principal secretary. There was no better incarnation of English Quebec's respectably alienated than these young Tories. As a group, they were obsessed with the eternal domination of Quebec politics by the Liberals, and like Mulroney they were hungry for the comforts and golden privileges that went with political power.

The conservative Anglo gentry of Montreal were considerably less stuffy than their Toronto equivalents, and they were also more interested in having a good time. Mulroney had Irish charm and conviviality in abundance, as well as an ability to convince whoever it was he was talking to that he believed in everything they did. According to friends from this time, all of

Mulroney's conversation was predicated, whether he was talking about fishing or politics, on exaggeration that they fondly understood to be exaggeration. It was an innate bent that quickly translated into career advantage. Mulroney made with ease the small transition from exaggeration to public relations pitch. Observers less charitable than his friends would come to characterize this glib hyperbole as a lack of probity. In those early years, Mulroney also imbibed the first law of Tory politics, an unequivocal partisanship that enjoined *on tire toujours sur les Rouges* – you always slam the Grits.

The Laval group made their way from Quebec City to the business, legal, and political world of Montreal in the mid-1960s, and Brian Mulroney went with them. One of their Francophone allies, Bernard Roy, helped Mulroney get his first job at the establishment law firm of Howard, Cate, Ogilvy. While Mulroney did not particularly stand out in terms of ability, he did possess certain natural advantages. First of all, there is his Irish background. The Irish are historic mediators between the French and English in Quebec, sharing a religion with one and a language with the other: there has always been much intermarriage between the French and Irish communities. In the politics of Quebec, Meighen or White, pure Anglos, could win a seat only on the West Island of Montreal, whereas Mulroney's political possibilities were broader. Then, there was his working-class background: Mulroney could move easily and amiably between workers and management. This was the key to his success in settling labour disputes on the Montreal waterfront in the mid-1960s.

The skills involved in such mediations were essentially those of impersonation. With his Baie Comeau background, Mulroney could call upon all the rugged tavern manners necessary to convince union leaders after a night of drinking that he was essentially on their side and that they should shave a couple of cents an hour off their wage demands. Dealing with management, he further developed the sleek gentleman's façade learned at St. Francis Xavier and Laval. (Only romantics from the middle class dress and behave like factory workers. Ambitious boys from the working class learn quickly the flat necessity of a genteel front to clothe the primitive appetites that drive the worlds of business and politics.) There was scarce doubt, however, where Brian Mulroney's allegiance ultimately lay: the route to money and high position was in acting for management, never the unions.

Of the Laval group, Mulroney was clearly the poorest and hungriest. The demands of high office in the late twentieth century are such that whoever wants it has to be driven by furies. Mulroney's father died just after Brian had gone on to Montreal. A friend from that time remembers the funeral at the family's modest apartment. Mulroney's father's pension was not going to go far, and he was faced with supporting his mother, younger brother and youngest sister. In those days, young lawyers didn't make much, and Mulroney's contemporaries were impressed with their friend's nerve when he told his law firm that unless his salary was raised he was going back to Baie Comeau. The firm came through with the salary bump. The friend recalls Mulroney's first suit, a matter of desperate concern because he could never get it to fit properly. In this context, the fifty pairs of Gucci loafers discovered in his Sussex Drive closet are perfectly understandable.

If there was a single key to Brian Mulroney's character, it was a hunger for success defined in the most unvarnished terms: big job, big house, a looker for a wife. Although he could mediate between business and labour, his loyalty was to the dominant power in any situation. Nor was Mulroney the sort to take a quixotic gamble. Staying firmly in the back rooms of Quebec Tory politics, he realized that a run at a seat in Parliament under either Stanfield or Clark was a loser's game. He couldn't afford to lose, not even once. He hadn't come all the way from Baie Comeau to place his bets on anything less than a sure thing.

When Mulroney decided to run for the Conservative leadership in 1976, his implicit promise to the party was so novel that they could not accept it: he was a bilingual Catholic from Quebec with so much of a winner's gloss that he offended their alienated instincts. In 1976, Mulroney looked to his party to have too much of the style of a Liberal. It took almost a decade of Joe Clark's mistakes to convince the Tories of his practical value. His success in the corporate boardrooms and political back rooms of Montreal was based on qualities more visceral than cerebral. He understood the art of the deal, he understood the art of pragmatic friendship known as networking, he understood the art of quid pro quo. When the American-owned Iron Ore Company of Canada hired Mulroney to become their local president, they knew they were getting a glossily packaged member of Canada's branch-plant class. He could finesse their labour problems in Schefferville and polish the company's image. After his experience on the Cliche Commission, he was well versed in the skills of vivid self-presentation on television. It was also Mulroney's pride that he could get on with anybody. In the province of Quebec he was supremely well connected. If the Iron Ore Company wanted to talk to the provincial Liberals, well, he could set up lunch with Robert Bourassa.

The Tory values of loyalty and self-interest could be mutually contradictory at times: it took the genteel virtue of hypocrisy to reconcile them. In 1982, Mulroney publicly shook hands with Joe Clark at the Ritz Carlton in Montreal while preparing the leadership campaign that would ultimately unseat Clark. Though he recruited Claude Wagner for the election of 1972, in 1976, when they were both candidates for the Tory leadership, the Mulroney camp leaked, through Peter White, information about Wagner's trust fund that ultimately eliminated Wagner from the race. Then there was the other major lesson of the greasy pole: suck up, kick down. At Howard, Cate, Ogilvy, Mulroney was known for his sucking up, his extreme deference to the senior partners and their wives and daughters. On the campaign stump, Mulroney raged defiance at picketing strikers and unionists. Neither was an act of personal preference, just obeisance to the social hierarchy as a practical ladder to success.

While the corporate arts of impersonation and slick self-presentation served Mulroney well behind the scenes, they seldom endeared him to the public once he moved into the arena of parliamentary politics. What was amiable and likable in a boardroom was unctuous and phony on television. It was felt that Mulroney gave up too much to his social self. The oft-made comparisons between Brian Mulroney and Ronald Reagan were ultimately false. The difference was seemingly between a proficient television performer and a lesser one. Yet, Reagan used all his considerable theatrical skills to propound a message he clearly believed. Where Reagan had the advantage of a simple creed – the American way – to communicate, Mulroney gave little evidence of having wrestled with all the devilishly elusive and complicated Canadian dilemmas of identity. He never mastered the accent of sincerity that is shaped, after all, by an inner loyalty to the truth of one's experience. Mulroney never gave evidence of much propensity to inner reflection. The actor's virtues of impersonation that served him well in labour mediation and corporate public relations left him with an actor's vices: attenuation of self, an immense vanity, and a desire to flatter and please the audience. The more sincere he tried to be, the phonier he seemed. Just as Reagan was well liked, no matter how outrageous the scandals that plagued his government, Mulroney would never be completely trusted, no matter what his government achieved. The electorate still looked to its leaders to provide a superior example in character. The noble self is boldly defined, its purposes clearly conceived and openly avowed. In odd ways, both Thatcher and Reagan could each lay claim to a noble self. But it often seemed that Brian Mulroney had achieved success at the cost of his integrity. In the federal election of 1984, though, it scarcely mattered. John Turner was much worse in every conceivable way. Universal rejection of the Liberals and Turner's blunders combined to relegate latent mistrust of Mulroney to the background. Nonetheless, the genetic defects of the Conservative animal were simmering in embryo waiting to hatch once it gained power.

After Turner's leadership victory at the Liberal convention in the spring of 1984, Mulroney and his party had difficulty recruiting the type of candidate they wanted in Quebec. Instead of high-quality men and women from the universities and the more prestigious law firms and corporations, the Tories, with a few exceptions such as Marcel Masse, could attract only low-level opportunists. Paradoxically, the pro-business fever of the early 1980s worked against the Tory recruitment program. A bilingual woman administrator, say, from the University of Sherbrooke with a Harvard MBA would be too engrossed in building up her own little company to take a chance on running for parliament. Consequently, many of the candidates that they did recruit were attracted to politics by its spoils and rapidly proved embarrassing to Mulroney in office. In addition, the Quebec Tory caucus was largely rural. Not only were they regionalists but their concerns were intensely parochial. They focused more on local issues – whether Hyundai would build a branch plant in their riding, who would sell the land, who would get the jobs there – than they did on national concerns. Quebec Tories cared little about federal nation building. As long as Quebec's interests were looked after, they were well satisfied. The rest of the country left them indifferent at best, and actively hostile at worst.

As prime minister, Mulroney sought to reconcile the various elements of his party; his program was never one of strongly held vision and conviction. Instead, he fashioned a patchwork of accommodation. The real split in the party was not left and right but pro- and anti-Dief. In contesting the Tory leadership, Mulroney had first wooed the Diefenbaker cowboys, such as Robert Coates, since they were the portion of the party most alienated from Joe Clark. The Diefenbaker cowboys most certainly had a strong vision of the country, one that had largely remained unchanged since the mid-1950s. Reactionary to the core, they were in love with capital punishment and censorship. They were anti-abortion and against bilingualism and the metric system. Mulroney knew that most of the country rejected their anachronistic and mean-spirited values but felt compelled, for political reasons, to mollify the cowboys by opening up their concerns for debate. So the electorate watched the spectacle of Mulroney dissenting from a motion to reinstate capital punishment, which members of his own party had introduced.

The Diefenbaker cowboys had proved embarrassing in another way. The scandal involving Coates and a B-girl in Lahr, West Germany, was less an example of yahoo lust run amok than the rebound of Coates' mistrust and dislike of the permanent civil service. After twenty-seven years on the back benches, Coates was determined in a particularly high-handed way to show the military bureaucracy at the Department of National Defence just how little he needed them. Almost immediately after taking office he alienated his senior civil servants. The subsequent scandal in Lahr must be seen, at least in part, as the successful effort of disgruntled bureaucrats to rid the department of an inadequate chief by leaking his indiscretions to an Ottawa newspaper.

Still, Mulroney's most powerfully interpreted maxim was "Ya dance with those who brung ya." He was most loyal to those cronies and pals whom he had met on his climb to power. Mulroney in office was like a 1920s Chicago Irish mayor: his best buddies and cronies would get plum jobs; those citizens shrewd enough not to have pissed him off over the years would be allowed to sweep up; those dumb fucks who made an enemy of the boss could goddamn well freeze in the cold.

Mulroney's fragile veneer of righteousness, however, could not stand one second of blame. When the Coates scandal hit, when Sinclair Stevens was accused of conflict of interest, when Michel Gravel stood accused of influence peddling, Mulroney, despite the combined reproach of opposition and media, would admit no wrongdoing. Instead of distancing himself from the culprits, Mulroney tied himself more closely to the scandals by his reluctance to acknowledge any sense of fault. Consequently, he was unable to assume the media stance Ronald Reagan had mastered, at least until Irangate, in relation to the scandals that plagued his administration. It was one of the Great Communicator's most original strokes, whether by accident or design, to appear to be just another citizen on Main Street making wry comment on the puzzling things that went on in that darn White House, and thus duck out of the line of fire. Mulroney's indestructible loyalty led him to take the assault full face.

Not surprisingly, Mulroney's allegiance to cronies did not go so far as to endanger his own prospects. As a result of the scandals of the first two years of his government and the resulting unpopularity of his leadership, Mulroney was forced to make peace with both the left wing of his party and the civil service. Derek Burney, recruited into the PMO as chief of staff in 1987, and Marc Lortie, appointed press secretary in the same year, were both recruited into the PMO from the Department of Foreign Affairs. But the prime minister called in the pros of the bureaucracy when he had little other choice. Like Diefenbaker and Clark, he had a free enterpriser's mistrust of government, seeing public servants as having worked hand in glove for too many years with the detested Grits. He also shared some of the resentment of perennial Tory outsiders who had suffered for years the condescension of a civil-service élite who looked down their noses at business. Like much else about Mulroney's government, his relationship with the civil service seemed hurried and improvised.

As for the corporate wing of the party, there was never any question that Mulroney would do his best to satisfy their desire in every way. Both his instincts to defer to power and his sense of stroking the hierarchy led to his abolition of the Foreign Investment Review Agency and the National Energy Program. The way to deal with powerful American financial interests was not to sit down and bargain hard but to appease and propitiate and assuage.

To a large extent, this instinctive program of Mulroney's was propelled (and with considerable force) by reaction. As far as possible, he endeavored to become the reverse image of the politician who, next to John Diefenbaker, had had the strongest influence on him: Pierre Elliott Trudeau. Strong leaders are, after all, infrequent, and Trudeau's political personality had been the dominant force in the country after mid-century. If Michel Gratton, Mulroney's former press secretary, is to be believed, the new prime minister was nearly fixated with equalling and surpassing the achievement of his predecessor.

If Mulroney possessed the psychology of the rising working class, however, Trudeau was a prime exemplar of the psychology of *noblesse oblige.* Trudeau's goals and aims, from the preservation of a bilingual centralist state, to the peace initiative of his latter career, all took the form of single-minded crusades that had profound inner meaning for him. While he devoted himself almost exclusively during the late 1970s and early 1980s to the referendum in Quebec and constitutional reform, he delegated the economic issues that would come to dominate the next decade to cabinet ministers like Marc Lalonde and Herb Gray. Trudeau was tough, decisive, visionary: he had large dreams for the country. Mulroney, motivated by the appeasing and propitiating instincts that had brought him to prominence, made Canada seem much smaller, an altogether more modest country in thrall to its provincial premiers and American and British allies. Trudeau was no plaster saint. Hardball patronage was a part of the game, and it was his pride that he could master the game in all its aspects. He did have the sense to entrust the messy work of patronage to Jim Coutts, Keith Davey, and Andre Ouellet, and preserve the high road for himself. Mulroney, however, liked nothing better than to play Godfather: few things gave him more pleasure than to distribute largesse personally, as if he was an alderman handing out turkeys at Christmas to poor families.

If Trudeau regarded high office as a knightly crusade, Mulroney had a more lunch-bucket approach: a job was a job. You kept the boss happy, you kept the customers happy. You did your day's work and you went home. Friday was payday. Their styles were different in another way. The early Trudeau shared something of the young man's sex appeal first brought into politics by John F. Kennedy. While Mulroney was far from being unaware of his own small-town Lothario looks, he was also that dullest of creatures, the reformed sinner. Sacrificing cigarettes and booze for power, he added only blandness to his unction. Mulroney contrived to be a celebrity without being a hero. No young Canadian boy or girl yearned to grow up to be just like him. Trudeau had been a romantic. Mulroney yearned to share something of that glamorous style and appeal, but his instincts leaned toward caution.

Confident of his own identity and vision, Trudeau practiced a kind of North American Gaullism in relation to the superpowers. He preserved the critical posture towards the United States that he had inherited from both Pearson and Diefenbaker. Domestically, his stance was one of continual challenge: his relation to the public was essentially embattled. Bilingual, cosmopolitan, cultivated, he reminded too many Canadians of their own inadequacies. Yet there was little doubt of Trudeau's ability to govern. By the time Mulroney came to power in 1984, Canadians took Trudeau's level of competence for granted. They assumed Mulroney would preserve this level and effect a national reconciliation as well. Mulroney assumed that he would naturally inherit the strong measure of respect that Trudeau had won for the person of the prime minister.

Both leader and country were mistaken. De Tocqueville wrote that power cannot sustain itself where reverence is lacking. Mulroney's street instincts served him well in the acquisition of power. They were much less useful in office. In Parliament, his platitudinous arguments lacked Trudeau's sharp intellectual focus and substance. Despite the partisan bombast, he was often like an actor struggling to play the role of a political debater. As the scandals unfolded, as Mulroney reversed himself on issues such as old-age pensions, the prime minister's greatest everyday task seemed to be the preservation of his own hard-won dignity, and he lost the country's respect. His promise, after all, was a material one: he would make first his cronies, next his business constituency, then the rest of the country, rich. Such materialism and careerism seemed to many a lowering of expectations and moral standards. Where Trudeau used pragmatic politics to achieve a nation-building ideal, for Mulroney practical politics was a goal in itself. Where Trudeau led and invited the electorate to judge his performance, Mulroney tried to give them what he thought they wanted. Trudeau pursued an aggressive style of leadership, unafraid to fight in the open those who disagreed with him. Mulroney attempted to preserve his corporate front of "civility" while, reportedly, his Baie Comeau instincts let loose tantrums and petty vengeances behind closed doors.

In part, this dilemma of public versus private self was one shared with Lyndon B. Johnson. In private conversation with reporters, Mulroney was said to possess funds of salty wit. When it surfaced publicly, as in his 1984 campaign remark "There's no whore like an old whore," about Bryce Mackasey's appointment as ambassador to Portugal, this cheery vulgarity appeared to discredit him. Yet like Johnson's, Mulroney's Snopes-shrewd, street-smart side was perhaps his most attractive. Although Trudeau had alienated many Canadians with his directness, others took it as proof of sincerity. Where Trudeau felt free to show the public many facets of his personality, Mulroney as a public presence rapidly appeared flat and one-dimensional and bursting with bad faith – just a voice in a blue suit. There were few sides to his character that he chose to show Canadians: the suspicion was that his was a nature without the complexity that could compel enduring interest. Whatever its initial appeal, Mulroney's much-vaunted "civility" soon wore thin.

Trudeau's critics' most insistent point was that he had created disunity in the country. Yet when Brian Mulroney took office, the conflicts between the federal and provincial governments were not automatically settled. Whoever sought to deal with them, whether Trudeau or Mulroney, was quickly stained by the country's enduring divisions. Lacking the Americans' unifying myth of *e pluribus unum*, Canada's internal disputes were too profound to be healed by the new prime minister's façade of "civility." Mulroney's instincts, honed in the corporate world, led him to replace Trudeau's national vision of the

Canadian state with a patchwork of short-sighted deals. Be it addressing simple problems like the F-18 maintenance contract or far-reaching issues like the Constitution (which he deemed solved by the Meech Lake Accord), Mulroney performed as a deal-maker. All the same, unlike Diefenbaker or King, he was no ditherer. Since his student days he had prided himself on his ability to get things done. He was determined to be decisive, and he was. The problem was that he undertook vast, transformative measures that promised to change the country altogether in a permanent way. Large decisions were taken without much reflection about their long-term consequences.

The most profound difference between Mulroney and Trudeau was found in their approaches to their own community, Quebec. Where Trudeau envisaged Quebec, however quixotically, as a province equal to others in a bilingual Canada, Mulroney subscribed to the decentralizing notion of Quebec as a distinct society. Trudeau simultaneously promoted Quebec's interests in Ottawa and fought against its secessionist urges at home. Mulroney instinctively appeased each and every Quebec demand. Just as he quickly conceded NEP and FIRA to Washington, Mulroney gave Quebec far more than it was expecting in jurisdiction over immigration and rights to nominate to the Supreme Court. Mulroney knew that his essential key to power lay in Quebec, and he was loath to deny it anything.

Trudeau's vision of the Just Society extended to more than notions of social equality. It also included the idea of a federal-provincial balance of power. Combined with Quebec's electoral strength, Mulroney's assent – never explicit enough to be a belief – to the doctrine of "special status" tilted the Canadian balance even further in Quebec's direction.

In the end, Mulroney found Trudeau's federalist notion of one Canada to be too much of a challenge, too much the quixotic dream. Mulroney's instincts led him back to a pre-federalist past. They told him you can't stray too far from nature. In society there were strong and weak, there were rich and poor – realism dictated that it was useless to intervene. In Canada, history had decreed two nations, English and French. The theory of "special status" insisted that it was foolish to try to transform this reality.

The drawback of Trudeau-style federalism is that it requires a leader as strong as himself to practise it. Mulroney's desire to propitiate strength, to genuflect to the dominant power in any situation, as well as his wish to repudiate Trudeau's example, all made him reluctant to confront either Quebec's self-assertion or that of the West. True to his background, Mulroney approached the balance of powers in Canada as a mediator, abdicating almost entirely his national role as the most important among the players.

Canadian party leaders tend to mold a country that mirrors their personality. Under Trudeau it sometimes seemed that the country's citizens ought to become the bilingual reproduction of its leader, and its cities cosmopolitan duplicates of Montreal. In all, Brian Mulroney was more like the average man on the street, more anonymous than his immediate predecessors. He was neither an exotic like Trudeau, a mandarin like Pearson, nor a cranky eccentric like King and Diefenbaker. He was mostly appetite and self-regard.

Ruled by Mulroney's branch-plant instincts, Canada relinquished its hard-won status as a medium power gained in two world wars and settled for the role of a satellite nation. Influenced by his propensity to placate and accommodate, the country regressed from its stance as a critical and independent nation back into the neo-colonial past. The lessons of the journey from working class to branch-plant prime minister are that, above all, the orders come from elsewhere. The lessons of the mediator, misplaced in a political context, are not to resolve issues decisively but to attempt to strike a compromise among irreconcilable contradictions. When a leader lacks a commitment to well-defined national standards and values, the result is an increasing lack of coherence in national purpose. Under Brian Mulroney, Canada became richer and more placid; it also lost its soul.

MEXICO

Just before he ordered his fourth *cuba libre*, the professor informed me that a man like him had to be careful about how much he drank. At first glance he looked more like a retired infantry colonel than a college teacher. He was a large man with close-cropped grey hair, a huge belly and an immense, shouting laugh. We had struck up a conversation at the patio bar of the small beach hotel and our talk of baseball and politics had eventually driven away the German couple sitting at the bar. A red sun was hovering like a ball of flame on the horizon at the edge of the bay. The evening was sweltering hot: the temperature was thirty-degrees in the shade. Now it was the end of the tourist season; outside the town, there were many small fires. The Mexican farmers were getting their fields ready for planting.

Now retired, the professor had taught all his life at a large mid-western university. His subject, Hispanic literature and history, obsessed him still, and he now spent his days travelling through Mexico, Spain, and Portugal. The professor had begun coming to Puerto Escondido thirty years ago, back when the town's main street was just a dirt road and there was no daily flight from Mexico City, just a bumpy unpaved highway, through almost impassable hills, from Oaxaca, eight hours away. He liked Puerto Escondido because there were no high-rise hotels, no package tours, no Texan yahoos. The visitors who came to the town were Europeans, Latin Americans, painters and writers, or those Americans like himself who had a special love for the country. The Mexicans themselves came here for the sea and the beach. The town was well named, in his opinion. "Hidden port." The professor was convinced the blessed anonymity couldn't last. Next year, or the following one, Puerto Escondido would be discovered and the barbarians would descend.

As the twilight deepened, we walked down the beach. The buildings that ringed the bay were shielded by large maternal palms, the hotels were small two-storey buildings; the restaurants were constructed of bamboo, with thatched roofs. The town lay south toward the equator along the Pacific coast from Acapulco. Starting out in life as a modest, bashful fishing village, Puerto Escondido had been forced by the needs of importunate visitors away from the bay, up a dry, dry hill until it met the highway from Oaxaca. Now it sported worldly little neon signs touting slick tourist shops that eagerly satisfied the insatiable tourist lust for Mexican silver and leather, and shrewd, small stands hawking T-shirts and beachwear. But Puerto Escondido even now did not lead the garish existence of a frankly commercial resort. Still tiny, the tourist town appeared demurely prosperous. There were few beggars and little crowding. The two blocks of main street that ran parallel to the bay had been closed to traffic. The houses and shops had a fresh coat of whitewash and bougainvillaea crawled purple and scarlet over the walls. At the top of the hill sat a church, whose bell was waking the townspeople to evening mass.

On the beach, fishermen, setting out in their boats, wore pastel swimwear. They had a South Seas air. The shore was strewn with their nets and the outboard motors were roped to the palms. As we walked, the professor delivered a monologue on the subject of Americans in Mexico. Gringos. When he had first started coming to the country in the years after the war, the visitors were serious people, studying the culture and getting to know the Mexicans. In those days, there were plenty of remittance men, whose families paid them to stay away. Then, a few years later, came the hippies. The professor didn't like hippies. They cared nothing for Mexico. They were just down here for the good dope, and to fuck on the beach. They didn't care if they met a single Mexican. Now, it was just a lot of wounded people, corporate and professional refugees, running away from their American lives, looking for something better.

We walked up from the beach into the town towards dinner. In the street, one of the pariah dogs almost went under the wheels of a taxi. I didn't want to see gory death before eating.

"Don't worry about it," said the professor. "Death's a big part of this culture."

Early the next morning I took a walk along the ocean front south of town, where the surfers were. The big beach is to surfing what Mont Tremblant is to skiing or St. Andrews is to golf. Out of an apparently calm sea, the surf, without warning erupted into swells the size of a house and broke onto shore with the roar of supersonic jets. This surfing beach was known as La Tuba or the "Mexican Pipeline." The surfers, blond young men from Hawaii and California, would ride the crest of a long wave, then nose their board back onto it as it broke, and then into another. When the surf unfurled in successive, contiguous waves like these it was said to be "tubing." Some of the surfers were professionals who made a living from tournament winnings and endorsements. Others were mere cultists and votaries of the sport, working at odd jobs until they saved enough to afford the fare to one of the great surfing beaches, like the Mexican Pipeline. The surfers were very young, some barely out of their teens, and each group of surfers seemed to have a video camera with them to record their feats. When they weren't surfing, they sat in the restaurant of a nearby hotel and drank beer and played cards, always scanning the sea anxiously for signs of their cult's godhead, the perfect wave. "Is it tubing?" Tom would ask Frank. "Nah," Frank would reply, "there's a couple of sets, but it's not tubing or anything." It was easy to make fun of these physical cultists, but the spiritual cultists were here too, resting up after peyote sessions and visions with the Indians.

On the beach closer to town, there were rocks, gnarled and sculptured as if they were made out of papier mâché. The surf itself could easily snap a leg or a back; the cross-tides and riptides could drag the unwary swimmer against these rocks. Planted in the sand was a sign that announced: *Playa peligrosa*, dangerous beach, *Cuidado*, caution. Every year swimmers were lost here. I respected the power of the sea far too much to attempt it: I had broken a leg in far milder surf.

There were other dangers on the beach, apparently. A sign on my hotel room door warned that the establishment could not guarantee the safety of its guests there after sundown. From time to time, I saw patrols of Mexican marines, a half-dozen soldiers in beige uniforms and full combat gear, casually slinging carbines and submachine-guns over their shoulders, making their presence felt on the beach. There had been a murder the other day in one of the restaurants along the shore, a knifing over a drug deal. Like the man said, death was part of the culture. The fishermen wore Sony Walkmans as they went about their work, and the bank and airline office in the town were equipped with computers, but Mexico remains a frontier society: *bandidos* still plague the countryside. The country's aficionados all had their war stories: a robbery at knifepoint, an attack in secluded ruins, a shooting incident. (There was another sign I had read in a hotel in Puerto Escondido that had the crazy poetry of mangled English. "In the event of fire or earthquake or any other sinister," it counselled with characteristic Mexican stoicism, "walk to the center of the garden and wait there quietly.") I knew from experience that in Mexico you had to carry yourself in a certain self-possessed way; there were situations you just didn't get into, if you were smart, places, unless you felt ready to handle big trouble, you just didn't go. But then, Mexico's dangers, if they didn't kill you, represented half the piquant spice of its appeal.

Watching the surfers was a guy in his forties, Tim. At first, he seemed like any other businessman on vacation. He liked Reagan, he didn't like liberals. He adored his wife and children.

Most such visitors came down to Mexico on one-week package tours. Yet Tim was on his own, on the loose in Mexico for an indeterminate period. "I just need a break," he said. He was staying at a campground on the beach, in a tent, even though he wasn't driving. He was travelling around by bus, hitchhiking, odd for a middle-aged businessman. He carried all his valuables with him all the time in a small blue knapsack that he never left out of his sight. Underneath everything he said was a hard edge, a rage just bubbling under the surface. He was one of the wounded; God alone knew what he was looking for.

That evening, in a restaurant in town, I ran into two girls from Seattle: Gloria and Shelley. I had come to believe that the west coast from San Diego to Vancouver had become Californian in its thinking. In the time it took to drink a few cold Coronas, I knew their life stories. Gloria was a tall girl with a tanned, athletic body, blond hair and a plain face, by contrast. Shelley was younger, childlike: she had a lobster-red burn from the sun. Gloria's beauty shop back home had failed. Now, she said, she worked in a restaurant. Shelley worked for an airline, "in communications." Baldly put, Gloria was a waitress and Shelley was a mailroom clerk. Back home, they were roommates, Shelley having moved in with Gloria after she got tired of supporting her saxophone-playing boyfriend.

Two more of the wounded, Gloria and Shelley were partying hard. They ordered more drinks. Despite their gaiety, however, the two girls were constantly and nervously solicitous of each other's well-being.

"How ya doin', baby?" Shelley asked Gloria every few minutes. "Mellow yellow," Gloria would reply.

Overhead, the ceiling fans turned slowly. The taped music endlessly played what I had come to think of as resort music: Jimmy Buffet singing "Margaritaville." Soon, the live entertainment appeared. It was a father-and-son act. The father wore long hair to his shoulders and a tank top. He had the deep tan and wasted look of the permanent expatriate. His boy, no more than twelve or thirteen, had delicate features and hair bleached white by the sun. The father played acoustic guitar, the son electric, and they performed soft Latin rock, music by Carlos Santana and Antonio Carlos Jobim. There was a novel in the story of an American father and son travelling around playing the bars of Mexico. In this story, the son would have to be a blazing, precocious virtuoso, his father the Leopold Mozart of Latin rock. Real life was more prosaic; the kid wasn't bad at all for a twelve-year-old but he still had a long way to go on the guitar, his father better only by a decade.

At another table was a group of surfers, the food piled up in front of them like they were feeding at a Big Ten training table. With them was Tim. Spotting the two women across the room, his face took on a hungry look that had little to do with gastronomy. The muscle in his jaw was voraciously working. He was waiting to be beckoned over and introduced. Soon, he had abandoned his surfer buddies and attached himself to the two women. While Gloria excused herself to make a long-distance call to her boyfriend back in the States, Tim told Shelley how much he adored his two children. It must have been the most pathetic, lame come-on she'd ever heard.

Returning to the table, the boyfriend pacified, Gloria wanted to move on to *La Tuba*, one of the town's discos. Tim did not want to go: Mexican dance clubs gave him bad vibes. Last night, a couple of young Australians had been followed back to their hotel from one of the clubs and robbed. But the girls' appeal was too strong; he tagged along anyway. On the way, Shelly noticed a game of hopscotch chalked out on the pavement and girlishly gathering up her skirt, hopped along. Once at the dance club, Gloria and Shelley were surrounded by a group of Mexicans. Waiters, fishermen, beach boys. They seemed to be the only two available women in town. It was a feeding frenzy.

La Tuba was a couple of chairs and tables fronting on the beach, a sound system and a dance floor, presided over by Silvestre, a large man with a moustache. He dressed Eurotrash-style and exuded a false *bonhomie*. Two German women, clad head-to-toe in high-fashion black, sat sipping coffee in chilly Teutonic silence. Some middle-class Mexican kids arrived and danced stolidly with one another. They didn't talk to anybody. Respectable Mexico remains a conservative Catholic society, and shaking your booty like Americans, like Shelley and Gloria, is viewed as vulgar. The other night some disapproving Mexican had thrown bottle caps at Shelley as she was out there slinging that thang on the dance floor. Now they were all vying for a chance to dance with her, then asking to go for a "walk" on the beach. Tim hovered on the edge of the crowd, clutching the blue knapsack to his chest as if afraid it would be snatched from him. He disappeared from sight for a few minutes, then reappeared, nervously. He didn't like the Eurotrash and the Mexicans at the club, but the loneliness was too much to bear.

I started to talk with one of Gloria's aspiring suitors, an off-duty waiter named Fernando. In his polo shirt and tan shorts, he was the preppiest-looking Mexican I had ever met. He too was eager to expound the ways of Mexico. He gestured contemptuously at the beach, the discos, and the restaurants. "This isn't Mexico," he said. "This is just gringos."

The next day, like a character in a novel by E.M. Forster, I went off with the professor to see the real Mexico. Authenticity of a sort was found up the parched hill away from the bay in the upper town on the other side of the highway to Oaxaca. The real Puerto Escondido was like a thousand other Mexican towns: dusty, dirty, chaotic. Once outside the city limits, you encountered rural life at its most primitive, and then the Mexican desert, badlands, stretched out forever. In the real town there was a school, a gasworks, a supermarket, government offices and a red-light district. None of it was picturesque or folkloric.

The old professor pointed out from the window of his car at the town's market. There was a story attached to it. He told me how the local government had decided Puerto Escondido needed a new market and built one, at great expense. Problem was, nobody went there because they still patronized the old place. One night, somebody or other, strongly suspected of having ties to the government, arrived at the old market and bulldozed it flat. Even then, nobody went to the new market, but just patiently rebuilt the old one. There it was in a nutshell: Mexico.

It was mid-afternoon, the heat was so oppressive that walking even a single step was a chore. We stopped for a beer in a cantina. In the back, a pig rooted in the garden. A few men sat around drinking *cervezas* and eating raw turtle's eggs. They promoted virility, it was said. The beers were served by a ten-year-old boy, wearing the checked trousers of a school uniform. The professor said: "The child-labour laws down here are very simple. All children work."

We went to another cantina. There, the professor introduced me to Antonio and his sister Juana, who ran the place. Antonio looked like the boxer Roberto Duran. He was a sailor and a diver. Like his two brothers before him, he was diligently drinking himself to death. He wore a blue tattoo of a mermaid on his chest and he had machete scars along his knuckles; another creased his forehead. Juana was buxom and had a flashing smile for every passing stranger. Her boyfriend sat with her at the table playing with a sharp knife, testing its long blade along his jeans. In each cantina, the professor announced himself with a booming laugh. *Haw haw haw.* It showed goodwill and friendly merriment, as if the Mexicans needed to be continually reassured of these qualities. Out in the dusty street, a VW Beetle passed, with twin loudspeakers affixed to its roof. The national elections were just a few weeks away. As always, the outgoing President had appointed his successor, and the Party of the Institutionalized Revolution would win. The VW was campaigning for the National Action Party, a small conservative party. Mexico had been a one-party state from the Aztecs to the Spaniards right up to el P.R.I. There was little democracy but many fine speeches at election time. Another failed revolution in Mexico to go with the failed revolutions in Russia and Cuba.

I had been coming to Mexico for twenty years. I still didn't know how I felt about the country. I was happier here than anywhere else, and for small reasons. The whitewashed walls, the red dirt, the smells and tastes, the tropical nights: everywhere you turned there were acute pleasures for the eye. There was also the salt air, the fresh-caught shrimp and fish. There was poetry in any country but it was much easier to come by poetry in Mexico. Yet I knew I would always be a stranger here. But sitting in this cantina talking in Spanish to this old professor and this drunken fisherman, I knew life to be open-ended and full of possibility and I was possessed by a wild sense of freedom. If this was not exactly happiness, it was something close to hope.

Yes, Mexico was paradise. But it was also an inferno. All those wounded men and women on the beach, fleeing the plagues and pollution and false values of North America, private and public, could only enjoy the consolations of Mexico through an act of willful blindness to its poverty and violence. But this country always had a knack of forcing the attention. My morning walk had evolved into a ritual. In the early hours before the sun rose high in the sky, the light was sharp and clear. It was cool and the smoky haze did not hang in the air. The surf was best around sunrise and I ran into Tom and Frank. They had news. Just a few minutes ago, they had been on the beach, working on Frank's board when they heard a pop, then a whiz, then a puff of sand between them as the bullet hit. Some bitter Mexican was shooting at them from the hills with a rifle. With remarkable sangfroid, they just kept on surfing.

Watching the National Action Party Beetle patrolling the meagre streets of the real Mexico, I was reminded of a scene I had witnessed in a beach restaurant the previous day. There was a wealthy Mexican family eating lunch. The mother was dressed more for an embassy reception than the beach: a white backless dress and high heels. One daughter wore a miniskirt, the other a jogging suit. They aped American styles perfectly. A small son, well-behaved, sat with them at the table. The father of the family sat apart, alone and inviolable in his regal male solitude. He looked something like the old Mexican comedian, Cantinflas, tall and skinny, with a dark moustache and a comfortable pot belly. While he was eating, he was approached by one of the vendors who hawked their wares on the beach. She was a shapeless young Indian woman with a stoic Oriental look. Vendors are a nuisance; everybody knows that. Cantinflas didn't say "No thanks" or "Not today" or utter any of the polite formulas of refusal. He didn't say a word, didn't acknowledge by even a tremor of an eyebrow the young woman's existence. He just kept gobbling his seafood with renewed gusto. The young woman stared at him eating for a few moments. Then, her face a mask, she walked away. There would be more revolutions in Mexico.

Suddenly, I was tired of the bars and the cantinas, the tourist town of Puerto Escondido and the real town. I had drunk too many *cuba libres*, too many *cervezas*, talked to too many wounded people. My friend the old professor was leaving that evening, moving on to a village high in the mountains. That afternoon I checked into a good hotel far away from the noise and chaos of the tourist town. In the Hotel Santa Fe everything was cool. Placid, discreet servants moved about in cotton embroidered Indian dresses. I sat under a palm by the pool and read Octavio Paz, a great poet who had resigned as ambassador to India when his government massacred hundreds of protesting students near Mexico City in 1968.

The next morning there were clouds in the sky, a quick shower. The summer rains were on their way; soon all the tourist visitors would be gone and myself with them. I sat with my coffee, looking out at the Pacific, savouring these lines of Octavio Paz, written in 1948.

Night falls on Teotihuacan.
High on the pyramid the boys smoke marijuana,
The guitars beat, husky.
What grass, what water of life will life
give to us
where can we unearth the word,
the measure that gives laws to hymn and
speech
to dances, cities, scales?
Mexican song explodes in a curse,
a many-coloured star whose light is

cooled,
a stone that blocks our doorways of
communion.
Earth tastes of earth, of earth that has
grown ancient.
Eyes see, hands touch.
Here few things are enough,
prickly pear and the spiny coral cactus,
figs in their hoods of leaves,
grapes with a taste that is a resurrection,
clams, stubborn virgins,
salt, cheese, wine and the bread of the sun.
From her dusky height an island girl looks
down on me,
a slim cathedral in a robe of light.
Towers of salt, the white sails of the ships
stand out against green pines of the shore.
Light is creating temples on the sea.

POSTSCRIPT 2007

Of course, Puerto Escondido was discovered by wealthy Canadians and Americans attracted by its low-rise charms. Malibu-style beach houses began to proliferate and the inevitable retirement condos. The surfing beach grew ever larger and it too began to have a Californian feel. The artists and painters who found the place moved inland or further down the coast.

SAUL BELLOW

Saul Bellow has cultivated a special place for himself. Since the publication of *Mr. Sammler's Planet* in 1970 he has personified the genteel reaction to the thundering savage freedom of the country's life. As Diane Johnson observed, it is the mission of Bellow's narrators to be at the moral centres of their books. This prize-winning, exemplary hero is the thoughtful and worried elderly person doing his earnest best against impossible odds to maintain old-fashioned humanist values and decent conduct in the face of urban violence, declining literacy, rampant greed, sexual anarchy, self-satisfied philistinism, debased media, crooked politicians, a trashy popular culture, degenerate ethics in the legal and medical professions, an academy that has failed to uphold genuine intellectual standards, artists who have turned their careers into sideshow carnivals, false philosophy, and death-saturated hedonism. Long story short, it's Saul Bellow versus The Decline of the West. So far it's been The Decline all the way, but Bellow refuses to weaken.

In *More Die of Heartbreak*, Bellow once again takes on the subject he defined much more eloquently in *Herzog*: the torments of campus love and marriage in America. That is to say, love and marriage and divorce, with all the half-states and ambiguous floating dilemmas found in-between.

Since *The Dean's December*, Bellow has contrived a unique novelistic approach with plots that offer little in the way of drama or suspense, limited action, compressed scope and vestigial characterization. In compensation, he offers a flood of ideas and observations: the novel as essay.

Bellow's meditative style is anything but austere: he is the master of a nervy colloquial voice that fairly dances with mother wit. All the same, late Bellow, as his most assiduous disciple, Martin Amis, has termed it, takes the longest of views. As in late Beethoven or Eliot's *Four Quartets*, all his characters' earthly squabbling is seen under the eye of eternity.

Not that *More Die of Heartbreak* is a work of serene Olympian detachment or autumnal serenity. What Bellow observes of Dostoevsky is equally true of himself: he is one novelist who works from his own troubled nature. Except for the odd peaceful interlude, the ladies are continually handing Bellow – this decent and humane man – one hell of a rough time. Women, he observes in a memorable phrase, "eat green salad and drink red blood."

The story of *More Die of Heartbreak* is easily told:

Benn Crader is a world-famous botanist living in an unnamed Midwestern city that bears all the earmarks of Bellow's Chicago. He is a widower exhausted by 15 years of embattled bachelorhood. For him marriage represents surcease from the emotional disasters of courtship, flirtation and rejection: the dating game carried on mercilessly from puberty till the grave.

What Benn Crader is looking for in marriage is a peaceful state wherein two human beings are "bound together in love and kindness," which he reflects, poor schmuck, "shouldn't be too hard to accomplish." Brilliant with plants, inept with women, Crader precipitately marries a predatory broad called Matilda Layamon. And Matilda proceeds to lay her man right out on the pavement, bleeding. Solely interested in the social status Crader's academic prestige can confer, she envisages a lushly furnished apartment where she can entertain visiting big shots like Henry Kissinger and Günter Grass. Her physician father, like Dr. Tamkin of *Seize the Day*, is a medical piranha and desires to ravage Crader's pockets to make this dazzling life possible.

Bellow invents a subplot involving Crader's nephew Kenneth Trachtenberg's difficulties with an S&M-loving airhead named Treckie, presumably after Star Trek. She is the mother of his child but refuses to marry him. Matilda, another prize bitch in Bellow's endless gallery, is offstage much of the time: for the reader, she is little more than a brutally oversized pair of shoulder pads. Similarly, Treckie has run off to Seattle. The novel's most intense connection is between the two men.

Accordingly, at the core of the book is the ongoing conversation between Benn and Kenneth about the larger implications of their woman trouble. Their talk, it has to be said, is morbidly fascinating: it is an aria of the defeated. "Knowledge divorced from life equals sickness," observes Bellow at one point. So, the dialogue between uncle and nephew is neither academic prattle nor men's-group whining; it represents nothing less than a prolonged disquisition on love by two of the disenchanted. The conclusion is that of two bitter old men. In their estimation, love is nothing less than "two psychopaths under one quilt."

Thomas Pynchon once observed of one of his characters that "women happened to him like accidents." Bellow's heroes demonstrate a comparable passivity; they are never pursuers, always the prey. Bellow has all the contempt for women characteristic of the traditional Jew. For him, it is relations between men that are spiritual and transcendent. Kenneth wants only to safeguard his uncle's gifts, "to protect him in his valuable oddity."

Matilda Layamon has a different agenda, the bitch. "The beauty and the charm were up front," writes Bellow. "Nobody was invited behind them to get a different perspective." Behind the mask is a rapacity up-to-the-minute and as old as Balzac. After he fails as an academic, Matilda demands Crader pursue a lawsuit concerning a family inheritance so she can buy a partnership in a brokerage.

(Direct reference is made by Bellow to Balzac's *Cousin Pons*, where another mild old gent is exploited by a ruthless family.)

Nor does Uncle Benn fare any better at the hands of other women. Each of them is more hateful than the other. A drug-taking socialite named Caroline Bunge makes her move. He almost marries the woman until he reflects that "during the act itself she would look and behave as if she was sitting in the Dress Circle at the opera and you were the starring tenor." A dumpy middle-aged neighbour appears at Benn's door and demands he do something about her sexuality. Treckie's mother presents an outrageous plan whereby poor Kenneth can get custody of his young daughter by marrying Mama herself, senior citizen though she may be. Bellow, in a wonderful turn of phrase, describes Crader as "dredged in floury relationships with women who could fry him like a fish if they had a mind to." At the end of the novel, the botanist flees to Antarctica where he can be alone with the lichen. One wonders, "Isn't there a single kind-hearted woman in all of Chicago?"

Bellow stands well outside any possible category. Although most of his characters are Jews, their experience is not especially particularized; it lies well within the American mainstream. The social world the late Bellow inhabits is that of the distinguished senior academic, the globe-trotting professor-emeritus, the "world-class intellectual." Too much inexplicable fuss is made of Benn Crader. Henry Kissinger and Günter Grass would certainly drop off to visit Saul Bellow, but never a botanist, no matter how distinguished.

Although Bellow himself would detest such *Ring Magazine*-style rankings, one question arises naturally in the circumstances. Who is greater, Bellow or Mailer? Since the two novelists represent a monumental study in polarity, no doubt the Ph.D. mills are already grinding on the subject. Where Mailer went to war and wrote about men in combat, Bellow stayed home and patrolled the home front. Where Mailer consciously abandoned his Jewishness all the better to encompass American society, Bellow insisted on it. Where Mailer strove unapologetically to become the egomaniacal literary King of New York, Bellow posed as a decent, modest chap in provincial Chicago. Where Mailer ventured out to explore the psychopathy of American life, Bellow stayed be-hind to man the burgherly barricades. Where Mailer became a kind of Mosaic prophet of youth rebellion, Bellow remained an apologist for the educated middleclass.

Herein lies the crux of Bellow's romantic dilemma. One British critic has observed that all of Bellow's novels could well bear the title of his first book, *Dangling Man*. His intellectual protagonists are far too dreamy and mystically inclined to make good, prosperous husbands. They are far too gentle to duke it out in the back alleys of the so-called real world of business, in the name of family life. (Children, Bellow justly observes, are the great excuses for scumball behaviour amongst the respectable. "Why do I do it? I do it for my kids.") At the same time, guys like Benn Crader are far too conventional to countenance any of the female inhabitants of the bohemias, high and low, available to them.

Nor does he appeal to these artsy women. The crotchety Bellow hero is in their view a killjoy, one dull Charlie. So he gets run over by suburban hard cases, *yentas* wholly out of sympathy with his spiritual nature. He mistakes respectability in women for decency and generosity, a woeful mistake. His protagonists dangle, essentially solitary, on the margins, forever hooking up with wrong numbers.

Still, James Joyce, who knew about these things, once made a remark that well applies to Bellow's quandary: the mistakes of a man of genius are merely the portals of discovery.

THE MURDER OF NANCY EATON

The third week in January was a bad time for Andrew Leyshon-Hughes. His mother and father, who belonged to a prominent family, were out of town, holidaying down south. Just seventeen and their only son, he was tumbling down a pitiless slope, suffering another one of his blowouts, sudden explosions into murderous violence. On Thursday, the boy phoned his Uncle William, and told him he needed help. They went to the General Hospital, on University Avenue, where a psychiatric resident spent about 15 minutes talking to him. The doctor pronounced the boy normal. He was suffering a case of teenage hormone changes, he said. Uncle William tried to describe the boy's violent history. The resident refused to talk any further.

Andrew's uncle then put him on a bus for a psychiatric hospital more than a hundred kilometres north, near Penetanguishene, near Georgian Bay. The boy had spent three months there the year before after another blowout. That time, he had stolen a car, driven up to Muskoka, broken into some cottages and he had shot up one cottage with a .22 rifle.

At Penetanguishene, after a group therapy session, he said he was feeling better and left the hospital with a girl named

Lisa. He took her to Toronto. They quarrelled. He then took refuge with a close friend, Nancy Eaton. She was twenty-three, beautiful and she was nicknamed "Tiger." He thought of her as his big sister. She worked as a real estate agent. She was also a descendant of the department-store founder and tycoon, Timothy Eaton, his great-great-granddaughter. Because he had nowhere to stay, she let him sleep on the sofa in her living room.

Early Monday morning, he woke at about eight, saw Nancy sleeping in her bed, picked up a knife from the kitchen, and stabbed her twenty-one times in the head, back, chest, hand and heart. He went to the refrigerator, took some eggs and started to juggle them, playing boyishly, and left the apartment, came back in six hours and raped the dead body.

In the fall of 1986, at Andrew's trial, an Ontario Supreme Court jury heard a psychiatrist, a teacher at McGill University medical school, suggest that, on the morning of the murder, Andrew had been a "crocodile man" (a reference to the portion of the brain that controls animal drives), a crocodile man because he was in a state of nature at its most savage.

Is there a satisfactory explanation for the murder of Nancy Eaton? We would like to think so but three fat volumes of medical records entered into evidence at the trial show that, far from going untreated, the doomed young man had been one of the most frequently examined human beings in the country, trotted by anxious parents from doctor to doctor from a very early age.

Something had gone wrong at the beginning: he'd been born with the umbilical cord around his neck, and there'd been a question of slight brain damage. At the outset, he fell behind in school, demonstrating "a mild learning disability." He often picked fights, and so he had few friends. Ernest was an accountant and Sarah was a trust officer. He would steal money from his mother's purse and from his au pairs. Because they had trouble keeping au pairs, Andrew was often alone. The marriage became a troubled one; the family home a permanent war zone; both parents began to avoid it. Once, when his mother reprimanded him, he ran away from home. Because he didn't return before midnight, she called the police. Andrew felt unloved, abandoned, left to the care of helpers. One drawing he did for a psychiatrist shows a child alone in bed. In an overemphatic hand, he wrote a balloon caption: "Why did he leave me alone? I'll kill him!!"

Frank Ervin, the McGill psychiatrist who testified at his trial about the reptilian brain, believed that middle-class parents are often reluctant to accept the notion of brain damage in their children; they want to believe that behaviour can be corrected by good old-fashioned willpower. Nevertheless, in such cases, society inevitably asks how much blame the parents must take.

Ernest Leyshon-Hughes, now a much-battered man who has suffered from a perforated ulcer, admits that he and his wife weren't the greatest parents. They weren't the worst either. His son would be angelic, personable, well behaved for months at a time. Then, the cruel transformation would begin. Normally neat, the boy would stop taking showers and dressing carefully. He would sleep all day and prowl at night. Then, the blowouts would come. They often occurred when the boy woke up. It was as if he was sleepwalking. You could pass your hand in front of his eyes, and there'd be no reaction. Just a blank. Another psychiatrist named Robert Carr said his play revealed a pitiless state of mind obsessed by war, control and attack.

In 1981, he stole the family car and escaped north from the city to his family's cottage. He stole a couple of bottles of alcohol, then came home. A year later, he headed north once more. Because he ran out of money, he robbed a small store at knifepoint. He got eighteen months probation.

One day, he beat up his mother. His father ordered him to leave the house. He went to stay with his uncle and aunt, Amy and William Jephcott, hunting and fishing enthusiasts. They had guns in their house, under lock and key. One day, he pointed a loaded gun at his aunt. Andrew had become unmanageable and his doctors were calling for help too. Lionel Solursh, yet another psychiatrist, recommended that Andrew be examined in Connecticut, at the Institute of Living.

There, an electroencephalogram revealed the possibility of temporal-lobe epilepsy. Keeping the boy in Connecticut cost $10,000 a month. His mother and father sought a second opinion and the boy came home. At Toronto Western Hospital, further E.E.G tests found "minimal non-specific abnormalities." He enrolled at The Annex Village, a progressive school. He was also hooking down hash, marijuana, speed and cocaine. That winter, a concerned teacher broke up Andrew's love affair with a girl, Stacey, phoning the girl's parents to denounce him. He stole Nancy Eaton's white Buick Skylark with the "TYGER" vanity plates.

The Leyshon-Hughes and Eaton families had had cottages beside each other on fashionable Lake Rosseau in Muskoka for years. Nancy and Andrew met as only children. She had known some troubled times as well. Somebody once called Nancy and Andrew "two lost souls." Nancy knew the boy had problems, and she knew how serious they were. When Andrew was released from Penetanguishene, she had phoned his father and asked him what was wrong with her friend. He said he didn't know. But if she was going to meet with him, please do it in a public place. Nancy was his best friend, confessor, big sister. Their conversation disappointed him. Like the uncle, like the hospital, like all, all, all the doctors. She couldn't help.

Nancy Eaton is dead, and Andrew Leyshon-Hughes is in Penetanguishene, probably for good.

ROBERTSON DAVIES: THE VIEW FROM HIGH TABLE

The language of Robertson Davies contains no term as consistently pejorative as the word "political." Francis Cornish, the hero of Davies' novel *What's Bred in the Bone*, tells a 1930s, New Statesman-style Marxist, "I hate your pet system and I hate fascism and I hate the system that exists." Davies is a skilled literary entertainer but he has more on his mind than keeping the pages turning. He is a didactic writer whose every book is full to bursting with moral lessons and maxims. Most of these lessons would not be out of place hanging in needlework in a Victorian parlour. Davies consistently assails the political as such in favour of a much-discussed religious and spiritual worldview. Nonetheless, he has an explicit notion of what society, particularly Canadian society, should be.

The fullest exposition of his political views is found, not in the novels, but in the seldom-produced play, *Question Time*. At the heart of the play is a dialogue between a Canadian Prime Minister, not unlike Pierre Elliott Trudeau, and an Eskimo shaman who has "a beautifully refined Edinburgh accent," a shaman who serves as the mouthpiece for Davies' reactionary social vision.

Davies' Prime Minister, like Trudeau, is cerebral, charismatic, progressive – qualities Davies finds repellent. The shaman, on the other hand, is no native primitive, but an Anglican clergyman in animal skins. He is one of those magicians, demons, and angels largely responsible for the patina of exoticism that gives Davies' work much of its popular appeal.

In *Question Time*, after a plane crash in the Arctic, Davies counterfeit primitive detains the glamorous, liberal politician "in a small not uncomfortable camp." The Edinburgh Eskimo proceeds to pronounce a few, long-cherished home truths. He is going to set the Trudeau-like figure straight.

Politics is a coarse art, Davies' mouthpiece tells the Prime Minister. Power is fleeting and men lost in high office are in need of instruction in the inner life, of the marvellous and irrational. One would be hard-put to name any figure, politician or artist, who so clearly bore the stamp of a markedly strenuous inner life as Pierre Trudeau, but we'll let that pass. Cataloguing the politician's sins and imperfections, the "shaman" finds that the PM "makes a God of his intellect" and his instinct for social justice contemptible. "The outcome of your compassion," says Davies' wise primitive, "is to make the weak powerful without making them strong."

As in most of Davies' work, the average guy in *Question Time* is represented by a couple of dumb slobs; America is viewed with traditional Tory Loyalist distrust. Progress, personal or collective, is an illusion. Democracy? "Black comedy, farce, and downright buffoonery." A free press? "The interviewer's squalid art." The sole Canadian prime minister meeting with Davies' approval: the wacko, table-tapping prince of equivocation, Mackenzie King. "When," asks the Eskimo, "have we had a stronger leader?"

The question arises: does Davies wish us to take these ideas at face value and in all seriousness, for there exists, of course, the distinct possibility that such blustery opinions merely are part of the quirky theatrical persona Davies has been cultivating since his early thirties. If, on the other hand, Davies means us to take his political notions as an expression of his ongoing educational endeavour, then I must view them with complete distaste.

In his vision of the British Canada at the turn of the century, there is no room for anybody not of Anglo-Protestant descent. In an early novel, *Leaven of Malice*, a young professor at a university not unlike Queen's University in Kingston, is marking papers, dolefully reading essays on Chaucer by students with names like Kaczabowski. The presence of the name itself is meant to be ludicrous. The grand canonical tradition of English literature as represented by Chaucer is one to which the Kaczabowskis clearly have no right: "Sighing, Solly tucked Kaczabowski into the middle of the pile, to come on him as a surprise later on. Picking up another, from Jean Thorsen, he found another reference in the first paragraph to our British heritage, a further hunt revealed that two more Scandinavians, a Pole, a three Russian Jews had claimed Chaucer as their own."

If those of non-British descent have no legitimate right to the literature of the mother country, then how about efforts to create an indigenous literature in the new land? Solly has strong opinions on this matter as well: "Why does a country like Canada, so late upon the international scene, feel it must rapidly acquire the trappings of older countries – music of its own, pictures of its own, books of its own – and why does it fuss and stew, storm the heavens with its outcries, when it does not have them?"

Callaghan, Richler, Atwood, Munro – your lives and works have been in vain – why did you bother at all?

Davies' picture of the world is bizarre cartography. The small Ontario town is fully present; so is London and Europe beyond. Toronto and Montreal and Vancouver barely exist. Quebec is a blank, Ontario is to be found about 100 miles off the coast of Liverpool. Yet, I must point out, Americans are wrong to see him as English; nor is he a simple colonial anglophile burdened with the simple snobberies of the type. No, the relationship of the British North American to the motherland is not at all one of simple admiration and respect but is racked with tortures of a particularly intimate sort; those, namely, of unrequited love.

Far from being exemplary heroes, Davies' Englishmen are often the villains of his transatlantic novels. In *Leaven of Malice,* Bevill Higgin is the bad guy; he is that depressingly familiar figure in Canadian life, the mediocre weasel of a Brit on the make, wielding his connection with the mother country as a spurious token of cultural superiority. In *A Mixture of Frailties*, Davies most passionate *cri de coeur* for the British connection, the villain, Giles Revelstoke, is a very literary composer who incarnates the creative English *daimon* but is nonetheless a seducer and a rake, a veritable Steerforth of the arts who preys on the small-town Monica Gall who is not an imperious beautiful American princess like James' Isabel Archer, but a grey little sparrow from a narrow deprived Canadian background who finds, like many other Davies' characters, that the British aristocracy is sybaritic, Bohemian, foul-mouthed, and none too honest in their money dealings. Davies reflects on Monica's relations with the tempestuous Revelstoke and his sluttish mistress, Persis. Her small-town respectability is outraged: "They never thought of her as one of themselves. She thought of them as Bohemians, though they would have hooted at so romantic and unfashionable a word, taking it as evidence that she was an outsider. But under their Bohemianism they were very English . . . Revelstoke himself was English of the Eton and Oxford variety, and of course the hateful Persis . . . There was a creature who managed to have the best of two or three worlds. To be the draggle-tailed beauty, with all the advantages of great and indestructible beauty, and at the same time to be able to become the well-bred lady – that was having it with jam and syrup at once."

But little Monica from Salterton, Ontario, has her revenge. In Davies' world, decadent Europe is not won over by extravagant American riches, as in James', but by solid dependable practical sense. Monica wins the dashing Revelstoke by her solid middle-class virtue, he conveniently dies, and the whole damn Bohemian panoply, including the promiscuous slut Persis, is gratifyingly scattered by scandal. Like other Davies heroines, Monica sensibly marries a much older man, the conductor Domdaniel, ripe with the wisdom of autumnal age, but not before he makes the following stentorian declaration: "Ah, I gather that the widespread notion that I am a Jew has reached you. As a matter of fact, I'm the second generation of my family to be baptized in the respectable bosom of the Church of England – just like that respectable fellow Mendelssohn."

That's a relief. Little Monica won't be bringing any disreputable Hebrew back to Salterton, Ontario, reeking of *gefilte* fish and socialism, setting tongues wagging.

Unlike the Jamesian expatriates, who will accept any cruel fate rather than return to the vulgarities of America, Davies' heroes, confronted by English arrogance, turn tail and retreat to Canada where they can condescend to their benighted countrymen. They become bulwarks of the WASP establishment: headmasters at Upper Canada College, officials at the National Art Gallery, senior professors at Trinity College, University of Toronto, Masters of Massey College. They become, in short, that insufferable figure in the country's cultural life, the Canadian with the acquired British accent and beard, the apostle of a culture whose importance has long ceased to exist, except in their imaginations. Davies' Britain is not that of Orwell, Pinter, Stoppard, Hockney or Bacon, let alone The Rolling Stones, but that of Galsworthy, Barrie, Thackeray and Dickens. But not the Dickens who had a reformer's passion and a vivid awareness of the lower depths. No, Davies attuned himself to the Dickens of coziness and sentimentality, not to *Bleak House* or *Little Dorrit* or *Great Expectations* but to *The Old Curiosity Shop* – Dickens at his most sentimental and quaint.

In book after book, Davies extols the wisdom of Polonius, the senior WASP, the voice of common sense and prudence. Unlike Stendhal, he does not offer worldly wisdom to men of the world. His mission is to console the top drawer of society, like a clergyman instructing an audience of tycoons on their duty, not to the underprivileged, but to themselves.

For Davies, who assents to much of the Christian message, if not to its organized institutions, a saint's heroic virtue is "too flashy, too spectacular." Jesus Christ himself is too much of a youthful radical. Calvinists are often too hard on themselves, Davies observes. "Forgive yourself for being human," he counsels.

Freud's psychology, rejected by Davies as too Jewish to be acceptable in WASP Canada, is dedicated to the liberation of human souls from the constraints and wounds of their origins and upbringing. Davies wants his characters to reconcile themselves to their upbringing while submitting to their origins: what's bred in the bone must out in the flesh, a profoundly conservative attitude.

Sex, clearly, is at the centre of Freud's moral universe and sex, after all, has long since ceased to be a pleasure or a problem for many of Davies' elderly protagonists. Compared to him, other explorers of the WASP psyche, such as John Updike, are almost pornographers. In *Fifth Business*, Dunstan Ramsay, headmaster at Colborne College (read Upper Canada College), reflects on the intense sexuality of the tycoon Boy Staunton: "It sounded like a sharp workout with the punching bag and I was glad I was not so abundantly endowed." Consequently, a marriage based on gratified mutual desire is seen by Davies as a species of lower middle-class vulgarity.

Nor is Davies in sympathy with those afflicted with the low itch of ambition. Rising in life may be the goal of most Canadians and Americans but Davies reflects that, "There's something to be said for knowing your place." In *Leaven of Malice*, another one of Davies' mouthpieces patronizingly counsels a dissatisfied young man, "Well, my friend, everybody is trapped more or less. The best thing you can do is understand your trap and make terms with it tooth by tooth."

The warden's advice to his prisoners.

What, then, constitutes his appeal?

In essence, Davies is the most recent exponent of what has been called the novel of resignation. As such he is not the inheritor of canonical authors such as James or Mann but the inheritor of that now-forgotten American middlebrow novelist, James Gould Cozzens. The point-by-point resemblances of Davies to the author of *By Love Possessed* are remarkable. There is the same Victorianism, the identical priggishness, the sympathy for the top dog. Cozzens' protagonists, like Davies, are always handing down advice, forever putting others in their place, should they have the bad manners to forget it.

The novel of resignation, as described by Dwight Macdonald in his famous essay on *By Love Possessed*, is an inversion of the story told by Tolstoy in *The Death of Ivan Ilyich* where the hero, successful in life and highly placed in society, is led by one sort of crisis or another to see how inauthentic his life has been and then rejects the conventional world and either dies or goes on to a new, more satisfactory life. As Macdonald points out, the lesson of the novel of resignation is to realize how awful a society is and then to accept it on its own terms.

The novel of resignation was a particularly popular middlebrow genre in the America of the 1950s. Sloan Wilson's *The Man in the Grey Flannel Suit*, Herman Wouk's *The Caine Mutiny* formulate the same message. "It is as if," writes Macdonald, "Tolstoy's *The Death of Ivan Ilyich* ended with the hero, after his atrocious sufferings, concluding that, as a high official of the Court of Justice, it was in the nature of things that he should die horribly of cancer, and that he must therefore bear his torment like a man for the good of the service."

Of course, one must occupy a comfortable seat in history to look back, not in anger, but in acceptance, and satisfied acceptance at that. There are few groups as untouched by the nightmares of the past as the Canadian small-town Anglo-Protestant gentry. Unlike our minorities from the Irish Catholic to Eastern European, their past is unlikely to raise much in the way of anger. (Davies' characters are remarkable for the way they glide over the horrors of the twentieth century from World War to Depression to World War. The sufferings of the victims are what happened to somebody else. But then, that's the first rule of middlebrow fiction: nobody gets hurt.)

The surpassing irony is that the spirit of the modern age, in all its wayward perversity, has found its celebrant in the man whose guiding genius was to avoid it, Robertson Davies. The desire for permanence after decades of wild change, the burrowing after roots, the outward conformism, are all striking characteristics of the post-Watergate era. That comfortable sense of Canadian isolation from the main currents of history served Robertson Davies well. His ideology of acceptance and resignation served as a kind of cloak of conformism, a one-size-fits-all grey flannel suit if you will, for all of those ambitious types of any sex or ethnicity seeking a career in the corporations. After a lifetime in the bush, his hour came nigh.

BLONDE AND BAD

We were sitting in the coffee shop of the hotel, waiting for the man from the newsmagazine to conclude his interview with Deborah Harry.

"Geez," the lady from the record company said to me. "Don't call Debbie 'Blondie' like that. She just hates it."

There are those who think of endless pleasure, glamour and money when rock 'n' roll springs to mind. I think of hotel coffee shops from coast to coast, all decorated like this one, in Day-Glo colours best suited to a nursery. I thought I had made what was only a natural slip, referring to Deborah Harry as Blondie, since she was in fact the blonde lead singer in the band in question, the other members being five guys named Moe. It was a common mistake. But nobody around her was going to let it pass.

In Harry's road manager's hotel room, I saw the man from the newsmagazine. He looked as if he had just gone head-to-head with the entire defensive line of the Pittsburgh Steelers.

"How did it go?" I wanted to know.

"Uh, all right," he said. And then, he fled.

Inside, the room displayed the unmistakable signs of rock 'n' roll life: the remains of last night's party, from overflowing ashtrays to empty champagne bottles, discarded clothes, leftovers of room-service meals, an unmade bed – unlimited chaos. There was no evidence of Harry or any other member of the band. Their road manager was simultaneously fighting off a cocaine nosebleed and hassling the newsmagazine's photographer. Deborah Harry would not have her photo taken separately from the band; nor would she have more than one photo taken that night while she was performing, because she didn't want some local *paparazzi* building a catalogue of unauthorized shots. Harry had a ferocious reputation when it came to the press: a recent cover story in *Rolling Stone* had portrayed her as Bitch Queen of the New Wave, a 40-carat press hater.

The photographer patiently explained that his magazine was going to need a selection of photos to choose from. The road manager remained adamant. This was not going to be fun.

"Where's the band?" I asked.

The road manager stanched his blood.

"Oh," he said. "They're having a meeting."

Trouble was brewing.

In a moment, the room was empty. There was nothing to do except look out the hotel window and think about how bored you were getting with rock 'n' roll. After a while, you found that celebrities weren't necessarily more thrilling offstage than someone you might have met at a supermarket counter. And pop music was definitely losing touch with its audience. No matter how outrageous the content or the performance or offstage behaviour, pop had become a predictable, stylized ritual of personalities and tours. As for the performers themselves, they were so embalmed by the music industry, so trapped by the parameters of limos, room service, fans, and roadies, you often felt, talking to pop music performers, that they knew and cared curiously little about the world outside show business. There was this huge, complacent indifference to everything but the record and the charts, the successful tour, the gossip about other musicians. Record sales had dropped, attendance at concerts was down. Where pop music once spoke to its audience in a fairly direct and moving way, it spoke now to almost no one's condition, nor presumed to, but contented itself with the self-proclaimed status of entertainment or recreation. As a result, I had come to the glum conclusion that an evening listening to rock, with few exceptions, was rarely more compelling than one in front of a television.

During the last couple of decades, pop music had gone from being an intentionally crude expression of disaffected teenagers to a hybrid quasi-art form (capable of the odd brilliant moment) to the homogenized, contrived product of superstars bigger than anything Hollywood had produced since the heyday of the studio system. For a while there, things were beginning to look bleak for all the "intellectual" critics of rock, the Greil Marcuses and Jonathan Cotts. It was becoming harder and harder to compare the latest rock 'n' roll flavour of the month to Faulkner or, indeed, to anything remotely artistic.

Then, just when everything was looking hopeless, across the sea from London, from which so many other musical styles had issued, came Johnny Rotten and the Sex Pistols and all the thrilling violence of punk. The rock writers from *Rolling Stone* and the *Village Voice* jumped on the first flight to the United Kingdom to get in on the new movement. Unlike the music coming out of the Los Angeles studios, it was "alienated," and every rock theorist took as his first principle, "If it's alienated, it must be Art." And there is nobody like your basic, semi-literate, south-of-the-Thames school leaver when it comes to alienation.

Of course the theorists, left-leaning veterans of the counterculture one and all, weren't satisfied with just good music; they had to have angry social significance as well. The Sex Pistols, with "Anarchy in the U.K." and their version of *God Save the Queen* were simply festering with social relevance. Pretty soon there seemed to be a whole new style taking over. The theorists jammed the magazines with essays on the Pistols, the Clash and such American counterparts as the Ramones, as well as on the socio-political-cultural import of dog collars and safety pins and the self-mutilation of their fans.

There were a couple of problems. First of all, punk rock was a commercial disaster in the United States: the playing was ugly, loud and inept. And then there was this: the punks meant it. They failed to understand that violence and anger went over very well in performance and on record just so long as one obeyed the rules of society and the music business offstage. The late Mr. Sid Vicious couldn't quite seize the notion that the punk routine was just another showbiz act – the result was the murder of his girlfriend and his own suicide. Nevertheless, a new movement had been announced, and nothing would stop its coming. The record industry recognized a fresh untapped market when it saw one.

Debbie Harry was a self-described ex-groupie, ex-junkie, ex-model, ex-waitress, ex-folk-rocker. In 1973, with a former art student, Chris Stein, she formed a group called the Stilettos that in 1975 became Blondie, named after the old comic strip and performing at the New York nightclub home of punk, CBGB's. Their first album, released in 1976, was a retro throwback to the music of the bad-girl groups of the early '60s, the wonderfully sluttish Crystals and Ronettes, with an overlay of Warhol-style high camp and whimsical perversity. In songs like "X Offender," the band's first single, Harry impersonated a sex pervert who falls in love with an entrapping vice cop; it was hilarious and deliberately provocative and erotic all at once. Although their first record won the band a cult following, it had little impact and they were forced to do most of their touring in Britain and Europe where punk rock had a larger audience. The follow-up album, *Plastic Letters,* was immersed in a kind of violent, tabloid reality, awash in kidnappers and hijackers. A third release, *Parallel Lines,* was more upbeat. It was lightweight, uncomplicated pop, minus the Warholian irony. The record became a best-seller, as did a single, "Heart of Glass," which Chris Stein had originally written as a James Brown funk number but had been reworked into a smash disco hit: *"Once I had a love and it was a gas . . . Soon turned out a pain in the ass."*

At this point, it probably would have been much easier for Harry and Stein to have cut the band loose and continued on as a single act starring Harry, directed by Stein – a white Ike and Tina Turner, minus R&B. Instead, Harry had shown commendable loyalty to her musicians, insisting on deflecting the media spotlight from herself, and onto the band. While it was true that Jimmy Destri co-wrote some of the band's material and that Harrison, Infante, and Burke were a pretty tight rhythm section, the media were interested only in the sexy blonde, Debbie Harry. To counter this perception, she even put out a lapel button saying, "Blondie is a group." But the attempts to shift attention to her backup musicians was doomed. There were hundreds of bassists and guitarists toiling in the rock biz, all but a few were entirely anonymous. Although the resulting resentment in the band was directed at the media rather than at Harry, it was a situation that showed no signs of changing, and one wondered how much longer Blondie could stay together in the face of it.

When the band at last walked into the hotel room that afternoon, they radiated the glow of unmitigated well-being which onrushing good fortune always seems to bestow. Debbie Harry was diminutive and rounded, not plump but broad-boned. She wore a white blouse, denims and sneakers, a pink rose in the lapel of her blouse.

After a wary greeting, she hurled herself across the unmade bed and began to pout. This woman really did not like reporters. One look and I could tell she was not about to enlighten me on the state of her inner life. Not one little bit. Shivering at the air conditioning, she pulled a blanket over her shoulders and buried herself in a copy of the lingerie catalogue of Frederick's of Hollywood from the years 1947-1973. In her mid-30s, Harry projected an appealing mix of diddy-bop toughness, haute couture elegance and hothouse fragility – a kind of cool sexiness that attracts and keeps firmly at a distance all at once. She seemed to have made a study of the iconography of blondes in American pop culture for the last half century, and as her moods changed you got a hint of Monroe, Harlow, Novak and Mansfield all chasing across her face. The comparison that returned most forcibly to mind was Monroe. There was the same *demi-mondaine* early career, the same exploitative pinup shots, the same reputation for difficulty. Just as Blondie's music recapitulates the pop genres of an earlier era, Debbie Harry's persona retrieved the earlier notion of the starlet, which had vanished from the movies and was present in television in plastic versions. Debbie Harry was a flat-out sex symbol, a deliberately provocative bad girl.

Chris Stein, on the other hand, was the most unlikely rocker ever. With his pale skin, owlish glasses, slight stoop and short hair, he looked less like a lead guitarist than a studious Jewish hospital intern. If Harry was Monroe, Stein resembled the other half of that unlikely couple of the 1950s, Arthur Miller. The brains behind the group, Stein deliberately kept a low profile; he let Harry have all of the limelight.

Harry and Stein attempted to manipulate the media in the same way as any Babbitt in a blue suit running for office. Problem was, they were babes in the wood when it came to P.R. Stein disliked the fact that a journalist had 100 percent control over what he wrote. Unless he moved to Red China, he was going to have a difficult time changing that. In her scuffling past, Harry had done some pretty raunchy photo work, semi-nude shots, to promote the band, which perhaps explained their determination to exercise control now that Blondie had achieved artistic respectability. Harry chatted long distance with Norman Seeff, a South African photographer much favoured by rock hierarchy. Maybe she thought reporters should be poodle dogs like fashion photographers. I mumbled something about hanging around for the rest of the day, if it was all right with him. In an elaborate display of democracy Stein okayed the notion with Jimmy Destri, the keyboardist, the bassist Nigel Harrison, Frank Infante, the rhythm guitarist and Clem Burke, the drummer. They were more than happy to claim their share of the publicity limelight.

Shortly afterward, Burke and Infante were awaiting the arrival of the limos that would take the group to the auditorium for a sound check. The two musicians were standing near the band's tour bus, when they were accosted by one of those barely ambulatory street crazies. This guy had his toothbrush in his pocket, all his earthly belongings in tow. Clem Burke in his rock star drag – the leather jacket, the 60s-mod electric blue shirt, the neo-Beatle haircut – drew the street-loony's attention as a bright ball of wool does that of a cat, and the man pounced, dazedly. He desired to find what this puzzling person in front him was, so, with absolutely no self-consciousness, he began picking at the flashy jacket with grubby fingers. For one bad moment, it looked like he was going to start sorting through Burke's neo-Beatle hair. However, an Irish New Yorker like Burke could take such minor lunacy in stride. Shrugging the loony off, he ducked into one of the waiting limos.

At the auditorium, 3,000 young fans had been waiting in the seats since early afternoon for a concert that was scheduled to start at 8:30. When Burke and Harrison ambled out onto the circular stage, expecting to test their instruments, the place exploded into wild cheers. Startled, they ran offstage, right into Debbie Harry, who had no idea how many people were waiting out front.

"We can't go out there," said Burke. An entire audience was out there waiting, he explained.

"But you gotta check your equipment." She was wearing a biker-chick outfit, a black motorcycle jacket with a silver skull in the lapel.

"You just go out there and give them a little wave and see what happens."

"They're not going to keep on shouting and screaming for a whole sound check."

"Yes, they are."

"It would be like having 3,000 people come to your rehearsal."

A compromise solution was reached. Stein and the other musicians could test their guitars without ever going onstage because of the wireless pickups the band used. Jimmy Destri put on one of the roadies' jackets and ventured out to tinker with his keyboards, unrecognized. In the meantime, the road manager's nose started to bleed again.

"Jesus," he said, "I'm going to check into a hospital."

"What happened to your nose anyway," I asked, mock-naive.

Before the guy could respond, Destri, having returned backstage, volunteered the opinion that the road manager had been having carnal relations with the devil and the bloody nose was the result.

After the improvised sound check, Stein and Harry went back to the hotel. Burke and Harrison and Infante weren't ready for anything so tame. Just across the highway, at the ballpark, 40,000 screaming, mindless fans were getting off on the likes of hard-rock bands like Nazareth and Aerosmith. Much earlier there had been a possibility of Blondie playing this gig. The band was curious to know whether Chris Stein had made the right move, especially since the punk band the Ramones were playing. Their limo sailed past the stadium security, the massed ambulances. Burke and Harrison checked out the crowd to see the progress of the New Wave movement amongst the masses, but the results were discouraging. The ballpark was a sea of denim – no punk styles in sight.

Burke spotted a couple he had met the previous night and called them over. After handing out two passes to Blondie's concert that evening he asked how the Ramones had gone over.

"Terrible, man," said the kid. "They lasted two numbers and three direct hits."

The Ramones, unlike Blondie, were practitioners of an anti-melodic punk style and had been hurried from the stadium stage with the aid of missiles hurled by the hard-rock crowd.

On the way back to the hotel, Frankie Infante, who'd been dying for a burger for hours, directed the chauffeur to pull up to a Burger Shack. Not only did Infante crave a burger more than almost anything else, he craved a greasy burger. So anyone who happened along Church Street that afternoon was treated to the sight of a long, black, sleek limousine crawling up to a grungy burger stand and waiting there while Frankie Infante from New Jersey bought a burger and fries.

Although these guitarists and drummers were all swell guys, the only personality of interest in Blondie remained Debbie Harry, no matter how she felt about it. Later that evening, just as the band left the hotel for the gig itself, I hustled onto the jump seat in Harry's limo, uninvited. She was lurking inside, her feet up, wearing an orange plastic jumpsuit and silver-glitter high heels. I shot her what I intended to be a big, hearty, friendly grin, to encourage small talk and camaraderie. What came out instead was a sickly, twisted grimace that died on the instant from an absolute lack of encouragement. On the way to the auditorium I rummaged about wildly for some straightforward journalistic inquiry but Harry's general demeanour did not seem to encourage questions. Every time I came near, her conversation ceased and a general chill filled the air. This woman was not fond of the increased scrutiny brought on by fame. Just what was she afraid I'd find?

Just then, a battered Volks pulled alongside the limo as it sped along the downtown streets, and a guy shoved the better part of himself out the window on the passenger side, his thin hair flapping wildly in the breeze. "Hey, Blondie!" He yelled at the top of his lungs, sticking his tongue out like some lust-maddened werewolf, "Hey, Blondie!" I guess he hadn't seen the lapel button. He didn't know that Blondie is a group. Deborah Harry gave him one quick, disgusted look, turned about three-degrees colder, and shut him out with one dainty touch of her finger on the power window.

What is it about blondes? Not natural blondes, the nursery school teachers, wheat and honey types, but the blatantly dyed babes. Why is it that when a woman goes out and dyes her hair blonde she unavoidably rings a whole carillon of male Pavlovian bells? Somehow, the blatantly artificial blonde lives in imagination as the scarlet woman, evocative of good, un-wholesome, dirty sex. Deborah Harry had plugged into this particular sexual myth like no other female rock performer of recent years, and she was still learning what it was to live day to day with the fallout. Again, Monroe could have told her a thing or two about the perils of life as a sex symbol.

Backstage, waiting to go on, Harry relaxed for the first time, possibly because she was surrounded by about half a dozen blonde lookalikes in the dressing room. There were the four blonde B. Girls and the two blonde Time Twins, both aspiring girl-groups. There was an odd, multiplying effect in the mirror-walled dressing room – one had the giddy sensation of being encircled by an army of buxom blondes. It was also somewhat striking that, in the company of these girls who looked remarkably like herself, blonde clones, Harry was the friendliest I had seen her all day. In the bad old days of *Time* magazine, it was said they had a casting technique when it came to profiles. If they wanted to interview John O'Hara, they would send along a recent Yale graduate who was trying to make his way in New York City; if it was Ernest Hemingway, it would be an avid hunter and fisherman. I now began to see that I was not the ideal person, in casting terms, to plumb the soul of Debbie Harry. What was needed was a blond girl who wore punk fashions and was just trying to break into the music business.

Just as she ran onstage, Harry had a notion of just how big the crowd was, and a look of absolute terror blew through her. There were 15,000 kids out there. She recovered instantly as she settled in front of the microphone, blew the crowd a kiss and singing in a clear, strong alto, kicked into a rapid-fire set of 14 tunes as the stage revolved around like a merry-go-round. There was a certain amount of irony at work here. Punk rock emerged as a reaction to the slickness and professionalism of mainstream pop music. Blondie was taking punk rock to larger audiences by playing this deliberately stripped-down style in a well-rehearsed, smoothly professional manner. Blondie's music was deliberately catchy, and as accessible as ice cream. Their ironic reworkings of lightweight pop material were taken straight by the kids in the audience.

Deborah Harry, though, was one of the most expressive performers in pop music. She didn't merely stand up there and sing but acted out each song as well, each phrase matched to a carefully nuanced expression. As the stage revolved, she struck pinup poses, jumped like a cheerleader, blew more kisses and finally rolled rapturously around the stage. There were a lot of young girls in the audience. They liked Harry's infectious sense of fun. When her show was over, the audience lit matches en masse. Afterward, in the dressing room, the band was in high spirits.

"Are they still yelling out there?" asked Stein.

"Yeah," said Destri. "They're yellin' 'We want our money back.'"

Harry gave a merry laugh as she entered the room.

"Aagh," she said. "The world's still spinnin.'"

As the limo edged through the departing crowd, Harry and Stein discussed the roadies, the upcoming gigs, dressmakers in New York, who they're going to send to the interview at the radio station in Buffalo. (You can imagine the pleased reactions when Clem Burke and Nigel Harrison show up instead of Debbie Harry.) Suddenly the car was besieged by scores of kids. It was an odd sensation, being inside a limo nosing its way through a tunnel of human flesh.

"Hey," Harry says, startled. "This is serious."

"Get the window up," Stein ordered the chauffeur as the kids started hammering on the roof.

"Hey, Blondie!" they shouted. "We love you, Blondie!"

This time Debbie Harry forgave the mistake.

"Hey," she said. "The Beatles! This is fabulous!"

Finally, someone, a fan, got it right: "We love you, Debbie! Come back soon!"

Then the chauffeur saw an opening and began to pick up speed, and the shouts of the crowd receded behind us.

POSTSCRIPT 2007

Blondie did in fact break up a couple years later, the quarrel between Harry and her backing musicians still unresolved. When the group was voted into the Rock 'n' Roll Hall of Fame in 2006 they were still feuding, right up on the stage during the nationally televised induction ceremony.

JAMES M. CAIN: POET OF THE TABLOID MURDER

One of the great illusions of literature is the identification of the personalities of novelists with those of the ciphers who populate the printed page. For example, James Mallahan Cain. Being the hardest-boiled of that quintessentially tough-talking trio that includes Dashiell Hammett and Raymond Chandler, many of Cain's readers concluded that the novelist spent a lifetime hanging out in roadhouses, listening to the death-row confessions of killers, and making up to pouting coochies in low-cut dresses and fuck-me pumps. In reality Cain, far from being a street guy, was that most housebound of creatures, the hard-working man of letters. And unlike Hammett and Chandler, he never in his life toiled for the pulps.

Cain, in the course of a long career, seldom pushed out from behind his big Smith-Corona except to indulge in his appetites for grand opera and gourmet food. The creator of Frank Chambers, the drifter hero of *The Postman Always Rings Twice*, and one of the toughest-talking narrators in the history of the novel, he was, in fact, a fellow of consummate gentility, his father for many years the president of Washington College, in Maryland.

The younger Cain had been intellectually precocious and, urged on by his father, he had finished college when barely out of short pants. After a botched career as an operatic tenor, Cain discovered his *metier* as a newspaperman, first on an army sheet in WWI France, then at the *Baltimore Sun*, finally as an editorial writer on the old *New York World*.

Successively, a protege of H.L. Mencken at *The American Mercury*, an associate of Walter Lippman on the editorial board of *The World*, the managing editor of the fledgling *New Yorker*, and a well-paid screenwriter during the golden age of Hollywood, Cain first won national attention for his coverage, in the *Atlantic Monthly*, of the West Virginia coal-miner's strike. His imagination triggered by the miners' dialect, he wrote a novel that he could not get published, followed by a failed play based on his experiences in the coalfields. It was the authenticity of "the American voice" that had caught his ear and his imagination and it was his determination to write in that voice – not the eastern seaboard voice of his genteel family – that was heard in Hollywood and so Cain moved to California, where he conceived the idea for *The Postman Always Rings Twice*, his most successful novel. "I make no conscious effort to be tough, or hard-boiled, or grim, or any of the things I am usually called," Cain wrote in his preface to *Double Indemnity*. "I merely try to write as the character would write, and I never forget that the average man, from the fields, the streets, the bars, the offices and even the gutters of this country, has acquired a vividness of speech that goes beyond anything I could invent."

There is a single theme at the heart of Cain's best fiction: his tough-talking characters are caught in a love triangle that leads to murder. A man falls for a woman so hot he's willing to kill for her. It is this torchy dame who became a stock figure in the pre-Code Hollywood of the early 1930s, a *femme fatale* usually played by Jean Harlow or Barbara Stanwyck, a mythic figure in whom sex begets violence.

Cain borrowed his signature theme from the real-life Snyder-Gray case, the most notorious murder trial of the 1920s. Ruth Snyder, the "Tyger woman," was a Long Island housewife who nagged her corset-salesman lover, Judd Gray, into murdering her husband, Albert, by bashing him over the head with a sash weight. The blundering lovers were quickly charged with the crime and lost little time in selling each other down the river and into the electric chair.

Cain set the story in a squalid roadside diner in California and made his doomed lovers far less genteel than Snyder and Gray – a hard-case drifter and a blowzy waitress. The lurid story would not have risen above its pulp origins had Cain not endowed it with profound emotional depth, a depth rooted in the persuasiveness of the language, an idiom stripped of false sentimentality as he makes the reader see how lust deepens into love and how love destroys them both. It is just this subtraction of sentiment from the dynamics of love that creates Cain's characteristic "hard-boiled" tone.

Making use of his journalistic experience, Cain also portrays the doomed lovers as social victims, helpless pawns in the games played by a corrupt criminal justice system and greedy insurance companies. In *Postman* and *Double Indemnity*, he teaches the reader as much about the insurance business as Zola ever does about coal mining in nineteenth-century France. *Mildred Pierce* tells you as much as you want to know about running a restaurant as does any contemporary memoir of a celebrity chef.

As for his most enigmatic title, *The Postman Always Rings Twice*, Cain offered several explanations. Most satisfying is that the postman stands for wicked Fate, which rings twice in the sense that Frank Chambers is acquitted of a murder he did commit and convicted of one he didn't.

Cain, as one of Hollywood's most highly paid screenwriters, couldn't handle success. On a five-year drunk, he made a disastrous marriage to the haughty Aileen Pringle, a fading silent movie actress and a former girlfriend of H.L. Mencken, and a collector of famous writers, a real-life *femme fatale*, and perhaps the model for Norma Desmond in *Sunset Boulevard*. Cain bloated up to a tidy 230 pounds on a binge from which he never quite recovered.

When he finally gave up journalism and screenwriting to concentrate on fiction, he never wrote another good novel. The latter part of his life is a terrifying record of a writer's powers failing, his refusing to give up, writing unpublishable novel after unpublishable novel. Finally, he returned home to Maryland and obscurity. "The poet of the tabloid murder" (in Edmund Wilson's famous phrase) died alcoholic, aged eighty-five in 1977.

Tom Wolfe, in the course of a panning review of Norman Mailer's Dostoevskyian murder novel, *An American Dream*, compared the book unfavourably to *The Postman Always Rings Twice*. Since then, there has been something of a Cain revival. Reread and recognized for what it is, a story that touches something central in American pop culture, Cain's best novel was filmed again with Jack Nicholson as Frank Chambers and Jessica Lange as Cora. It is now clear that James M. Cain's *noir* sensibility has left a lasting mark on movies and literature.

WAYNE SHORTER: WEAVER OF DREAMS

Since the late thirties, the saxophone has been the pre-eminent solo instrument in jazz. While there have been virtuoso improvisers on other instruments, especially the trumpet, it seems the saxophone has best conveyed the sensuality of the music, best captured its hothouse moods, from sexual urgency and frenzy to a not unpleasant sense of voluptuous exhaustion. As the movies have sought to convey either weariness or obsessive eroticism, they have leaned heavily on musical soundtracks that feature jazz saxophone.

Because of this pre-eminence, the strongest saxophonist of his day has often become a culture hero, especially among young blacks, who become disciples of his style and his approach to his instrument. This tradition started with Coleman Hawkins and Lester Young, the President of the saxophone, and it can be said to have reached its apogee with the incomparable Charlie Parker. Bird's influence was so strong that for upwards of a quarter-century after his appearance on the scene, young saxophonists copied his style virtually note for note in a way that can only be compared, in other arts, to the influence of T.S. Eliot on poetry (you can still hear Eliot's phrasing, his intonations, in someone so generationally removed as Sylvia Plath), and Matisse.

After Parker's death, there was some question as to who would inherit the saxophone mantle. It seemed that shortly before his dying, brought on from heroic excesses with drugs and drink, Parker had anointed Sonny Stitt. But somehow Stitt never achieved the kind of indisputable status that Parker possessed; his playing was too similar to his mentor's and there was that immutable rule of jazz saxophone that the reigning king must be decisively original.

For a while, then, it looked like Sonny Rollins would emerge as the leader of the new generation but, despite the extrovert virtuosity of his playing, there was something too diffident about Rollins' presence on the jazz scene to qualify him as the reigning influence. He was always withdrawing from sight to practice, to refine his style and contemplate. During one of these periodic removals, Rollins' claim to be the most important saxophonist of his generation was usurped by a musician who had undergone a long and arduous apprenticeship before he emerged with a transcendent style of his own. This musician, of course, was John Coltrane. For a while there, in the late sixties, with Trane, it was Charlie Parker all over again, and then some. All the young saxophonists played like Coltrane. Older players like Jackie McLean and Art Pepper, who had formerly worked within Parker's style, changed their playing to accommodate Coltrane's pointillistic approach.

John Coltrane eventually became far more than a saxophonist to black Americans. Today, he has the stature of a spiritual leader. After Coltrane's death, there were many fine saxophonists around, but no undisputed champ. But then, one player began to assert himself and become the most prevalent influence on young players, but in a curious and reluctant fashion.

That saxophone player is Wayne Shorter. It seems that every good young sax player who comes through town, including Branford Marsalis, imitates Shorter. This is itself curious because Shorter is a chameleon, a singularly diffident musician who blends into the musical surroundings where he finds himself. For instance, when he was playing hard bop with Art Blakey, Shorter's style was an amalgam of Rollins and Coltrane, using something of Rollins' buzz-saw sound combined with Trane's modal sheet of sound. He also had Rollins' sense of composed structure in his solos and Coltrane's open harmonies.

It is, however, Shorter's playing while with Miles Davis that most influences saxophonists of the present. While harmonically liberated, his concept is more restrained than the avant-gardist excesses of Ornette Coleman or Eric Dolphy. Shorter's approach is angular, elusive, subtle, suffused with an effete melancholy. His greatest innovation is to dispense with the headlong sense of rhythmic frenzy that generally distinguishes jazz saxophone. Hard-core jazz aficionados often complain that his music fails to swing, but then, neither does Debussy, with whom he has a lot in common. Shorter's introverted music floats cautiously in space, misty and dreamlike, conjuring up images of midnight-blue landscapes. The medium is the saxophone and the mood is the message. Shorter's playing is all mood.

All the same, saxophone heroes always have a message that is more than musical. Coltrane was the voice of black power and inspirational Afro-American spirituality. Shorter's concerns are more reflective. He concerns himself with the dream-life of black Americans, their inner life, like the rest of ours, inextricably mingled with the dreams of Hollywood. Shorter, in one of his interviews, described how his music has been inspired by many films, especially nightmarish science fiction and horror movies, among them, *The Red Shoes*, in which a ballerina sells her soul to the devil in exchange for artistic mastery; in his mastery of the jazz saxophone, Wayne Shorter suggests a looming menace, a whiff of regret, the onset of dread. It is the pre-eminent saxophone sound of our time.

THE BLADE IN THE MIRROR

When Draper felt a craving for the drug, it was rarely his own doing. He would be in a bar somewhere downtown with someone like Hutchison and the subject would come up, and then he would become conscious of a slight, almost intangible itch in his nose and then he could visualize the white powder glittering up from its silver foil and he could almost sense the bitter, sharp taste you got when it dropped from the nasal passage to the roof of your mouth – and then he knew he had to score. Let's not be coy, Draper felt like getting high and raising some quiet hell. Hutchison never called the drug cocaine but blow or toots or lady, and he was always ready to score just so long as he had someone like Draper to pay the shot. Hutchison was one of those marginal types who subsisted on the edges of the city's film and recording industries, working as a driver or an extra or sitting in on guitar or back-up vocal there, and doing a little bit of everything to paper over the dry patches in between. When he was working, he lived high; when he wasn't, his life became a dismal routine of unemployment and scrounging loans. But if you wanted something that had an illegal tinge to it, especially along the line of illegal drugs, he was the guy.

As far as Draper himself was concerned, he liked the rush of scoring almost as much as he liked the drug itself. There were genteel cokeheads who would only buy from friends and refused to leave their comfortable living rooms and glasses of white wine; but for Draper there was something about dipping into the demimonde world of the dealers and observing, in a quietly superior sort of way, their lame little cloak-and-dagger maneuvers, their fugitive slang, that amused him no end. So, in the afternoon, Hutchison would decide that the mood was right and that Draper had the price in his pocket. Then, he'd take a handful of quarters to the bar's pay phone and start to hunt around. "Anything happening?" he would ask, or, "Got any cassettes?" if the dealer was connected to the music business. If the calls proved fruitless, they would set off, in one of the many vintage cars that seemed to pass through Hutchison's hands, for one of the city's boutique strips.

The glossy shops would remind Draper of a Near Eastern drug bazaar. You would enter and the girl behind the counter would be trying to unload some 1940s nostalgia item or a punk glitter creation on a customer, or else she would be on the phone, trying to fob off her bank manager or accountant, hoping to keep what was usually a wispy and insubstantial enterprise from going down the tubes altogether. Hutchison, a brawny sort, would be wearing one of his fancy Mexican shirts, dark slacks, cowboy boots. He would saunter in, Draper in tow, wait until she had finished with the customer or bank manager and then half-kiddingly gather her in his arms, and ask if the old man was in and then, sotto voce, whether there was anything going on. Most of the time, even if it were late afternoon, her old man, Chuck or George, or whoever it was, would be asleep, having sat in on a session all night, or having helped out with a friend's renovation for 48 hours straight. Then they would say their good-byes and trail on to the next boutique somewhere down the block and it would be the same story, the customer or the bank manager and the fanciful clothes and Herb or Bobby in the back of the place asleep.

The girl behind the counter would tell them what shit was around at this moment and that what her guy Herb had was great while what that drip Chuck had down the street was terrible, and how friends of hers had scored from Chuck and how unsatisfied they were and how Draper and Hutchison should never trust him. Sometimes Herb would be reputed to have some great crank and no blow at all and then they would need to repair to yet another bar and decide who they were going to patronize when he finally woke up: Herb with his crank or Chuck with his blow.

Crank, amphetamine, didn't interest Draper. Its low-rent, trailer park connotations were too much for him. Hutchison, on the other hand, had no loyalties to any particular drug. He would take high-quality crank over low-grade blow any time. If there was nothing of high quality around he would settle for low. More than anything, he was just interested in getting ripped. As they sat sipping beers, he explained that for a drug connoisseur, such as himself, pure crank was infinitely preferable to cocaine that had been stamped on or badly diluted; that, unlike cocaine, pure amphetamine, when snorted, presented no after-effects. Draper was adamant. To him, cocaine evoked the high life of the 1920s, luxury living on the Côte d'Azur, while amphetamines evoked some scrawny creep shooting up in a room in Parkdale. Then, there was the matter of whose word you were going to trust, Chuck's or Herb's.

In the end, it usually boiled down to who woke up first. Chuck's apartment was littered with old pulp magazines from the 1940s and there were African masks on the wall. Reggae pounded dully in the background. Chuck didn't have much to say, even though Hutchison kept up his line of ingratiating patter, kidding him along. The dude was professionally suspicious. Chuck was tall, in his late twenties with frizzy black hair, and he bore the chief distinguishing marks of the heavy cocaine user: his every other sentence was punctuated by a heavy, sniffling *thnnump*, as if he were fighting off a bad cold, and dark circles hung beneath his eyes, giving him that half-attractive, half-sinister look of romantic decay.

Draper was sufficiently familiar with the drug life that he knew that a social charade had to be acted out, the illusion maintained that a couple of friends were just dropping over for some conversation and, oh yes, don't you just happen to have some white stuff hanging around that just happens to cost an arm and a leg and which can land you seven years in the pen? The drug life consists of an elaborate, formal, Mandarin ritual. So, before anything else could be discussed, Chuck reached down with elaborate nonchalance and produced a plastic cellophane bag of marijuana. Draper could immediately tell by the way that Chuck lovingly separated leaf from twig that this wasn't any of your homegrown, weak-tea marijuana but the real item, powerful and dangerous. When the tightly rolled cigarette came around to him, he knew that he could not just take one nervous puff and pass it on, that would be to fail a crucial test of cool. Instead, he took a deep, strong pull and then held onto the joint, as the others had, regarded it meditatively, thoughtfully, as if this were the equivalent of a wine-tasting session, then took several more equally deep lungfuls and only then passed it on. In so doing, Draper proved that he, too, was truly and deeply absorbed in travelling to the reaches of outer space. What's more, he knew that it was one of the imperatives of cool that you not talk much but communicate instead in meaningful nods and enigmatic flickers of expression. To a dealer one didn't know too well, this communicated a suitable dignity and reserve; most of all, an enigmatic countenance communicated the notion that you knew how to keep your mouth shut, for in the fugitive, clandestine drug world the worst thing you could have was a loose mouth.

Only after the ritual smoke was over, and both Draper and Hutchison were completely blasted, could the subject of cocaine be broached. Yet another test of cool was comprised of the ability to function as if nothing had happened when you were barely able to stand. (Draper had heard of Montreal types who preferred to pull bank heists while loaded on LSD. Now there was Gallic elan!) Then arrangements were made, money changed hands and Chuck went out to meet his supplier. Hutchison prudently made it a point never to deal with the large wholesalers, even if he was buying weight, never to know who they even were, but to always deal with the small fry like Chuck. That way, he was convinced, there was less chance of taking a bust since police interest was bound to lie primarily with the wholesaler. As a mere consumer, provided one took a few elementary precautions, the odds of arrest were pretty long. As long as you didn't bring drugs across borders, didn't deal yourself or didn't in some way draw unnecessary attention to yourself, you were almost entirely safe, barring some woeful fluke of bad luck. Only lames took a bust.

There was just one feature of these expeditions into the drug world that irritated Draper and that was the waiting. You had always just missed the dealer or he had to wait for somebody himself. There was always some reason that you ended up waiting in a seedy pad for hours making dimwitted small talk. After an hour, when Chuck did not return, Draper lost patience and he left Hutchison, trusting that his 300 bucks would not just vanish.

Several hours later, Hutchison appeared at Draper's stylish apartment with a couple of grams. A small mirror and a razor blade which Draper kept were produced. Hutchison took the silver-foil packet from his pocket and carefully and lovingly spread it out on the coffee table. There the cocaine lay, white and powdery as fresh December snow. Using the flat surface of the blade, Hutchison lifted a small portion of the drug out of the silver foil onto the mirror. Then, chopping up the lumpy imperfections so that the powder was even finer and thus easier to nose, he divided it into four good-sized lines. Draper produced a plastic straw, saved from a take-out milkshake carton and cut down to size, and bent over the mirror. The popular mythology of cocaine demanded that one use the crispest of high denomination bills for the occasion, but to Hutchison this was the mark of the novice show-off. He loved to tell the story of one newly flush movie actor who ostentatiously turned on a room of friends in London, some of whose luck wasn't running as good as his own, using a £20 note, which came back transformed into a £1 note, as if by sorcery. As far as Hutchison was concerned, the plastic straw, cut in half, was more practical and less vulgar.

It was a dealer's pride, the decisive component of his very identity, that his product was the best. Just as Chuck's grass was of the first quality, so was the cocaine. The effects of the drug were notoriously subtle. Unlike marijuana or the other hallucinogens, cocaine did not produce a powerfully self-evident alteration of consciousness. In fact, the inexperienced may at first wonder what the fuss is all about; that is until they learn to perceive the drug's effects. This time, however, it hit Draper like a soft blow on the head, rendering him near speechless for a few minutes. Then his mood suddenly shot upward, he felt himself exploding with energy and confidence, physically stronger, years younger. His nose and palate were numb and dry but vodka and tonic helped. The drug went fiendishly well with alcohol. Draper suddenly felt like phoning up friends he hadn't spoken to in months; he wondered if there were any good parties on that night. In its effects, coke is just about the opposite to marijuana, which takes you into the depths of yourself, nor does it lead to much sage reflection. Draper went over to his audio system, selected the loudest, heaviest rhythm 'n' blues he could find, cranked up the volume so that walls trembled, then pounded around the room with a blithesome tread, a strange apelike contortion that he passed off as dance. Hutchison emitted a low, devilish chuckle, just on general principles. It was good blow. Ten minutes later the effects had vanished. It was time to do another couple of lines if they wanted to keep the buzz. Draper knew they would end up doing the drug until all they had was gone: cocaine is not something that encourages a sense of moderation.

Draper could remember the first time he had encountered the drug. It was almost a decade ago and it was the tail end of the hippie era. He was living with a bunch of friends in a house on Avenue Road and the place was one of those intercontinental way stations of the time that seemed to extend through Toronto from New York to London to Athens and Paris and Mexico City; the kind of house where a friend or a friend of a friend could always be assured of a bed and sympathetic company. One morning near dawn there was a knock at the back door and when Draper stumbled from his bed to open it, there was a remarkable Australian blonde, Diane, whom he had met in Greece and who had previously surfaced in Toronto. They had edged toward a love affair but that's where it stayed, on the edge, despite her rangy beauty. Diane was a trifle over-liberated for Draper. Now here she was again, fresh from the airport, attired entirely in pilgrim's white, barefoot, and clutching an attaché case filled with druggists' vials of pharmaceutically pure cocaine that Diane had in some unimaginable way brought through customs. Diane was as naive a flower child as ever trod the Yellow Brick Road to Wonderland. She had bought the drug in Afghanistan and she had smuggled it into this country, not with any rapacious idea of profiting herself but as a love gift for a certain sub-Manson-ish fellow for whom she cherished an unrequited passion, one of the freelance charismatics of the period, half-gangster, half-prophet.

The first time Draper had tried cocaine had been nothing short of hilarious. Versed in the hashish culture of the time, schooled in cannabis' qualities as an enhancer of all the senses, Draper and his friends had prepared an extravagant meal, only to find, after they had sampled the drug, that their taste buds had become wholly anaesthetized and the experience of fine dining was not unlike introducing large chunks of cardboard into your mouth. When Diane couldn't locate her wandering charismatic, she began, in the spirit of Love and Peace, to give away great gobs of the stuff, worth thousands of dollars.

The resulting scene was wild. Night and day Draper's house began to fill up with every manner of strange creature. The word was out . . . free cocaine! Day after day, utter strangers would knock at his door, panting to meet the legendary benefactress. Finally, Draper, who had little by little dwindled into a state of battered paranoia, expecting the narco squad to come smashing through the door at any second, demanded Diane either move or sell off what remained of the drug. He put out feelers in the dope underground, looking for somebody who was interested in buying a largish quantity of cocaine. What happened next served to immerse him in a trough of paranoiac despond more intense than anything that had gone before. Accustomed to the relatively innocuous dealers of marijuana, Draper was entirely unprepared for the parade of hoodlums who dealt in cocaine, often as not African-American studs up from Manhattan, sporting black-velvet suits and silver-headed canes, feral sorts looking to take off anything not nailed down and willing to pack heat to do it. My God! Real criminals!

When Diane's supply was finally used up or sold off, Draper dismissed the whole thing as an anomalous incident, just a sport of chance. In the years that followed, unwitting pioneer that he was, Draper began to notice how cocaine was entering his world in a big way. It was the sort of black dude he had met in his kitchen at Avenue Road who was getting his picture on the cover of magazines in the U.S., a new kind of outlaw hero. People he knew began to take regular trips to Bolivia and Colombia for the drug and legitimate enterprises were funded on the proceeds. It was rumoured that many an establishment in the city's burgeoning restaurant scene and many a boutique had raised its initial financing from a trip down South America way, and that many a mini-mogul in the city's flourishing real estate trade maintained his cash flow dealing cocaine.

If marijuana had been the characteristic drug of previous decades, it was cocaine that now set the tone. Where marijuana encouraged its users to mellow out and lay back, cocaine encouraged its users to go out and take the world by the horns. It gave them the confidence of two shots of scotch but at the same time left them in absolute precise control. The drug made you sharp-edged, hard and cool. For those ruthless entrepreneurs of the self who now emerged, it was no small help in achieving their ends. If there was a project that demanded 48 hours of non-stop work, then cocaine could buy you that time. If a presentation had to be made for which you had to be exact, witty, and aggressive, cocaine could do that for you, too. And the chances were slim that anybody who might disapprove could tell you were in the evil grips of an illegal drug – the symptoms were that hard to detect.

From time to time, Draper's work took him into the world of extreme lives. He would find himself in the back of the limo as this week's greatest band would pull up to the backstage entrance of one of the city's arenas. The groupies would be lined up in their exotic finery of electric greens and blues, a whole sociological spectrum from the funkiest street chicks to the most refined private-school graduates, achingly beautiful some of them, just nervously waiting for the nod from one of the boys in the band. And the guitar player from New Jersey or the drummer from Birmingham or Encino, on the crest of the evanescent wave that is pop fame, would nod his head and indicate to the hulking road manager, with regal largesse, which of the girls was to be put on the list of guests allowed backstage. Once admitted to this preserve of the glorious, if transitory, few, the girl would likely as not march straight up to the stringy-haired guitar player from Jersey or the toothless drummer from Birmingham and say, "Is there anything I can do for you in Toronto?"

"Uhhh, sure, darlin'," the drummer would mumble, uncertain.

"I mean is there anything I can do for your nose in Toronto?" the girl would say. And that, too, was a feature of the rock life, everybody wanted to turn the stars onto cocaine. That, and sex, was their link, their point of contact with all that celebrity, all that money, all that adulation.

The groupie would dutifully set off on her errand and after the show would return to the band's hotel suite where the most oddly assorted group of people would be waiting, tight friends for this one night. There would be record label people and visiting musicians from other bands who were passing through town and the groupies, and those rare members of the press who the boys in the band felt comfortable around. They would all be waiting on the pleasure of Jimmy from Birmingham who was holed up in the bathroom, giggling, inviting the chosen in there one by one to have a toot. This was one aspect of drug ritual that Draper came to hate – its resemblance to high school. Jimmy the drummer would invite the privileged, blessed soul, if he or she was cool enough, into his bathroom and they would share their little drug secret. What was most important was that some of the people outside the door not be invited in. When Draper's turn came he would go in and close the door after him and there would be Jimmy, who in all likelihood would be dead or back playing bars in a year, doling out the drugs. Here it was, the privileged moment of contact. More often than not, Draper actively disliked Jimmy from Birmingham, but he was, all the same, willing to snort his coke.

Draper could almost chart the course of the drug as it moved from the high Bohemia of international showbiz down through the reaches of the yuppie middle class, the altogether respectable dinner parties where the cocaine would appear with the brandy, a kind of jaunty after dinner mint. There, occasionally protesting, occasionally embarrassed, the sort of people who would never dream of breaking the law in other circumstances or of buying the drug for themselves would be initiated in its use. They would profess to feel nothing at all, then protest that the drug did nothing for them, failing to notice that they were talking a mile a minute, coke-rapping, babbling on witlessly. Or else a network television producer would notice that his on-camera host was showing exceptional stamina in getting through a gruelling shoot. When asked the secret of such endurance, cocaine would likely as not be the answer and, of course, the producer would have to give it a try and pretty soon he'd be coke-rapping away, disclosing some pretty, uh, personal things about himself, fully believing that he had just discovered truth and beauty at the end of a tiny spoon.

Draper would get calls from a gay friend confiding that a particularly dishy young man was coming over for "drinks" and did Draper know where there was some blow to be had. Or a Bay Street lawyer, representative of one of the city's stuffiest law firms, would be down in New York on business and the archetypal black dude would sashay up to him near Times Square and shove a matchbox full of the stuff close to his nose as a sample. When, snuffling it in, his mood considerably improved, the cautious man from Bay Street agreed to make a buy but the coke proved to be ground aspirin. Pretty soon, Draper was noticing that if the girls behind the perfume counters in department stores weren't wearing born-again crosses, they were wearing silver chains with miniature coke spoons dangling, and radios all over town had Clapton chanting "Get high, get high, get high," and the crowd screaming back, "Cocaine!"

After a while, Draper observed that the drug stood as a mark pure, old-fashioned status, an indication that you could afford to throw away $500 as part of an evening's entertainment. Still, there were dissenters. "Christ," the aspirin-duped lawyer told him one night, "for that kind of dough I can get a real meal plus a whore, you know what I mean?"

One year Draper was working out on the east coast and it was his birthday and a bunch of friends phoned him from their cozy booth at a restaurant on Bloor Street. Over the line came the clink of champagne as they toasted him, followed by manic giggling and snuffling sounds as a number of lines were snorted off the glass-topped table, just to show him what he was missing back home.

For Draper himself, after an initial period of enthusiasm, the drug did not represent a particularly large presence in his life. It was just something, like soggy quiche, that seemed a permanent feature of life in the city. Things stayed that way until he met Joanne. When Draper first met her, she was riding high, coming through town playing a famous nightclub. She was astonishingly beautiful, she had a throaty blues voice like Dinah Washington's, she had a record out on a major label, and she had a whopping advance. Her life seemed to be all limos and the best hotel suites and a seemingly endless amount of the very finest cocaine. But the road gets lonely even for a rising star, and someone introduced her to Draper one night and there followed one week of sizzling room-service romance and almost one year of a long-distance telephone "relationship." By the time Draper got around to visiting her in Los Angeles, the album had proved itself a stiff, had sold three and one-half copies, and the major label had cancelled Joanne's deal. She still had the booty from her brief instant of glory, the house in the Hollywood Hills and the antiques and the Mercedes, but now she maintained it all by dealing blow to the household names she had met in her heyday.

Things began to fall apart the moment Draper got to Hollywood. In the first place, an affair maintained over the long-distance wires is made of pretty flimsy stuff. Then there is the small matter of sex. Although cocaine has a reputation as an aphrodisiac, Draper found that, in Joanne's case, constant use proved it to be the exact opposite. She was all up in her own head most of the time; blow deadened the sensual impulse. So sex with Joanne was now disappointing, beautiful though she might be. Draper had laid out his thousand dollars' worth of air fare to come to southern California; he wanted the beach, he wanted fun in the sun. Instead, Joanne got up at 5 o'clock in the afternoon, reached over to her bedside table for her vial and her spoon and that's how they got up in the morning. Then there was the matter of Joanne's fast-vanishing career as a vocalist. In an effort to reverse this skid, she was making a demo with the studio musicians in Hollywood and some of the household names were in the studio singing back-up. Folks liked Joanne and everybody was rooting for her to come through but Joanne couldn't sing: cocaine is not good for the pipes. She had begun the session singing in a head voice, a kind of falsetto and for a half-hour she had good control of a sort of tasty break in it, Berlin cabaret-style. After that, her voice degenerated into a whisky howl, a straight gin-mill screech and that was the end of the session – and you can't get much down on tape in a half-hour. The household names departed, shaking their heads.

All this time, Joanne was telling Draper that she was immune to the effects of the drug but, in the depression that followed the abortive session, Draper tried to put her straight. Listen, he told her, I'm telling you, baby, that you're not immune, that stuff is insidious. You can't get a full articulate sentence out of your face and it isn't very attractive. You're coke-rapping, Draper told her, and you have one subject and one subject only and that is ME ME ME. The whole thing is egomaniacal, it's narcissistic and frankly, sweetheart, you're boring the shit out of me.

At that point, Draper was faced with the classic junkie's partner dilemma. If someone you care for is wired to a drug, do you leave, try to wean them off it or get down in the hole with them? For the shortest period imaginable, Draper got down in the hole. Joanne had decided, that in an effort to save her voice, she would move on to the needle. Draper had injected cocaine just one time and it was one of the worst experiences of his entire life. The next morning he was filled with a self-loathing worse than anything he had ever known. He stood in the shower with a pounding headache, feeling he could throw up forever. He felt every one of his thirty-odd years and he knew he was no longer young, that youth had indeed fled. Looking at the huge malignant bruise on the inside of his left arm, looking at the needle marks, he did not at all like what he seemed to be turning into, nor did he like the trashed-out, burned-out future that the needle marks promised. *O, Lord, stop hooking me up with these lame women*, he thought. That day, without leaving a note for Joanne, he headed for the airport and went home.

Six months later, he was coking and drinking in his apartment with Hutchison, who had a pretty good needle story to share with him. He had been on a film out west and he had been shooting cocaine. Hutchison was a character of gargantuan appetites. He was the sort of guy who liked going out for breakfast and having eggs, waffles, bacon, sausages, a small steak, fries, five slices of toast, then wash the whole mess down with a half-dozen Margaritas and finish up with a fat spliff. So with petite department-store clerks sniffing the stuff, it would be a point of honour for him to start using a needle.

Hutchison had been riding high on the Hollywood North film boom, working a lot and making plenty of money. He had been out on the Prairies on a film set, shooting cocaine all the while, when he decided that he had bugs growing under his skin. This is classic formication symptom; it's in all the textbooks, under "cocaine psychosis." In the bestial grip of this delusion, he informed the backwoods sawbones that he had been travelling in the tropics and had picked up some evil bug out there, which was in fact moving around horribly under his skin. Well, even without cocaine, Hutchison was a forceful kind of gent. Behind it, he was nigh unstoppable. He convinced the small-town doctor that he really did have bugs crawling around just under his skin, and, fu-uck, the guy operated on his arms and legs, leaving long, livid scars. For a few days afterward, Hutchison was relieved of his terrible itching, then he realized what he had done to himself and decided to pass on the needle for a while. Cocaine was truly insidious, and the worst to be said about it was that it could have you savagely in its grip and you would never know it, that is until you brought something upon yourself that was unimaginably grotesque.

By the time Hutchison left that night, he and Draper had finished all the cocaine. Draper was still wired to the teeth but it was late and there was nowhere to go. He was beginning to feel as if his body had somehow disappeared and he was left with merely a brain and a nervous system, a head on a stick. When he finally managed to fall asleep that night his dreams were lurid, iridescent and somehow hideously obscene. Then they all at once resolved themselves into an explosion of colour, a shattering spinning whirlpool. When he awoke next morning, Draper was in rough shape. He was not only hungover but the after-effects of the cocaine were worse than that time in Hollywood with Joanne. His head felt encased in cotton wool, he had a bad headache, his thoughts seemed to form themselves in slow motion, he had trouble getting a breath, the world was a grey, dismal place. Worst of all, his nerves were shot. Horrible nameless creatures were rising to the surface of his mind and Draper didn't like the look of them at all.

He wrote his symptoms off as just another hangover after another evening's debauch and ordered himself to take it easy on the blow. But, in the weeks that followed, they seemed to stay with him, refused to go away. He felt taut and jumpy, the smallest sound made him start, and worst of all, he was beginning to be unable to glance at a razor blade or knife or stand in a high place without feeling the reckless urge to take it to his wrists or jump. What only happened to lames like Joanne was happening to him. *Not only do I have the coke jitters,* he thought, *I've got the coke horrors as well.*

Every encounter began to be an agony for him and he would scream inwardly as each second crawled by, as he waited for whoever it was to go away so he could be left alone with his fear. It began to occur to him that he was losing his mind. He began turning down cocaine when it was offered. The only thing that seemed to drown those shapeless creatures when they swarmed up at him was scotch and he began to drink a lot of it. What was happening? He was more or less happy with his life – he just wanted to kill himself. He rejected the notion of looking for help amongst the head-shrinkers. The last thing he wanted was to sit in an office and have some geek in a white coat and a mustache sit behind a desk and examine his psychological deficiencies, his moral abnormalities. There was no great Freudian secret why he or anybody else used cocaine: it was available and its effects were pleasant. That was it, baby. He felt that if he could just get away from things, get away from that fast cocaine tempo, the nameless fears would recede, he would stop feeling as if his brain was being squeezed tight in some invisible vise, and his nerves would recover. The rough ride would smooth out.

He had a sister living in the countryside near Kingston. He asked her if he could visit for a while, just to relax, but he made a point of keeping to himself just how bad things were with him. In the back seat of her Volvo he replied in monosyllables to her questions, his hands balled into agitated fists, his jaws clenched. That evening he quickly excused himself after they ate and went to bed. *Country air and sunshine*, he thought, *that's the remedy.* The next morning the sun was shining but Draper was still in thrall to his demons. He felt like jumping up and screaming, smashing his head against the brass bed-frame. Outside, there was a slight breeze blowing through the fields. *Be cool*, he counselled himself, *you've got noting to worry about, all you've got to do is lie back in this warm bed.* Sprawled amongst the pillows, he had a chance to think about how he had ended up in such awful shape. Only a fool would deny that cocaine had something to do with it. The Spaniards, who had first encountered the South American Indians who chewed the coca leaf, had considered its effects "a demonical illusion" and now Draper was willing to consider that they were right. He wasn't a man to indulge in illusions. He had observed Joanne in their grip and despised her for it. Now he knew he himself was no better. That would change.

After a couple of weeks Draper began to feel himself recovering. His nerves were steadier, the beasts seemed firmly lodged in his subconscious and no longer floated so ominously to the surface. He had beaten them, all by himself. As he made ready to return, he didn't pretend to himself that he was giving up cocaine. Too many people he knew talked a blue streak about the evils of the drug, the bad things it did to people . . . just before they did another line. It was just too much a part of his world to be avoided. There were already rumours that the drug whose vogue would eclipse cocaine was heroin, and that was something else entirely. What would he do, Draper wondered, when the day came that Hutchison or another friend showed up with another kind of white powder? Of course, heroin was where he drew the line. It was for lames. Yet, at the same time, he thought, m*aybe just once, just to see what all the talk was about, that was all.*

Acknowledgements

Cronenberg Goes to Hollywood and **The Fixer** appeared in *Saturday Night.*

Glenn Gould at 45, **Ad Nouveau Meets Art Nouveau**, **Mexico**, and **The Blade in the Mirror** appeared in *Toronto Life.*

The New Class, **No Way**, **Marie-Josée**, **Henry Miller**, **Stephen Vizinczey**, **Miles Davis**, **James M. Cain: Poet of the Tabloid Murder**, and **Wayne Shorter** appeared in *The Globe and Mail.*

Brawling for Peace, **Blonde and Bad**, and **Echoes of Woodstock** appeared in *Weekend Magazine.*

The Angry Journey of Trevor Berbick and **The 66 Percent Solution** appeared in *Quest Magazine.*

The Murder of Nancy Eaton appeared in *Chatelaine.*

Saul Bellow appeared in *Books in Canada.*

Robertson Davies: The View from High Table is reprinted from ECW Press' *The Bumper Book.*

Morley Callaghan's Toronto *Noir* is the introduction to *It's Never Over,* Exile Editions.